Horse Sense in American Humor

THURBER: A SELF-PORTRAIT

Of humorists, Mr. Thurber says: "They lead . . . . an existence of jumpiness and apprehension . . . . have a genius for getting into minor difficulties: they walk into the wrong apartments, they drink furniture polish for stomach bitters, they drive their cars into the prize tulip beds of haughty neighbors. . . . ."

Horse Sense in American Humor

From Benjamin Franklin to Ogden Nash

BY WALTER BLAIR

The University of Chicago

New York
RUSSELL & RUSSELL

817.09
B 635h
102796

PREFACE

I

THIS book is about horse sense, the horselaugh, and the ways the two have worked together in America. For almost two centuries the best way to make an idea tasty to most of the people of this country has been to serve it up with a sauce of native-grown humor and horse sense. Because they have loved to laugh and because they have thought horse sense was the best kind of truth, Americans everywhere have welcomed an idea served up with such a sauce.

Of all the sorts of writing done in the United States, our native humor has been the one enjoyed by the most kinds of people. In early days people of all classes paid as much heed, almost, to the salty sayings in their almanacs as they paid to the Bible. Later, when the daily or weekly newspapers came along, farmers, mechanics, tradesmen, men in government, and white-collar workers—all were likely to turn quickly to the funny columns. Clippings of good things from these, yellowed in billfolds, were passed around so often that their edges became curled and frayed.

In time, after the humor had been put between book covers, the common man might be talked by smart agents into buying histories, travel lectures, or doctor-books; but the books he bought without pressure salesmanship and then re-read to pieces were such as Davy Crockett's *Autobiography*, *Artemus Ward's Book*, or Bill Nye's *Remarks*. The most widely and deeply loved characters in the world of print were not those in highbrow plays or novels but the muddy-booted heroes of lowbrow humor—men like Josh Billings, Mr. Dooley, and Will Rogers. And when the man in the street quoted from memory something he had read, nine times out of ten it would be a specimen of this humor, like Crockett's "Be sure you're right, then go ahead," or Mark Twain's "Differences of opinion make a horse race." Down through the years, in other words, humor has come as close as any kind of printed matter to being the literature of the people.

II

The reason why horse sense worked so well with this much-loved humor to shape American ideas becomes clear when one considers what our people mean by "horse sense." To our general way of thinking, horse sense is the same thing as common sense, homespun philosophy, pawkiness, cracker-box philosophy, gumption, or mother-wit, and it is, therefore, permissible to use these terms interchangeably.

Some Americans may have had the lowest idea possible of this sort of sense—that it is, as one dictionary puts it, "ordinary, normal, or average understanding," without which a man would be insane. According to this definition, unless a person is doomed to idiocy, this would be the sense God gives him at birth. Most Americans, however, have thought too highly of common sense to define it as just a quality saving a man by a hairline from idiocy. They feel that no one can say anything kinder about a person than "He's got horse sense."

The reason is that the term, in our more usual meaning, stands for "good, sound, practical sense." A man blessed with mother-wit in this meaning of the words, Americans

think, is lucky in that he can handle whatever problems he
has to face—deal with them properly. He does not have to
look into a book to find the answers, does not have to ask
anybody on earth what to do. He can solve his own problems because he was born with a long head on him, he has
"been around," and he has learned everything he can from
experience. When he gets into a new situation, he whittles
his problem down to its essentials, sees how it compares with
situations in his past and how it differs from them, and then
he thinks out what he should do—figures out the right
answer.

Horse sense, as Americans use the term, is not only a way
of thinking; it is also, of course, the name for the kind of
ideas a man gets by thinking that way. So when a man with
gumption puts into words a truth he has ciphered out, another man with a good mind will say, "That's horse sense."
The mother-wit remark will probably have a form that
shows the way its author came to hit on it. It will not be
bookish, because he will not have depended on stuff in
print to help him get the idea or phrase it. It will be short,
because everything that has no bearing on it will have been
hewed away. More likely than not, it will show that its author has based it on life itself, because it will refer in a
figurative way to a deep lesson he has picked up while
working in the fields or walking the highways of the world.
When, for example, old Miguel de Cervantes, the Spaniard,
said "Make hay while the sun shines," he called to mind
how rain ruined hay when the farmer left it standing too
long, and his experience helped him bring out something
wise about doing any important job as soon as the chance
offers. Seeing how sound this idea was, generations of com-

mon men have been glad to remember the saying and to follow it if they could.

Another way we use the term makes it possible for us to say of someone, "He's got uncommon common sense." Though such a sentence might puzzle a foreigner, it could give no trouble to most people in this country. Everybody would know that a man with uncommonly good horse sense would be one who had been born with a better than ordinary mind, that he had not let book learning muddy his thinking, that he had had many experiences and had caught on to their meaning, so that he had become unusually good in figuring out what to do at any time. Such a man would have a way of saying things that would make people agree with him—the great mass of men of gumption, at any rate. Most Americans would point to Lincoln as a fine example of a great man of this sort.

III

Common sense was not invented in America, nor did this country manage to get patents on it. Long before America was settled, people had seen its value. Nevertheless, there is some reason for claiming that mother-wit had a better chance here than elsewhere to do things. When Tom Paine wrote what was perhaps the smartest piece of propaganda ever produced here (and was wise enough to give it the title *Common Sense*), he pointed out that things were so different on these shores that Americans had "it in their power to begin the world over again." In another work he stressed the need for horse-sense thinking to cope with the brand-new problems of the New World: "When precedents fail to spirit us, we must return to the first principles of things for information; and think, as if we were the first men that thought."

And so well—knowingly or unknowingly—did our people follow this advice that, when sound observers from abroad looked at the United States with keen eyes, it struck them that ours was peculiarly a land of homespun philosophy. Alexis de Tocqueville, the brilliant young Frenchman, for example, after traveling widely here in the 1830's, said that the common-sense way of thinking was a national philosophy. He said:

I think that in no country in the civilized world is less attention paid to philosophy than in the United States. The Americans have no philosophical school of their own; and they care but little for all the schools in which Europe is divided, the very names of which are scarcely known to them.

Nevertheless it is easy to see that almost all the inhabitants of the United States conduct their understanding in the same manner, and govern it by the same rules; that is to say, that without ever having taken the trouble to define the rules of a philosophical method, they are in possession of one, common to the whole people.

To evade the bondage of system and habit, of family maxims, class-opinions, and, in some degree, of national prejudices; to accept tradition only as a means of information, and existing facts only as a lesson used in doing otherwise and doing better; to seek the reason of things for oneself, and in oneself alone; to tend to results without being bound to means, and to aim at the substance through the form;—such are the characteristics of what I shall call the philosophical method of the Americans.

But if I go further, and if I seek among these characteristics that which predominates over and includes almost all the rest, I discover that in most of the operations of the mind, each American appeals to the individual exercise of his own understanding alone. . . . . Every one shuts himself up in his own breast, and affects from that point to judge the world.

A second observer who might be quoted was a German who left Germany because he did not like the place and settled in America because he preferred its ways—the great Carl Schurz, who in time did much for his adopted country. In a letter Schurz wrote to another man of German blood during the Civil War, he mentioned "that characteristic, God-given trait of this people, sound common sense." His speaking of the trait as if it were not only peculiar but also precious showed Schurz was getting the American point of view.

A third observer was an Englishman, the widely traveled and greatly learned James Bryce, whose *The American Commonwealth*, published in 1888, is one of the best studies ever written of living and thinking in the United States. After reading many books and talking to people in all walks of life over here, Bryce had much to tell of our smug faith in the brains of our people, of our confidence

that the people are sure to decide right in the long run, a confidence inevitable and essential in a government which refers every question to the arbitrament of numbers. . . . . If you ask an intelligent citizen why he so holds, he will answer that truth and justice are sure to make their way into the minds and consciences of the majority. This is deemed an axiom, and the more readily so deemed, because truth is identified with common sense, the quality which the average American is most proud of possessing.

Bryce also wrote a penetrating passage which pointed out how Lincoln's common sense made him a great leader in this country.

IV

Beginning with the days of Benjamin Franklin and coming down to the present time, this book tells the story of the literature in which our racy humor and horse sense have been blended to persuade or enlighten the people of this country and which, in one way or another, has appealed to our love for home-grown laughter and our almost religious faith in mother-wit. It shows how the authors of this literature developed and used horse-sense humor—how they adapted it to the opinions they held, to the changing times, and to the changing audiences which they wanted to influence. In other words, it shows how this humor, though in some ways always the same, in other ways differed from period to period in what it tried to do and how it tried to do it. As a result, the chief task of this study is to explore changes in the form of what has been, by and large, the most efficient kind of appeal to the American mind.

This story is of interest for several reasons. Obviously, it emphasizes one of the lasting American beliefs—the one the *Nation*, in 1870, called "our blessed American faith in the sufficiency of born gumptions." It shows the fine artistry of writings which, though some pedantic scholars have sniffed at them, form a body of literature wisely loved by our people. And since these writings were so beautifully fitted to the times that begot them, looking at them carefully ought to teach us much about our people and our past.

WALTER BLAIR

CONTENTS

LIST OF ILLUSTRATIONS

CHAPTER I
Early To Rise

The learned fool writes his nonsense in better language than the unlearned but still 'tis nonsense.

He is no clown that drives the plough, but he that doth clownish things.

—POOR RICHARD SAUNDERS

I

FOR the trouble he caused them, Benjamin Franklin has been hated by many Americans—among them Mark Twain. Franklin, Twain told the world in 1875, was a "vicious" fellow who "early prostituted his talents" to cooking up sayings sure to give little boys of all later ages trouble and sorrow. Mark took lusty cracks at the way Franklin would "work all day, and then sit up nights, and let on to study algebra by the light of a smouldering fire, so that all other boys might have to do that also, or else have Benjamin Franklin thrown up at them."

He got down to cases and told stories of how, every day, the memory of Franklin caused children to suffer. Any time a boy behaved like a boy, he said, up would pop a snarling little proverb of old Ben's to stop the fun. If, say, the youngster bought himself two cents' worth of peanuts, his father would get off the one about a groat a day being a penny a

1

year, and all the joy would be gone from those peanuts. "And," said Mark, his anger boiling up as he looked back at his own blighted childhood, "that boy is hounded to death and robbed of his natural rest, because Franklin said once, in one of his inspired flights of malignity—

> Early to bed and early to rise
> Makes a man healthy and wealthy and wise.

As if it were any object to a boy to be healthy and wealthy and wise on such terms."

In spite of Mark's harsh words, Franklin was really much more of a good fellow than a spoilsport. Franklin did, of course, preach thrift. But for all his kind words in its favor, frugality, he himself had to allow, was "a virtue I never could acquire myself." He was strong for vegetarianism, too, but as a little story in his *Autobiography* tells, his will weakened, when, on a sea voyage, he got hungry.

. . . . being becalmed off Block Island [he said], our people set about catching cod and hauled up a great many. Hitherto I had stuck to my resolution of not eating animal food; and on this occasion, I considered . . . . the taking every fish as a kind of unprovoked murder, since none of them had or ever could do us any injury that might justify the slaughter. All this seemed very reasonable.

But I had formerly been a great lover of fish, and when this came hot out of the frying pan, it smelt admirably well. I balanced some time between principle and inclination: till I recollected, that when the fish were opened, I saw smaller fish taken out of their stomachs. Then thought I, "If you eat one another, I don't see why we mayn't eat you." So I dined upon cod very heartily and continued to eat with other people, returning only now and then occasionally to a vegetable diet. So convenient a thing it is to be a *reasonable creature*, since it enables one to find or make a reason for every thing one has a mind to do.

He turned out sayings like "Eat to live, and not live to eat," and "Drink water . . . . and leave the dry belly-ache in the punch-bowl," and he did a fine job of talking up exercise; but more than once he ate and drank so heartily and walked so little that he was laid up with the gout. The story he in time told of his life showed that his notion that honesty was the best policy had been based on experiments with its opposite; and the gossip of his day showed that the way he carried on with women was not exactly puritanical.

What people—Mark Twain and others—have thought about Franklin has been wrong in another way. Not only has he been given better morals than he really had; he has also been given less "book larning." Many, if they were told that Franklin was a well-read man, would deny it. He was the sort of fellow, they would claim, who had no truck to speak of with books—a man who used his natural-born sense to think out any problem he had to solve. But scholars of Franklin can, with no work at all, draw up a long list of heavyweight authors he had read. Say two such scholars, Messrs. Mott and Jorgenson:

He seems to have been acquainted with portions of Plato, Aesop, Pliny, Xenophon, Herodotus, Epictetus, Virgil, Horace, Tacitus, Seneca, Sallust, Cicero, Tully, Milton, Jeremy Taylor, Bacon, Dryden, Tillotson, Rabelais, Bunyan, Fénelon, Chevalier de Ramsay, Pythagoras, Waller, Defoe, Addison and Steele, William Temple, Pope, Swift, Voltaire, Boyle, Algernon Sidney, Trenchard and Gordon, Young, Mandeville, Locke, Shaftesbury, Collins, Bolingbroke, Richardson, Wheaton, Watts, Thomson, Burke, Cowper, Darwin. . . . .

The list goes on through twenty-five more names, "to suggest only the more prominent," the authors say considerately. It is easy to believe their summary: "Such a catalogue tends to discredit the all too common idea that [Franklin] the untutored tradesman was torpid to the information and wisdom found in books."

From a picture made in Paris

BENJAMIN FRANKLIN IN THE ROLE OF A COONSKIN PHILOSOPHER

How did Franklin, then, come to be known both as a copy-book hero pained by wing-sproutings and also as a stranger to books? The answer, of course, is that he was given his misfit reputation because people confused the author with the fellow he made up—Poor Richard of the almanacs. Poor Richard was both good and unlearned, people reasoned; Poor Richard was Franklin; therefore Franklin, too, was both good and unlearned. This is about as logical, to be sure, as it would be to expect Pearl Buck to be the same person, say, as a Chinaman in *The Good Earth*. But, absurd though such an idea of Franklin may be, it is a compliment to his skill in using horse-sense humor.

Looking at Franklin's writings, one can see that Poor Richard stands for only part of the pioneer work his clever creator did in the field of homespun humor. In Franklin's writings, as a matter of fact, although they came early, there are hints of nearly all the later developments in this humor. Notably he made use of both the horse-sense character and the fool character, who were to be stand-bys for humorists for a long time.

II

Franklin created his first horse-sense character—an unschooled person, amusingly wording ideas in humble phrases—in 1722. The date is worth noticing, because at that time the liking of Americans for such a character was not nearly so keen as it was to be later. For one thing, horse sense itself did not rate so high then as it did in the years to come. For another, the ideas people had about style led them to think better of the highfalutin word-embroideries of scholars than of the hayfield talk of bumpkins.

The feeling people had about knowledge and style was of long standing. In the times when the early settlers had started forest-rimmed colonies on these shores the general belief had been that, since learning led straight to knowledge, bookish men were the best to run the Colonies. In 1722, this imported notion was still widespread: most men who had high places in America could rattle off Latin and Greek as fast, almost, as they could English, and men who had read few books were generally in low places.

Therefore, many of the leading English and American writers had a grudge against writing which was not—as they were likely to say—elegant. In England the most admired author was Alexander Pope, who polished his lines until they sparkled like brilliants. In America one of the literary leaders was the learned Cotton Mather. Mather's ideal writer, as he described him in 1726, "could not have writ as he does if he had not read very much in his time." "And his composures," the critic went on (he meant compositions), "are not only a cloth of gold but stuck with as many jewels as the gown of a Russian ambassador." So Mather felt that anyone who used the language of a farm hand—or even, say, of a bewigged, coffee-house wit—must be doing it simply because he knew no better. It could not be because there was anything of value in this low style of writing.

The job Franklin had in 1722 made it seem unlikely that he would find time to write at all. Apprenticed to his brother James, who was the publisher of a newspaper called the *New England Courant*, the sixteen-year-old boy had enough chores to do, it would seem, to keep him hustling. A sort of one-man newspaper plant, he set up the *Courant* in

type, he ran it off the press, and then he peddled it to subscribers. Somehow, though, the boy did snatch time for
writing. He himself has told how he secretly scribbled out
his first piece in a disguised hand, how he sneaked it under
the printing-house door in the dark of night, and then how
he stood at his printing case the next morning and greedily
listened to his brother and the other contributors to the
paper as they praised it.

For two reasons, the chances that this "Dogood Paper"
and others which followed it (as others did) would be homespun humor might seem to be rather small. Franklin at the
time was enthusiastic about a number of the more genteel
literary men then admired—so enthusiastic that each day he
skimped his food at lunch time to snatch a few minutes for
dipping into their pages, nor each night did his aching bones
keep him from staying up late to read more. The same Cotton Mather who had such a good opinion of jeweled prose
was one of his favorites. So were several authors—coffee-
house Addison and Steele, for example—whom Mather
thought informal, but who actually were far more formal, as
a rule, than most moderns. These last two authors the boy
complimented by copying, shutting his book now and then
and trying to come up to their standard in his rephrasing of
their ideas. Moreover, he was at an age in life when imitation came naturally.

As would be expected, his first attempts did have many
echoes of the writings he had been enjoying—especially of
the genteel *Spectator* papers, which Addison and Steele had
put out in England. From this British series he took the idea
of playing a part when he wrote, using the first person but
making the "I" in the papers a kind of person very different

from young Ben Franklin. Like his English models, the boy would make clear that this writer was an observer, standing on the sidelines and chatting about life—a "spectator." Also like the English stylists, young Ben gave his character a few close friends with whom to talk. Finally, he picked up from the *Spectator* some hints about subjects he might treat.

But the interesting thing about the *Dogood Papers* was not that they had so many echoes in them but that they had so few. The "character" who wrote them, the language in which they were written, and even the ideas they gave voice to were acclimated to America in a day when most writing done over here could hardly be told from British models, except that it was worse.

The reason for his cutting loose from the ways of writing then in fashion is not hard to find. Looking at the boy's background—in addition to his own good gumption—we can easily find forces which pushed him toward writing as he did. Both the Boston of the day in which the papers were written and the kind of articles published in the paper for which he wrote them helped to shape his style.

Boston in 1722, as an impressed map-maker boasted, had all of "42 streets, 36 lanes, 22 alleys, near 3000 houses; 1000 brick, rest timber; near 12,000 people." Its people were having trouble with pirates and with the Indians of the near-by forests. All this may push the town into the distant past; but Boston had not a little in common with any modern city. Notably, the town was split by a quarrel about a very up-to-date problem.

In politics this quarrel set the Governors and the Council against the House of Representatives. The Governors, of course, were men of property, and the Council—the upper legislative body—was drawn from the aristocratic families and well-to-do merchants. Against them in many conflicts were the members of the House, who as a rule spoke for the little storekeepers, the farmers, the laborers, and the growing crowd of mechanics. Not only in politics but also in commerce the same sort of division appeared; as a mason wrote in the quaint spelling of the day: "In 1722, aboute this time there was great disputing aboute perogative and property. The rich oppress. The poor complain." Even in that far-off day, in other words, the Have-nots were beginning to complain against the Haves. And when the poor complained, they were not likely to express themselves very well, because the people on their side were not likely to be very well trained in putting ideas into words.

The *Courant*, as a rule, sided with the cornhuskers and the leather-apron men. It slapped at the owners of great houses and the corrupt politicians, who (it said) stole money from the pockets of honest laboring men. As time went on, this paper put out by Franklin's brother won more and more of a name for itself as a champion of the lower classes.

Because they wanted to catch the ear of the workmen for whom they were speaking, the *Courant* authors worked up a style of writing which would be plain even to the uneducated. They worded their pieces, as one of them said, "in a very easy and familiar manner, so that the meanest ploughman . . . . may understand." So much, in time, did they go in for the common way of putting ideas that learned men in near-by Harvard began to snap, in print, at their "low" and "insipid" style of writing. After a while, too, the *Courant* writers' revolt came to be against more than a way of using words: it was, in the end, against the way of thinking that took for granted that a man's learning largely decided the value of what he said. The radical idea that a man could have good ideas even if he had horny hands actually got into a sentence written in 1721. "Say not who hath written," said the author, "but consider what is written. . . . . Say not that he is a mechanic, and an illiterate man; for there is good metal sometimes under mean soil." The very pen names some of the *Courant* authors used showed their friendship with the Have-nots—names like Timothy Turnstone, Ichabod Henroost, Homespun Jack, and Betty Frugal.

When young Ben Franklin, then, started to write for his brother's paper, he knew, in addition to the writings of Addison and Steele, with their somewhat conversational but also rather formal style, what his brother and others on the *Courant* were doing—putting their ideas into phrases something like those of clodhoppers and even going so far as to hint that bumpkins were acute. And the most important influence on his writing, in so far as it was to be new, was the influence of the Boston newspaper for which young Ben was writing.

This influence led him to draw a character with horse sense and to let her express herself in a style less embroidered than Mather would approve. The character in question— Widow Silence Dogood—let it be known in her papers how she stood in the current Boston controversy. Since, she said, in her very first paper, people in those days had to know about an author—"whether he be poor or rich, old or young, a scholar or a leather-apron man, &c . . . . it may not be amiss to give a short account of my past life and present condition. . . ." The little life-story which followed made clear that she was poor, that she was friendlier to the leather-apron man than to the scholar, and that she was of the farm rather than of the town. Her sniffs at the block-heads who had Harvard diplomas, her biting talk about the wide open spaces in college men's skulls, and her way of specifying that she went most for "all useful and desirable knowledge" showed she was on the *Courant* side, depending on gumption for her ideas and arguments. And the stands she took against "arbitrary government and unlimited power," against certain religious attitudes, and even against the showy clothing of the rich dames of Boston were the stands of Franklin's paper.

The way she put these ideas was not elegant. Barred from her writing were the many literary allusions then in fashion; and the widow actually made fun of the British passion for prettifying essays with sentences "in the learned languages, which," she said, "will not only be fashionable, and pleasing to those who understand it, but likewise be very ornamen-tal." Slang found its way into a couple of papers she wrote, and she was not above telling an earthy little joke or throw-ing in a humble aphorism or two. Her answer to a corre-spondent who asked her to scold womankind for loafing is a fair sample of her style.

As for idleness [she said], if I should *quare*, where are the greatest number of its votaries to be found, with us or the men? it might I believe be easily and truly answered, *with the latter*. For, notwithstanding the men are commonly complaining how hard they are forced to labor, yet if you go among the women, you will learn that *they have always more work upon their hands than they are able to do*, and that a *woman's work is never done*, etc. But however, suppose that we should grant for once, that we are generally more idle than the men . . . . , I desire to know whose fault it is? Are not the men to blame in maintaining us in idleness? Who is there that can be handsomely supported in affluence, ease and pleasure by another, that will chuse rather to earn his bread by the sweat of his brows?

Except for one word of Latin, this paragraph is written in language in keeping with the widow's education. The homely proverb and the biblical phrase are within the range of her understanding, and her ideas come from her own head rather than from books. Such was Franklin's first horse-sensible character—chatty and worldly-wise Widow Dogood, with her generally unlearned style.

III

More famous, of course, as a man of gumption, was Franklin's Poor Richard, whose sayings were printed in a series of almanacs beginning in 1732 and going on for a quarter of a century. This worthy, as people were to remember him, was less clearly drawn than the widow had been. One almanac had a little rhyme in it in which Richard spoke vaguely of his living out in the country with his wife and of his being temperate, charitable, pious—a reader of books which pointed the way to virtue. His wife sounded uninteresting: she was "careful"—whatever that meant— and she evidently lived pretty much the quiet life he did.

But Richard, as he said, had a habit of "scattering here and there" through his annual booklets "some instructive hints in the matters of morality and religion." These little hints were easy to remember—worded simply, as they were, and full of homely comparisons. Not a few of the aphorisms were so brightly stated that Americans made them part of their daily talk, as, for instance, those about the groat and about early rising which so annoyed Mark Twain. Others seem to be just as worthy of remembrance, for example:

By diligence and patience, the mouse bit in two the cable.
The sleeping fox catches no poultry. Up! Up!
The used key is always bright.
If you'd have it done, go; if not, send.

People who think this Poor Richard a rather dull fellow, given only to talk about climbing the ladder in business, will be pleasantly surprised to find he could also talk in quite another strain. As Mr. Carl Van Doren points out, what made the biggest and most lasting hit with American readers was not the whole collection of Poor Richard's sayings but a selection from them, made in 1757—a culling which had to do with getting on in the world. This selection, called "The Way to Wealth," Franklin's most popular single work, had the bits in it his countrymen have most enjoyed recalling— the sentence sermons which urged a successful, if rather dull, life.

Elsewhere in the almanacs, however, Poor Richard talked of matters more to the taste of people who, for some reason or another, are not hagridden by the hope that they will make heaps of money. For instance:

> An old young man will be a young old man.
> Fish and visitors smell in three days.
> Let thy maid-servant be faithful, strong, and homely.
> Keep your eyes wide open before marriage; half-shut afterwards.
> Marry your son when you will, but your daughter when you can.
> There's more old drunkards than old doctors.

There is a racier flavor in these than in the better-known sayings.

In spite of the differences in tone between such aphorisms as these and those more commonly quoted, there is a consistent philosophy behind both. Whatever its origin (and several sources for it other than the early *Courant* writings might be mentioned), it was the philosophy which Franklin by now had found he himself liked best and which he held to through life. To his thinking, morality and practicality were very much the same thing. If a man wanted to know what he ought to do, he had better not worry too much, Franklin thought, about the rules for living he found in dull books. His concern, instead, ought to be with the way things actually worked out in the world—the things he himself had learned concerning the fitting of means to ends, by keeping his eyes open and his wits about him.

This great American philosophy was that of horse sense or gumption or mother-wit—call it what you will—and Franklin created Richard Saunders to be its exponent.

Poor Richard, as the kind of words he used showed, was a man of little book learning but much rich experience. His experience made possible his wise remarks about life— whether those remarks were in line with general moral standards or not and whether they dealt with money-making or sex, long visits or the buncombe about temperance. He figured out what would work, he told his readers—and that was morality for him and for them. Poor Richard became known and respected by the thousands of buyers of his almanac because he could give them news, in a witty way, of his useful discoveries.

IV

After Franklin, many a humorist, taking advantage of the American liking for such a preacher, was going to use a similar sort of person as his mouthpiece—men like Josh Billings or Mr. Dooley or Will Rogers, to cite only three of many such lay preachers to be treated later in this study. Not only would a man like Poor Richard be useful to drive home general ideas about living; in addition, he would get a great deal of attention when he dealt with political affairs. Franklin himself, pioneering again in this field, made use of a horse-sense character in some of his writings to put across political ideas.

Another example of such a device may be worth a glance, a paper published in 1766 in France and England, "On the Price of Corn, and Management of the Poor." The very first paragraph showed that the author—who signed himself, perhaps rather too learnedly, "Arator"—was playing the same kind of part as Franklin: "I," he wrote, "am one of that class of people, that feeds you all, and at present is abused by you all; in short I am a *farmer*."

Not only did Arator make himself known in this early sentence. Later in the letter, to show he knew what he was talking about, he told how he had come by his knowledge. Books had had nothing to do with it. He was, he said, a man who had traveled a great deal in his youth, looking at the results of laws in various countries. Using his own two eyes, he had worked with the fine brain the good Lord had given him to think out the best way for a government to treat farmers. He had seen how different policies worked; he had suffered himself. Therefore, he could say what worked—what was expedient and therefore right. He set down his notions in the simple words of a forthright farmer who had no nonsense about him.

His attack was on the government for taxing the export of certain farm products. This tax had been set up for two reasons—that manufacturers might produce goods at lower prices and that the poor might be helped by it. As to the first, Arator had his doubts:

I have heard my grandfather say, that the farmers submitted to the prohibition on the exportation of wool, being made to expect and believe, that, when the manufacturer bought his wool cheaper, they should also have their cloth cheaper. But the deuce a bit. It has been growing dearer and dearer from that day to this. How so? Why, truly, the cloth is exported; and that keeps up the price.

Now, if it be a good principle, that the exportation of a commodity is to be restrained, that so our people at home may have it the cheaper, stick to that principle, and go thoroughstitch with it. Prohibit the exportation of your cloth, your leather, and shoes, your iron ware, and your manufactures of all sorts, to make them all cheaper at home. And cheap enough they will be, I will warrant you; till people leave off making them.

Some folks seem to think they ought never to be easy till England becomes another Lubberland, where it is fancied that streets are paved with penny-rolls, the houses tiled with pancakes, and chickens, ready roasted, cry, "Come eat me."

Thus Arator, arguing in the way natural for a keen-minded common man, put out an early example of talk about political subjects made persuasive because it was based on mother-wit and written in salty, barnyard phrases.

V

Franklin, as has been said, also should have credit for the early use of another kind of character who was going to be used time and again by American humorists eager to get converts to their ideas—the fool character. In a country like democratic America, where gumption was thought to be the common property of the voters, if authors let characters speak who had no native wit, the idea was that the readers would see at once that the things such characters said were nonsense. Hence, in time, many a numskull (like Lowell's Birdofredum Sawin or Locke's Petroleum V. Nasby) was going to take a wrong stand and be laughed at for his lack of mother-wit.

When we look for an example of such a character in Franklin's works, we find one turning up, in—of all places— *Poor Richard's Almanac*. The reason is (as Mr. J. F. Ross made clear as recently as September, 1940) that Franklin started his almanacs with a conception of Poor Richard very different from that which later became famous. And just as British models had helped him a great deal with the *Dogood Papers*, they helped him draw this character also.

Jonathan Swift, rather than the American's earlier idols, Addison and Steele, gave Franklin the hint for his new character sketch. Back in 1708, Swift had played a practical joke which had caused quite a stir. A shoemaker by trade, John Partridge, who had done well as the publisher of an almanac in London, had been the butt of the joke. In February, 1708, Swift had put out a pamphlet prophesying Partridge's death: "Having consulted the star of his nativity, I find he will infallibly die on the 29th of March next at eleven at night of a raging fever; therefore I advise him to consider of it and settle his affairs in time." Partridge, who was a bit of a fool, had taken pains in the next issue of his almanac to deny that he was dead. Swift had written a devastating reply, backing his own claim and announcing that he could not be held responsible for any silly corpse that walked around calling itself Partridge.

Franklin, starting his almanac, stole Swift's general plan of action. Canny businessman that he was, the American put in the place of the English Partridge a person who could be killed off with more profit—a rival American almanac-maker named Titan Leeds. Richard Saunders, the person Franklin invented to edit his almanac, confessed in the Preface to the first issue that he had decided to put such a book out in order to make money. He went on,

Indeed, this motive would have had force enough to have made me publish an almanac many years since, had it not been overpowered by my regard for my good friend and fellow student Mr. Titan Leeds, whose interest I was extremely unwilling to hurt. But this obstacle (I am far from speaking it with pleasure) is soon to be removed, since inexorable death . . . . has already prepared the mortal dart . . . . and that ingenious man must soon be taken from us. He dies, by my calculation made at his request, on October 17, 1733, 3 hours, 29 minutes P.M.

Leeds, it seems, did not know the story of Partridge well enough to learn a lesson from it. Like the butt of Swift's joke, the American astrologer came out with the claim that he was not either dead. Thereupon Poor Richard, like his model, turned out a fine argument proving that his victim, "whatever he may pretend . . . . , is really defunct and dead." Perhaps his most amusing proof was that "no man *living*" could write such horrible stuff as appeared in Leeds's almanac.

Franklin's most important debt to Swift, however, was not for this trick but for a way of drawing characters. In what he had had to say about Partridge and Partridge's wife, the earlier writer had drawn two characters very neatly. As Mr. John F. Ross has noticed, Richard and Bridget Saunders owed much to them:

Both Swift and Franklin sketch in the characters by a few lively details rather than by elaborate accounts. Both use a natural, homely, comic realism, effectively suggesting the domestic life of the philomath, the every-day human beings behind the title-pages of almanacs. Just as our imaginations are set to work by the implied efficiency of Mrs. Partridge with the cudgel, so are they set to work by Bridget's determined threat "to burn all my Books and Rattling Traps (as she calls my Instruments) if I do not make some profitable Use of them."

In addition, Richard and Partridge have much in common. Both are poor, needy men, frankly preparing their almanacs not so much for the honor of the stars as for their livelihoods. Both reveal entertaining glimpses of the practical problems of the craft. Both are favored with wives who must be supported; and the wives themselves are of much the

same type—Bridget's practicality, talkativeness, vigor, and deter.nina-
tion are decidedly reminiscent of Mrs. Partridge's "pretty distingu·shable
voice" and handiness with the cudgel, and both wives seem to be more
practically energetic and forceful than their husbands.

Now the surprising thing about this picture of Richard—
for those who know the man only by his modern reputation
—is that he was not gifted with much horse sense. He was a
clown in a farce rather than an oracle of wise sayings. And
in his early years, at any rate, although the pages of his
almanacs were dotted with acute remarks, it would have
been hard to guess how they got there, unless, perhaps, his
quarrelsome wife Bridget or some keen printer had slipped
them in. Some of the sayings in the almanac were very definitely out of character for Richard. Advice about going to
bed early, for instance, would have been very poor advice for
an astronomer to follow.

But the characters of the astronomer and his wife, dimly
drawn from the first, tended, as time passed, to fade from
view. The almanacs came out at intervals of a year, and
much could be forgotten between the appearances of the
shadow characters both by the author and by his readers.
By design or by chance, as the years passed, Bridget
Saunders died or disappeared, and finally Richard sank
without a trace. Without a trace, that is, of his old self: a
new Richard, somehow the concocter of grand horse-sense
sayings, took his place. The two characters labeled Poor
Richard, then, illustrate both of Franklin's valuable inventions in the horse-sense field. The earlier one, being a dim-
wit, could be depended on to say foolish things. If he talked
about ways of living or about politics, an intelligent reader
would be likely to find his arguments very strong—for the
other side.

VI

The fool Richard of the earlier almanacs, like the wise Richard of the later almanacs, became a mouthpiece for Franklin in political battles years after his almanacs had stopped appearing. He had a new name and a new guise, and he had more immediate jobs to do than before, but he was really the same character—one who pointed the way to right opinions by saying the wrong things.

The stupid character, to cite one example, was useful in a piece of propaganda published in an English magazine in 1773, when Franklin was over in London doing his best to get better treatment for the Colonies. In an opening paragraph of this article, the supposed author, "Q.E.D.," described himself as "a modern simpleton." Then, in the paragraphs that followed, the fool character gravely gave rules of the sort forecast in the title, "Rules by which a Great Empire May be Reduced to a Small One."

The writer showed his idiocy by comparing this process of whittling down an empire to a simple and homely act. "A great empire," he said with the solemnity of an owl, "like a great cake, is early diminished at the edges." Evidently proud of himself for hitting on such a pretty little simile, Q.E.D. took care to use it again, gloating over the bright idea that the leaders of the empire could so handle affairs that they would be like "a wise gingerbread-maker, who, to facilitate a division, cuts his dough half through in those places where, when baked, he would have it *broken to pieces*."

More stupid, however, than the way Q.E.D. preened himself on his silly way of prettifying his sentences, was the whole idea behind the essay. In a day when everybody with natural-born sense took for granted that the bigger an empire was, the better, to deny this marked a man as a fool. Here was such a fool offering twenty lines of action, carefully listed, one after the other, for bringing about the very result his readers least desired.

What Franklin counted on, of course, was that these readers, seeing that the writer was a simpleton, would realize the more easily how silly his advice was. That advice was exactly along the lines of British foreign policy, and the wily American propagandist knew that one of the best ways to discredit that policy was to have a numskull, in all seriousness, speak highly of it.

VII

Franklin's invention of the horse-sense character and the fool character and his discovery of the way each of them could be used amusingly for preaching either a way of life or a political principle were his great gifts to the American humor of gumption. Other developments were going to take place before this kind of humor began to take its most memorable form. Two such developments were to be of particular importance: (1) the greater use of the language of the hayfield and the shop and (2) the more detailed drawing of character.

Franklin did, to be sure, break away from the showy style beloved by hordes of his contemporaries. He had sound notions about the simplicity of good writing. "The words used," he said, "should be the most expressive the language affords, provided they are the most generally understood. Nothing should be expressed in two words that can be as well expressed in one; . . . . but the whole should be as short as possible, consistent with clearness. . . . ." Nevertheless, Franklin was not one to go very far in the use of local phrases or of the slang creations which have given the American language so much gusto. A patient graduate student, checking all the words Franklin used between 1722 and 1751, has had to make the pathetic confession that only nineteen of them "were discovered to be pure 'Americanisms,' and of these, six are the names of herbs or grasses; one is derived from the name of an American university, and one from the name of an American state." Franklin's work, in those days of elegant writing, might seem rather like American talk, but it really was much more bookish.

Furthermore, even the more vivid of his characters—the Widow Dogood or the stupid Poor Richard or the wise one —were drawn with only a few strokes of the pen. He would have had to add many details about them to give them real vividness—details about the way they looked, the way they acted, the way they lived.

Before Franklin had been in his grave very long (he died in 1790), some of the writers for newspapers and almanacs had begun to be much more daring than he had been in their use of Yankee language. The *Old Farmer's Almanac*, started in 1793, for instance, came much closer than Franklin ever had to giving homespun advice in corn-patch language. Reading the pages of this earthy annual, a farmer might find himself asked "How does your hay spend?"— might be told not to follow the example of Squire Thimbleberry who would "pinch his own hay," which "ain't of the best quality," that he might sell hay in the spring. In 1801, a hayseed in an almanac told a lady who had said her dress was a sack: "I vow, I have heard of a pig in a poke, but I'll swamp it, if ever I saw a sow in a sack before." In another place a poet, rhyming in the words of a bumpkin, would sing that his loved one was "tall as a haypole" and had lips "as sweet as molasses," or would carol:

> Miss Sal, I's going to say, as how,
> We'll spark it here tonight,
> I kind of love you, Sal, I vow,
> And mother said I might.

Along with this descent into the realms of homely speech went a development of more vivid characters. Writers began to distinguish between the dry-spoken Yankee, for instance, and the tall-talking frontiersman or between the hot-headed Virginia aristocrat and the poor white trash who were beginning to squat on the frontier. Before long—in the political exploitation of Davy Crockett, say, during the first third of the nineteenth century—the picturing of the fool character and the man with gumption by means of American speech and new-found ways of drawing character were to prove of greater value than anyone in Franklin's day had expected.

CHAPTER II

Davy Crockett: Horse Sense on the Frontier

Mr. Speaker:—*The broken fenced state o' the nation, the broken banks, broken hearts, and broken pledges o' my brother Congressmen around me, has riz the boiler o' my indignation clar up to the high pressure pint, an' therefore I have riz to let off the steam of my hull hog patriotism . . . . without the trimmins. The truth wants no trimmins, for in her clar naked state o' nature she's as graceful as a sucking colt in the sunshine. Mr. Speaker! what in the name o' kill-sheep-dog rascality is the country a-comin' to? Whar's all the honor? no whar! Whar's the state revenue? every whar but whar it ought to be! . . . .*

Tharfore, I move that the only way to save this country is for the hull nest o' your political weasels to cut stick home instanterly, and leave me to work Uncle Sam's farm, till I restore it to its natural state o' cultivation, and shake off these state caterpillars o' corruption.

—ALLEGED SPEECH IN CONGRESS OF REP. DAVID CROCKETT (TENN.)

I

IN THE late 1820's and the 1830's a man named David Crockett posed for much more detailed portraits of a homespun character than the mere sketches in the writings of Franklin and in the almanacs which came later had supplied.

Crockett represented the host of movers westward—the frontiersmen who, through a century, left one meridian of

24

longitude after another behind them as they opened new lands. He qualified geographically as a representative, because he was born in a log cabin in a part of Tennessee not long before taken from the Indians and because he grew up with the wild country. But he was typical of these movers in an even more important way. The frontiersmen had more to do with making gumption a national religion than any other single group. Thanks largely to them, candidates on the common-sense ticket before long began to win national elections. Anyone, therefore, who really represented these scattered settlers had to be strong on common sense. Davy, who in one way or another had as much to do with the triumph of the western brand of gumption as almost any man, was an ideal representative. He played no small part in the raising of horse sense from the status of a local peculiarity to that of a national virtue.

Many people who have heard about Davy only recently may wonder what he ever had to do with horse sense. If you are in the right neighborhood, ask an Ozark mountaineer about Davy, and he may say, "Davy Crockett? Sho, he's still huntin' in these parts. T'other day I heerd tell how he went on a hunt a long piece from his cabin. He slept out in the woods, and when the sun come along in the mornin', he took a long jump onto hit, thinkin' hit'd land him at his clearin' in no time. He'd forgot, y'see, that he was west o' his cabin, not east of hit. Well, he jest hung on, traveled fer twenty-four hours an' saw the hull world. Next morning, he jumped off at his doorstep afore his old woman had breakfast ready."

This is typical of the stories still told about Crockett in some of the cabins of the South. In other words, Davy today, more than a century after he became famous, is talked about as if he were still around, as if he were a superhuman backwoodsman who hangs his powder horn on the crescent moon or jauntily climbs aboard the sun. There does not seem to be much sense in that. And in his own time the yarns told about him were even more nonsensical. In the 1830's and 1840's a series of almanac stories, some of them written by Crockett's one-time neighbors, gave Davy a biography which, pieced together, went something like this:

Even when he was born, Davy was the biggest infant that ever was and a little the smartest that ever will be. But, watered with buffalo milk and weaned on whiskey, he grew so fast that soon his Aunt Keziah was saying it was as good as a meal's vittles to look at him.

His boyhood was notable. The family used his infant teeth to build the parlor fireplace. At eight, he weighed two hundred pounds and fourteen ounces, with his shoes off, his feet clean and his stomach empty. At twelve, he escaped from an Indian by riding on the back of a wolf which went like a streak of lightning towed by steamboats.

Before long he met the first of many sweethearts, a girl sizable enough to win his admiration. She was bigger than a whiskey barrel, and when Davy put his arms around the creature, it was like hugging a bale of cotton. Another of his girls was Lottie Ritchers of Gum Swamp—a streak of lightning set up edgeways, and buttered with quicksilver. But the girl who finally wore his wedding ring first attracted his attention by flogging two bears while Davy looked on.

By the time he married, Crockett had got such a name, among the animals themselves, as a hunter, that some would die when he just grinned at them, and others, looking down from a tree and seeing him reach for his gun, would holler, "Is that you, Davy?" Then when he'd say, "Yes," they'd sing out, "All right, don't shoot! I'm a-comin' down."

Nevertheless, he liked the varmints, and some he tamed almost beyond belief—among them a pack of ravenous wolves, the white steed of the prairies, and an alligator named Long Mississippi. His favorite pet, though, was a bear, Death Hug, raised from a cub by Mrs. Crockett. The Crocketts treated him just like one of the family: he used to sit up at table with them. The bear often helped Davy get his holler gum tree boat down the Mississippi—he'd sit in the stern with a pipe in his mouth and a flag in his paws, dangling his tail in the water to steer the boat.

When friends told Davy the country would be ruined if he didn't go to Congress, he mounted his pet alligator and rode up to where a rival candidate was speechifying. The other candidate hollered murder and ran, and was never seen afterward; so Crockett won the election. He taught the bear and the alligator the polka, so they'd be at home in society, and went to the Capitol with them.

In Congress, Davy's speeches were thunderbolts, but when re-election time came, Davy was as independent as ever. He told the people of his district, "Elect me or not, as you like. If you don't elect me, you can go to hell and I'll go to Texas." So a little later, Crockett was riding his bear to Texas, outrunning a thunderbolt.

Some say Davy got killed at the Alamo, but the fact is he gave Santa Anna an awful licking. Then, riding Death Hug from place to place, he wrought havoc among the enemy armies.

What happened to him after that is rather indefinite—the details anyhow. He got up into Oregon, that's sure, because there are stories about what he did there. And he did some ocean traveling, and had some trouble with cannibals—but not much trouble. When he died, if he did, no one knows.

A preposterous life-story like that would seem to be as far from common sense as anything could be. It seems, one would say, to be a typical creation of the famous liars of the old West, who passed hours by campfires genially man-handling facts. To while away long evenings these old-timers told tall tales about strange critters like, say, the Big Bear of Arkansaw. In the famous hunting yarn about him, the Big Bear, when a bullet smashed against the front of his head, just "shook his head and walked down from the tree as gently as a lady would from a carriage." When the huge var-mint finally was killed, it took five men to load his carcass on a mule: his skin covered a whole bed and "left several feet on each side to tuck up." That was how big the Big Bear was. And other animals and even men—according to the camp-fire yarners—were just as astonishing. If the whoppers of wilderness yarn-spinners gave the only clue to the characters of frontiersmen, one might easily pass the West by in a study of homespun philosophy.

But before the lies were concocted, there was a real David Crockett, born in Tennessee and reared there—a flesh-and-blood man who was killed by the Mexicans in the Alamo out in Texas in 1836. And there was a quirk of western character which made frontier voters think well enough of this real Crockett to elect him and re-elect him to the state legislature and to the United States House of Representatives. It made no difference to them that he was poor, that he was appallingly uneducated. They thought he could get along because they guessed he had good horse sense. This fact suggests the paradox of Crockett's renown: he won fame and office because he had horse sense; he remained famous because of the nonsense associated with his memory. How this came about is an interesting story.

II

Historians have found that often, when men left settled parts and started life in the little clearings they had chopped out of the backwoods with their axes, their ways of thinking changed. "Common hardships, common poverty, common ignorance, and the utter inability to get any more out of life than coarse food, coarse clothes, and a rude shelter," as one scholar says, "reduced all to a level of absolute equality which existed nowhere else." Some rose above this level. But, if a man climbed above others in the West, it was not because he had learned more from books. It was because he knew more about following signs, outwitting Indians, or making crops. As a result, many frontiersmen sniffed at the mere mention of book learning—were suspicious of all kinds of books, including lawbooks. The back-country man liked to decide for himself how he should behave, regardless of what Blackstone said. When, in 1728, the aristocratic William Byrd, II, Esq., of Westover, Virginia, got into what was then the corn-pone section of North Carolina, he made the horrifying discovery that there, as he said, "every one does just what seems good in his own Eyes."

Even when enough people had settled in a district to make a government necessary, they preferred one they set up themselves to meet their own needs to a government set up by learned lawyers. A petition by western Virginia frontiersmen at the end of the Revolution to start a state of their own dressed the idea in juicy language. They wrote:

> Some of our fellow citizens may think we are not yet able to conduct our affairs, and consult our interest; but if our society is rude, much wisdom is not necessary to supply our wants, and *a fool can sometimes put on his clothes better than a wise man can do it for him*. We are not against hearing council; but we attend more to our own feelings than to the argumentation of others.

In many of the workings of frontier government, faith like this in the gumption of the average man made havoc of older ways of governing. One old pioneer remembered that early western judges hated to instruct juries. This was, as he said,

> a clear departure from the practice of the judges in England and most of the United States; but the new practice suited the circumstances of the country. . . . . I knew one judge, who when asked for instructions, would rub his head and the side of his face with his hand . . . . and say to the

lawyers, "Why, gentlemen, the jury understand the case; they need no instructions; no doubt they will do justice between the parties."

In such a section an electioneering candidate was likely to bring up issues which anywhere else would be irrelevant. Candidate Earth, in a frontier story, shouted to the voters:

Now, gentlemen, don't you think they ought to make me sheriff? I say, if Bob Black has floated farther on a log, killed more Injuns, or stayed longer under water than I have, elect him; if not, I say what has he done to qualify him for the office of sheriff? Did any of you ever know him to call for a quart? I never did; I have known him to call for several half-pints in the course of a day, but I never did know him to step forward manfully and say, "Give us a quart of your best." Then I say again, what has Bob Black done to qualify him for sheriff?

One of the ways in which Crockett was typical of the West is illustrated by the story about his first governmental job in the book which purports to be his autobiography. This book shows that he reached manhood in a thinly settled part of Tennessee after suffering only four days of schooling; then, as a man, he went to school about a hundred days. "In that time," he says, "I learned to read a little in my primer, to write my own name, and to cypher some in the three first rules in figures. And this is all the schooling I ever had in my life. . . . ."

This untaught man was living with his second wife and their children in a clearing on Shoal Creek when, about 1818, the people of the district decided they had to have a temporary government. "So," he says,

we met and made what we called a corporation; and I reckon we called *it* wrong . . . . we lived in the backwoods, and didn't profess to know much, and no doubt used many wrong words. But we met, and appointed magistrates and constabules to keep order. We didn't fix any laws for them, tho'; for we supposed they would know law enough, whoever they might be; and so we left it to themselves to fix the laws.

Appointed one of the magistrates, Colonel Crockett carried
on his work in a way which would have horrified any lawyer
but which seemed to him sensible enough. When he wanted
to judge a man, he would say to his constable, "Catch that
fellow, and bring him up for trial." This seemed a proper
way to do things, he says, "for we considered this a good
warrant, even if it was only in verbal writings."

In time the legislature gave the district a more formal
government, and Crockett, now in the office of a squire, had
the task of writing out warrants and recording proceedings.
It was a chore which was, he said, "at least a huckleberry
over my persimmon." Helped by his constable, though, the
squire in time learned to put everything in writing. Nevertheless, his way of working was still a trifle irregular. When
the constable was out somewhere and saw that a warrant
would have a good effect, "I told him," says Davy, "he
needn't take the trouble to come all the way to me to get
one, but he could just fill out one; and then on the trial I
could correct the whole business if he had committed any
error." This irregularity and others did not trouble this
frontier officer a whit. His story of his squireship ends with a
smug summary:

My judgments were never appealed from, and if they had been they
would have stuck like wax, as I gave my decisions on the principles of
common justice and honesty between man and man, and relied on natural born sense, and not on law learning to guide me; for I had never read
a page in a law book in all my life.

From that time the Colonel moved onward and upward,
winning offices in campaigns which would have ended in
dismal beatings anywhere except in a place where book
learning was thought less of than mother-wit. When, for in-

stance, in 1821, he ran for the legislature, he had read no newspapers, had never seen a public document, could not make a speech about governmental affairs. But his neighbors knew he had made his way along blazed trails just as they had, that he could kill enough "varmints" to feed his family and even some of his neighbors, and that he had done his share in discouraging Indians. This tall hunter in buckskin could knock down plenty of squirrels at a neighborhood hunt. Between horns of chain-lightning whiskey, he could tell good stories. So the number of votes they gave him more than doubled the votes for his rival.

When he ran for the next session, he walked into a meeting and said to the crowd: "I don't want it understood that I've come electioneering. I've just crept out of the cane to see what discoveries I can make among the white folks." But he gave voters chaws of tobacco and drinks of whiskey, he told some more good yarns, and he won again. In 1827 he ran for the United States Congress, told more funny stories, passed around horns of corn whiskey to possible supporters, "not to get elected of course," he said righteously, for that would be against the law; but just . . . . to make themselves and their friends feel their keeping a little." And after the votes were tallied, the Colonel scurried around and borrowed enough money to get to Washington, to serve in Congress.

Not long after this a French visitor, in America to study democracy, was a passenger on the steamboat "Louisville" on the Mississippi. After talking to some Tennesseeans on board, he made his way to his stateroom to write about his newest shocking discovery:

When the right of suffrage is *universal*, and when the deputies are paid by the state, it's singular how low and how far wrong the people can go.

Two years ago the inhabitants of the district of which Memphis is the capitol sent to the House of Representatives . . . . an individual named David Crockett, who has no education, can read with difficulty, has no property, no fixed residence, but passes his life hunting, selling his game to live, and dwelling continuously in the woods.

His competitor, a man of wealth and talent, failed.

Again today, they [my fellow passengers] assured me that in the new western states the people generally made very poor selections. Full of pride and ignorance, the electors want to be represented by people of their own kind. Moreover, to win their votes one has to descend to manoeuvres that disgust distinguished men. You have to haunt the taverns and dispute with the populace; that's what they call *Electioneering* in America.

III

The Frenchman, De Tocqueville, made one or two mistakes in this paragraph about Crockett. This is not surprising, since he had heard about the man from readers of the press of the day, and already such readers were beginning to be misled by stories about the Colonel in scores of newspapers. In time the real Davy was to disappear into a thicket of such stories, and, after a century, scholars who tried to follow him into the tangled growth were to come out with strange tales of what they had found there.

Writing about Crockett in Congress, some of these historians were to say that along the old trail they had found traces of more than one Davy Crockett—traces of two Davies, or three, or even four. Mr. Claude G. Bowers, for example, says: "The present generation scarcely realizes that there were two Davy Crocketts—the man of the woods and the fight, and the less admirable creature who made a

DAVY CROCKETT AS HE WAS PICTURED IN THE ALMANACS

rather sorry figure in the Congress." And the late Vernon Louis Parrington lists and describes four distinct species of the genus Crockett. It is possible, after watching Davy's story unfold in the newspapers, to go Parrington two better. There were, it seems, six Davy Crocketts.

This sounds fairly mysterious but is not really so. It is simply a way of saying that there was one real Crockett, and in addition there were five pictures of the man, all of them different and all labeled with his name. Any mystery about the matter disappears when you skim through the pieces written about him in newspapers and elsewhere, not bothering too much with statistics, simply noticing the different ways the backwoodsman is pictured.

Of course, the Crockett, the flesh-and-blood being who was born in Tennessee, who married, had children, and went to Congress, was the real article. People who saw him with their own eyes—more than six feet tall, broad shouldered, red cheeked, black haired, dressed in buckskin—had no difficulty in believing that he was not an impalpable spirit. An old gaffer who had heard him speak at a barbecue in the Big Hatchie district in the late twenties had no doubts, two score years later, about having heard a speech which was "plain and sensible . . . . , with now and then a dry, witty allusion to his educated opponents, which would bring thunders of applause."

This Crockett puzzled none of the people who saw and heard him; but, shortly after he departed for Congress, newspaper wags began to print tales about him more fictional than factual. In other words, the reporters wove together fiction with facts about Davy and started quite a gallery of portraits.

It was a fiction of the time, for instance, that, just as all Scotchmen were stingy, all frontiersmen were both wonderful in their capacity for drink and boastful in their talk. Jokes were based on the idea that Westerners were so fond of liquor that they spent most of their waking hours bending their elbows. When they woke up each morning, said the stories, all had eye-openers; then they had phlegm-cutte and then they nursed mint juleps the rest of the day. A man who had nothing to drink until after eleven o'clock in the morning won the insulting frontier nickname of "an elevener." And, perhaps partly because they spent so much time swilling, partly because they were just naturally rambunctious, frontiersmen always introduced themselves to strangers (in stories) with a boast, perhaps like scores of such flapdoodle challenges printed here and there, perhaps like those in Nimrod Wildfire's story, as it was told in a jokebook published in Kentucky:

I was ridin along the Mississippi in my wagon, when I came acrost a feller floating down stream . . . . in the starn of his boat. . . . . Mister, says he, I can whip my weight in wild cats, and ride straight thro' a crab apple orchard on a flash of lightning. . . . . Says I, ain't I the yellow flower of the forest? And I'm all brimstone but the head, and that's aquafortis! . . . . My name is Nimrod Wildfire—half horse, half alligator, and a touch of the airthquake—that's got the prettiest sister, fastest horse, and ugliest dog in the district, and can out run, out jump, throw down, drag out and whip any man in all Kentuck!

Such a swap of remarks, in the lore of the day, conventionally preceded a fight.

Shortly after he became a national Congressman, several newspaper yarns showed Crockett behaving exactly like a jestbook frontiersman. In one about a stump speech, after saying he was a candidate, Davy went on:

Friends, fellow-citizens, brothers and sisters: Carroll is a statesman, Jackson is a hero, and Crockett is a *horse!!*

Friends, fellow-citizens, brothers and sisters: they accuse me of adultery, it's a lie—I never ran away with any man's wife, that was not willing, in my life. They accuse me of gambling, it's a lie—for I always plank down the cash.

Friends, fellow-citizens, brothers and sisters: they accuse me of being a drunkard, it's a d——d eternal lie—for whiskey can't make me drunk.

This story, of course, simply fits the Colonel into a joke pattern. It might easily have been cooked up by any wit who knew only two things—that Crockett was a frontiersman and that frontiersmen had a name for boasting and drinking. Another tale, supposedly in the words of the Tennesseean, told how, when he stopped at a tavern in Raleigh on his trip to Washington, he found a crowd of fellow-guests blocking his way to the hearth:

. . . . I was *rooting* my way 'long to the fire, not in a good humor, when some fellow staggered up towards me, and cried out, "Hurrah for Adams." Said I, "Stranger, you had better hurrah for hell, damn you, and praise your own country."

Said he, "And who are you?"

"I'm the same David Crockett, fresh from the backwoods, half horse, half alligator, a little touched with the snapping turtle—can wade the Mississippi, leap the Ohio, ride upon a streak of lightning, and slip without a scratch down a honey locust—can whip my weight in wildcats . . . . and whip any man opposed to Jackson."

While I was telling what I could do, the fellow's eyes kept getting larger and larger. . . . . I never saw fellows look as they all did. They cleared the fire for me, and when I got a little warm, I looked about, but my Adams man was gone.

The very wording shows that this is after the same model as the almanac story; and another version of the yarn is still closer to the original.

These stretchers about the Congressman make clear how, in the public prints of the day, caricatures were drawn of Crockett which showed a person very different from the real man. At first, probably, they were just tossed off for the fun of it, without any motive. But in time journalists awoke to the fact that invented anecdotes like these could be used for political purposes. That was the start of the multiplication of Crocketts—important because it showed many newspapermen what they could do by exploiting the American liking for homespun wisdom.

IV

Crockett went to Washington for the first time in 1827. At the time the followers of Andrew Jackson, another Tennesseean, were still growling about the way Congress had made Adams president instead of Jackson in 1824. The Jacksonites were going strong in a drive which was to carry Old Hickory into the White House in the next election.

The canebrake Congressman made himself known as an outspoken follower of Jackson soon after he reached the Capitol. As Miss Rourke, his best biographer, says:

He attracted attention at once. He . . . . became quickly known in Washington as the "coonskin congressman." No one at all like him had appeared in office; he aroused great curiosity. His tall figure was striking. His casual speech was often repeated because of its pithy center. Tall talk was easily attributed to him. . . . . Such stories [as the one about Davy in the tavern] were printed in many eastern newspapers of the time, and they all stressed Crockett's loyalty to Jackson.

Not being bothered by facts, the anti-Jackson papers naturally pictured Crockett as a low fellow, and the pro-Jackson papers, as a grand person. Stories in papers of both parties agreed on certain qualities of his—that he was uneducated, that he talked tall, that he was funny. But in anti-Jackson papers, because he had these traits, the man was pictured as a rambunctious clown of the canebrakes—and it was implied that Old Hickory, in the White House, would be just as awkward. Papers which supported Old Andy, on the other hand, showed the Congressman as a horse-sense backwoodsman, who used his boastful talk and his humor to put enemies in their places.

A good example is offered by two tales of how Davy, shortly after he went to Washington, dined with President Adams at the White House. An anti-Crockett reporter put into print this story (as he said he had heard it from the Congressman) about the affair:

I stepped into the President's house—thinks I, who's afraid? . . . . Says I, "Mr. Adams, I'm Mr. Crockett, from Tennessee." "So," says he . . . . and he shook me by the hand. . . . . I went to dinner, and walked around the long table, looking for something that I liked. At last I took my seat just beside a fat goose, and I helped myself to as much of it as I wanted. But I hadn't took three bites, when I looked way up the table at a man they called *Tash* [attaché]. He was talking French to a woman on t'other side of the table. He dodged his head and she dodged her's and then they got to drinking wine across the table. If they didn't I wish I may be shot. But when I looked back again, my plate was gone, goose and all. So I just cast my eyes down to t'other end of the table, and sure enough I seed a white man walking off with my plate. I says, "hello, mister, bring back my plate." He fetched it back in a hurry . . . . ; and . . . . how do you think it was? Licked as clean as my hand. If it wasn't I wish I may be shot. Says he, "What will you have, sir?" And says I, "You may well say that, after stealing my goose." And he began to laugh. . . . . Then says I, "Mister, laugh if you please; but I don't half like such tricks upon travellers. If I do I wish I may be shot." I then filled my plate with bacons and greens; and whenever I looked up or down the table, I held to my plate. . . . . When we were all done eating . . . . I saw a man coming 'long carrying a great glass thing . . . .

stuck full of little glass cups. . . . . Thinks I, let's taste them first. They were mighty sweet and good—so I took six of 'em. If I didn't I wish I may be shot.

The Representative from Tennessee was so riled by this caricature of him as a genial but stupid boor that he wrote to two of his friends who had been at the dinner, asking them to testify that it was "a slander." He wanted their word that it was perpetrated by "enemies, who would take much pleasure in magnifying the plain rusticity of my manners into the most unparalleled grossness and indelicacy." Congressmen Clark of Kentucky and Verplanck of New York quickly produced for the press testimonials that, as one of them said, his behavior at the dinner was "perfectly becoming and proper."

In the pro-Jackson papers of the time there appeared a different story about the same White House function, probably just as untrue as the slander which so irked the frontiersman. It was supposed to be an account, in the words of the Colonel, of a talk he had after the dinner, in the White House drawing-room, with the President's son. It told how this young aristocrat had tried to lead his guest on with questions about pastimes in the backwoods. "I know'd he wanted to have some fun at my expense," said uneducated but canny Crockett. So he strung out a yarn about the four classes of people living on the frontier. As he told about the first class, "the quality," he got in a little satirical dig at the President's son, who had been much criticized by the anti-administration press for bringing a billiard table into the President's mansion. This stratum of western society, he said, "have a table with some green truck on it, and it's got pockets, and they knock a ball about on it to get it in the pockets." Then, as he told about the other three classes, he stretched the truth more and more, until, he said, "the whole house was convulsed with laughter"—presumably at the expense of the dude who had foolishly tried to trick the backwoodsman. The tale had touches as indelicate as the one which so roused Crockett's ire; but there is no evidence that he was bothered by its untruth.

By contrast with the real Crockett, who was presumably created by God, the other Crocketts were created, then, by anti-Jackson papers and pro-Jackson papers, for political purposes. One of them was a westernized version of a fool character like that which Franklin had used to discredit, by his advocacy of them, the hateful policies of the British; the other was a westernized version of Poor Richard or of the rustics whose wisdom drawled in the almanacs. These propagandist versions of the frontiersman were just getting established when the real Davy did something which caused both sets of political journalists to bring out new canvases and start new pictures of him.

He changed sides—joined the anti-Jackson forces. In the period which lasted from January, 1829, when he went over, until 1836, when he died, newsmen who had been for him turned against him, and those who had attacked him earlier decided he was all right. So both groups proceeded to make up fresh sets of yarns accordingly.

The pro-Jackson papers, in this period, turned their old picture of Crockett—the picture of a bumptious but canny frontiersman—to the wall. In its place they hung a very different picture. The new portrait took some of its details from the earlier anti-Jackson portraits: it showed Davy, "the coon killer, the Jim Crow of Congressmen, the buffoon of the House of Representatives . . . . the authorized Whig jester." Thus the *New York Times*, in one vituperative editorial, spoke of him. The *Washington Globe* emphasized the man's grossness by ironically calling him "Dainty Davy."

But the Jacksonians added some new touches to the sketch, which made the backwoodsman not only stupid and clownish but also vicious. James K. Polk, for example, wrote for the Tennessee newspapers a series of five articles, signed "Several Voters," pieces so concocted that they seemed to come from Davy's constituents. They held that Crockett did not do his duty—that he had often missed House meetings, that he had done "literally nothing" for the poor people in his district. Further, they constantly stressed a point all the party newspapers were making—that the stupid Congressman had allowed himself to be bought and used as a tool. Similarly, the *Washington Globe*—the official Jackson organ —played up the way the opposition had signed up "mercenaries from every rank and class," with Crockett as the "first recruit." Many times they spoke of "David Crockett & Co.," using a phrase which gave the idea of organization on a commercial basis. Jackson, now in the president's chair, in his correspondence, stormed at his enemies and "crockett their tool" and frequently used the "Crockett & Co." label.

The anti-Jacksonites in turn set up a picture akin to that their rivals had once drawn but with the earlier suggestion of their subject's shrewdness greatly amplified. He now became a homespun oracle, outraged by the horrible carryings-on of the party in power and able to attack them with telling digs because he was so blessed with horse sense. Aphorisms headed "Crockett's Latest"—shrewd japes at the Jackson crowd—came out in many newspapers.

Hand in hand with the campaign to show that Davy was wise went a drive to show that, contrary to reports (some of which the anti-Jacksonites themselves had started) that he was a wild and woolly Westerner, he was a normal gentleman. A "respectable gentleman of Tennessee" wrote the *Jacksonville Banner:*

I apprehend very many have entertained erroneous opinions of the character of Col. Crockett. He is indeed a specimen of the frontier character, but a very favorable specimen. He is an honest, independent, intelligent man, with strong and highly marked traits of originality, which renders him very interesting and agreeable. . . . .

The *Philadelphia Courier*, in a story about the Colonel when he stopped off in Philadelphia, wanted readers to know that he was dressed like other men—"in dark clothes," Byronic collar, and white hat. He went from Columbia, said the *Columbia Spy*, "leaving persons who expected to see a wild man of the woods, clothed in a hunting shirt and covered with hair, a good deal surprised at having viewed a respectable-looking personage, dressed decently, and wearing his locks much after the fashion of our plain German farmers." An Elizabethtown, Kentucky, newspaper, in its report of "the Hon. David Crockett's" visit, took up the refrain:

Many conjectures were afloat relative to his personal appearance: some supposed that he would not appear as a very man, but . . . . would assume the form of some comical or hideous monster. It is needless to say that such were disappointed [in their expectations]. He seemed to us to resemble very much the appearance of other great men—shrewd, intelligent, and graceful; with a commanding, lofty aspect, and a dignified, manly countenance.

Late in 1833, the Congressman from Tennessee sent to the newspapers an announcement. He was very angry, it said, about the way he had been misrepresented in a book which had brought together many newspaper stories about him. He was therefore going to write an autobiography, to "strive to represent myself, as I really am, *a plain, blunt, Western man*, relying on honesty and the woods, and not on learning and the law, for a living." In February, 1834, he had his Preface ready, and it, too, was sent to the papers. It repeated the charge that people had been so misled by portrayals of him that they had "expressed the most profound astonishment at finding me in human shape, and with the *countenance, appearance*, and *common feelings* of a human being. It is to correct all these false notions, and to do justice to myself, that I have written." When the book, *A Narrative of the Life of David Crockett*, came out, the *Boston Transcript* said:

This is the Simon Pure edition, which the Hon. Member from Tennessee felt compelled to write and publish, to protect his extensive reputation . . . . from the roguish wags of the Capitol, who described the adventures of the gallant Colonel in so many ways that he hardly knew himself.

The piece makes clear that the *Narrative* was part of the campaign of the anti-Jackson forces to show Davy was a normal man, very worthy of respect. This "plain, homespun account," as it is called in the Preface, was, in other words, a full-length portrait of the Crockett who had been drawn in friendly newspapers. The same politically useful character appears not only in the *Narrative* but also in *An Account of Col. Crockett's Tour in the North and Down East*, published in Philadelphia in 1835. Here is a blunt, honest man, pathetically lied about by enemies—a man so chock-full, however, of mother-wit and humor that he can laughably state the obvious case against his rivals in politics.

Many times the author of the *Narrative* makes his autobiographical account a springboard for political arguments.

In chapter vi, for example, the Colonel stops his story of
how, when he had fought under Jackson against the Indians, he had rebelled against orders, to draw forced parallels between the past situation and the contemporary rebel-
lion against Jackson's unreasonable bank policy. Or, in
chapter ix, Crockett tells how, when he almost died, "I
might easily have been mistaken for one of the [President's]
Kitchen Cabinet, I looked so much like a ghost." The very
end of the book underlines Crockett's political independence:

> Look at my arms, you will find no party hand-cuff on them! Look at
> my neck, you will not find there any collar, with the engraving

> MY DOG
>
> ANDREW JACKSON

The *Tour* tells about a trip the Westerner took during the
spring of 1834 through the cities of the Northeast under the
auspices of the anti-Jacksonites, speaking at each stop to
huge crowds who shared his political views. Many pages are
taken up with speeches in which certain notes are struck
again and again: "I am a plain, uneducated backwoodsman, and find some embarrassment in making an appropriate speech to such an intelligent audience as that in
————. . . . . I am from the far West, and have made but
little pretensions of understanding the government, but one
thing I know. . . ." This beginning, synthesized from two
speeches, is a typical one.

Crockett's partisans, of course, asked readers to believe
that the Crockett shown in these two books was the real

article. "Veracity," said one newspaper firmly, "is stamped on every page." But the matter is open to doubt. Like a Huey Long or a Maury Maverick of today, the public figure of the man is so well fitted to politics that one suspects that the character is at least partly assumed. In fact, anyone looking for the originator of the tradition of the "just folks" politician in America will do well to study the case of the Coonskin Congressman.

And all the credit, in the end, will not go to Davy, since both books clearly were touched up by collaborators (both of whom have been identified) who wanted to make the writings politically useful. An inevitable result is that wherever, almost, you look for the real Crockett you are baffled. Go to the congressional records of the time, and you will find speeches which obviously were doctored up before they were printed. Get hold of the letters written in the Colonel's own hand, and you will find, first, that they justify the suspicion that his other writings have been thoroughly edited and, next, that they do not offer any sure basis for guessing at his character.

V

Hence, as I have said, historians have difficulty in dealing with Crockett's life. Very good historians can dig into the documents and come up with bewilderingly different findings. "Restless, assertive, unsocial, ... obsessed with the faith that better land lay farther west, cultivating a bumptious wit . . . . ," says one, "he was only an improvident child who fled instinctively from civilization." He was "the incipient poor white," says another, with "the elements of decay in him." Another finds that he was a brave hunter, an efficient farmer, a far-seeing legislator, and a heroic warrior. Still another cannot explain him except as a split personality.

If competent modern historians, sifting the evidence, have such a time of it, we may be sure that the people of Davy's day had even a worse. Here were a whole batch of pictures of the man, all of them very different. They were different, of course, because the writers of the day—apparently without the help of Franklin—had hit upon the greatest of all tricks for swaying American opinion—the appeal to common sense. From now on canny politicians as well as writers for a huge public were to take complete advantage of this appeal. The writers had depended upon the American love of gumption, had expected horse-sense readers to turn against Davy when he was shown as a clown, to back him when he was pictured as a log-cabin prophet. But the people were too pawky to be misled permanently by such journalistic tricks. What it appears they sensed, finally, was that the Crocketts in print were a mess of contradictions. So they painted their own picture of the man—a picture which did not look so messy to them—and chose to forget the other pictures.

An Englishman, Captain R. G. A. Levinge, traveling through Kentucky about a decade after the Tennesseean's heroic death at the Alamo, learned there about the Crockett who was to be immortal. He said:

Everything here is Davy Crockett. . . . . His voice was so loud that it could not be described—it was obliged to be drawn as a picture. He took hailstones for "Life Pills" when he was unwell—he . . . . fanned himself with a hurricane. . . . . He had a farm, which was so rocky, that, when they planted corn, they were obliged to shoot the grains into the crevices with muskets. . . . . He could . . . . drink the Mississippi dry—shoot six cords of bear in one day. . . . .

This was the lasting Crockett, the mythical demigod whose fantastic life-history as it was unfolded in the almanacs was sketched at the beginning of this chapter.

This Crockett had little or no political value, and the happenings in his comic career jumped from the green earth into a backwoods fairyland. Is it possible to think of this rider of thunderbolts as a natural product of minds that worshiped gumption? I believe that this hero of frontier fantasy is such a product, in two ways.

First, these yarns originated by fireside tale-tellers or written down to be enjoyed by fireside readers are escape literature of a kind likely to be peculiarly attractive to farmers and woodsmen. Their demigod hero, in a way, is less notable for his tremendous abilities than he is for his limitations. Another demigod might have used his superhuman powers to create a great symphony, a great work of art, or a great epic; he might have set up a perfect system of government under which all men were free and happy; he might have enlarged human knowledge—but not Davy. The nonsense about Davy showed him licking with ridiculous ease the stubborn physical world with which frontier folk had to battle by means of common sense. Sickness, rocky farm land, cold, rambunctious neighbors, Indians, and varmints —the pests of the common-sense world—were the effortless conquests of this campfire creation. Even the fantasies of frontier folk, in other words, were given practical chores to perform.

In the second place, the picture of this mythical Crockett was a horse-sense victory over the jangling details in all the different cartoons. As folklorists would say, it was a "rationalization"—it made a "rational" story about Crockett by winnowing away a host of contradictions in the pieces about him. The one interesting quality of character which turned up in all the newspaper skits—the one element of consistency —was the mythical element. The boasts of Davy in any of the stories, "whiskey can't make me drunk; I can wade the Mississippi, leap the Ohio, ride upon a streak of lightning," and so forth, were talk fitting for a superhuman being. Regardless of his political tie-up, Crockett showed his wisdom or his clownishness partly by making similar boasts. Even the *Narrative*, Crockett's official autobiography, used ways of talking more fitting for a creature of fantasy than for a common man—a man (to quote his own words) whose "love was so hot it nigh to burst my bilers"; who—if his sweetheart accepted him, "would . . . . fight a whole regiment of wild cats"; who got "so mad that I was burning inside like a tarkiln, and I wondered that the smoke hadn't been pouring out of me at all points." Other phrases in the book told about strange critters the coonhunter encountered—critters more at home in fantasy than in actuality. The Westerner told, for instance, how he met a woman "as ugly as a stone fence . . . . so homely that it almost gave me a pain in the eyes to look at her"; how he spied "a little woman streaking along through the woods like all wrath" or a bear so big that "he looked like a large black bull."

What the people did, then, was make Davy's boasts come true—carry him to the kind of imaginary world which went well with the kind of beasts and people his tall talk described. Temporary things such as changing political ties vanished, but the one abiding element—strangeness—remained. As early as 1832, the legend-makers had begun to develop this lasting version of their hero. The apotheosis was suggested in a news story, widely reprinted, which read:

APPOINTMENT BY THE PRESIDENT.—David Crockett, of Tennessee, to stand on the Allegheny Mountains and catch the Comet, on its approach to the earth, and wring off its tail, to keep it from burning up the world!

The *Narrative* was written not only as a protest against political misrepresentation but also as an antidote to the legendary picture already being sketched. Ironically, it stimulated legends: the women, for example, whom Davy had dismissed in a few phrases in the book, were given complete life-histories in the almanac tales. There they were fit companions of Demigod David; they wore hornets' nests garnished with eagle feathers for Sunday bonnets; they could wade the Mississippi without wetting their shifts; they could outscream a catamount or jump over their own shadows.

The folk mind, in short, refusing to be misled by the political propaganda draped around Crockett, in time made known the People's Choice for immortality—the only consistent character it could find in a stack of contradictory portraits. And today, if you get far enough away from paved roads and roadside pop-stands in Tennessee and Kentucky and sit by the fire with backwoods yarn-spinners, you will learn that this Crockett, somewhere or other, is still carrying out his boasts in superhuman ways.

CHAPTER III

Jack Downing—Common Sense in Imagination

We have a rule here that "all just government derives its powers from the consent of the governed." So, if we've got to look round and govern the world, hadn't we ought to get the world's consent first? And, as you want to take hold of Russia first, I s'pose she is the first one we ought to ask consent of. And if the Russian will consent that we shall hold him back, we'll hold him back and run the risk of it.

—Major Jack Downing, Downingville, Maine

I

TODAY a pen-and-ink artist who wants to picture in a cartoon a figure standing for the American people has no trouble: he simply draws a symbol everyone will recognize—Uncle Sam. But a hundred years ago or so, before Uncle Sam had become such a stand-by, the cartoonist would have used a figure better known at the time—the pawky, impudent Yankee, Jack Downing. If it is mentioned that Downing wore a high hat, a bat-wing collar, a swallowtail coat, and striped trousers, it will be clear that even when, in time, Uncle Sam took the Yankee's place, the old man turned out to be Jack himself dressed in Jack's old clothes but wearing a white goatee. Downing made such a hit with the people of his period, partly because he showed new uses for the homespun character, partly because he was so embroiled in the stormy national fights of the days of Andrew Jackson.

A year after Davy Crockett went to Washington, the people of the United States elected Jackson their first president. There had been presidents before, of course, but the people themselves—by their own votes—had never before this really had a chance to decide who would live in the White House.

Jackson, like Davy Crockett, was from the Tennessee frontier; Davy had fought Indians with him. His nickname, "Old Hickory," showed that he had lived the kind of a life that made him the idol of Westerners. Tall, red haired, fiery tempered, in his youth he had given more than he had taken in fist fights and in duels. He had led the hunters of old Kentucky in the Battle of New Orleans. Later he had been an honest and brave statesman. The people remembered this story of Jackson's life at election time and were pleased to think it showed he was one of them. They remembered too, probably, the uncanny gift the old soldier had for putting their exact ideas into words. No American statesman before Lincoln had a brain which worked more in harmony with the common sense of the people than did Andy's. So, when the people had a chance to speak, they voted Jackson into the presidency.

March 4, 1829, he walked over from Gadsby's Hotel to take the oath of office on the rotunda of the Capitol. His mop of hair was no longer red: time and worry had turned it white. He was a wrinkled old man with deep-set eyes, and his wife's recent death had made him look even older than he was. Lean, towering, carrying himself like a soldier, he delivered his address and then repeated the words of the Chief Justice while the great crowd listened in respectful silence.

Soon after the speech ended, a celebration started, the like of which Washington had never seen before. Jackson was the people's man, and the people had turned out to welcome him. The city was crowded with men, women, and children—farmers, mechanics, and frontiersmen. They set up a thundering howl and surged toward the flag-draped table on the rotunda. Jackson had to fight his way through them to get to his horse. When he rode to the White House, they cheered again and pushed after him. Finally, they fought their way to the White House, where they behaved in a way that nauseated the old fogies who saw them.

One-horse-town politicians, buckskin-clad hunters, farmers and mechanics in linsey-woolsey, poor whites, mulattoes, and Negroes in rags jammed the doors and bulged through the windows. As soon as waiters came into the room, thirsty celebrators grabbed all the glasses of orange punch off their trays. Black eyes and bloody noses were passed around impartially. Men in muddy boots stood on satin-covered chairs. Women fainted. When news spread that tubs full of punch had been set on the lawn, clots of the crowd eddied from the doors and rushed for them. Groaned a conservative judge: "The reign of King Mob seemed triumphant."

When, in time, the mob went away, Old Hickory paced the floor, his battered corncob pipe trailing smoke behind it, and talked with his friends about organizing his administration. Ready to help him in Washington was an unusual group of advisers—a "Kitchen Cabinet," as it was called. From the very beginning of his presidency, knowing that these unofficial aides to the President had much to say about his policies, his enemies did not fail to make an issue of them. They did their best to pump up the suspicion of the voters that there was something villainous about these hangers-on helping the President.

There was much talk of such Kitchen Cabinet men as Amos Kendall, Major William B. Lewis, and Isaac Hill. A visiting Englishwoman heard a great deal about Kendall, in a minor government job, but, she said, "The moving spring of the Administration; the thinker, the planner, the doer; but all in the dark." The prematurely white-haired, sallow-faced man was the ghost writer of the President and the party. Major Lewis was an old friend of Jackson, who moved into the White House with him, visiting the President's apartments whenever he felt like it, even when the old man had his nightcap on. He talked with Jackson as man to man; and he had at his fingertips data about all the men important in the politics of the day. Little Isaac Hill had risen above lameness, poverty, and a lack of formal education, to a Kitchen Cabinet post: all his pent-up venom made him a driving force against the enemies of Old Hickory.

In both the official cabinet and the Kitchen Cabinet was Martin Van Buren, so crafty a politician that he was nicknamed the "Little Magician." A tiny, bald-headed man with fuzzy sideburns and a perpetually beaming smile, he worked in suave ways for his chief. Many a night Jackson and he sat around in their shirt sleeves, puffing pipe smoke and deciding on party policies. Old Hickory scouted the suggestion that this adviser was slippery, feeling that "Van" used the same way of solving problems as the President himself—just plain gumption. "I say to you frankly," Andy told

a senator, "that Van Buren is . . . . a true man with no guile.
It is said that he is a great magician—I believe it, but his
only wand is common good sense which he uses for the benefit
of his country." People in every section knew that Van was
Jackson's right-hand man, chopping off heads, hiring office-
seekers, snaking bills through Congress. They knew, too, before long, that Andy had decided he wanted Little Van to
follow him as president.

II

During Jackson's second year in office this political setup
and all the comedy it provided got into a series of letters,
written in farmer lingo and signed with the name of Jack
Downing. They came out in newspapers all over the country. According to these letters, Jack was a Yankee hayseed
who had footed it from Portland, Maine, to Washington to
try to land a political job. The President had taken a liking
to him and had made him an unofficial adviser, and now
Jack was blabbing the news about hilarious happenings in
the Kitchen Cabinet. Chuckling readers knew that there
was really no such person as Downing—that some clever
humorist had invented him as a mouthpiece for amusing
satire on politics and politicians. No one, of course, supposed that the letters were anything more than a passing
fad—no one guessed that Jack had started something in
American humor which was going to last for more than a
hundred years.

Certainly Jack's creator, Seba Smith, had not cared a
tinker's dam about fame when, in 1830, he had begun writing the Downing letters. He had been much more interested in such a simple thing as bread and butter. He was in
Portland, it was midwinter, and the little newspaper he had

hopefully started about three months before was dying of
poor circulation. From the start Smith's *Portland Courier* had
had to fight for its life. It was a daily paper in a time when
most newspapers were weeklies; and, furthermore, Smith, a
good-natured man who was made uneasy by bitter arguments, was putting out a nonpartisan sheet, even though he
knew Maine people were partial to cantankerous political
journals. Three months had used up nearly all the money
Smith could sink, and the editor scowled and tried to figure
out a way of keeping his sheet alive.

Looking at other papers, he saw that most of them were
holding readers by doing something he had decided not to
do—printing hot and furious pieces on politics. The Maine
legislature in Portland was carrying on in a way which had
inspired a squabble not only in Maine but also in the rest of
New England. The trouble was that the two parties were
almost evenly balanced, and the equally divided representatives were destined to lash out at one another six whole
weeks before they could organize and get down to the business of passing laws.

Smith saw that he would have to take advantage of the
wide interest in this squabble if he was to catch new readers.
How could he do this without taking sides? Maybe he remembered how Franklin had made up characters who spoke
for him. It is possible that he called to mind some of the
farmer talk in the almanacs of the day or some of Davy
Crockett's yarns in the newspapers. Or perhaps he happened to recollect how a New York man, a few years before,
had written some funny letters signed "Jo Strickland,"
which had shown up a rumpus in the New York state legislature. Somehow, at any rate, he hit on a plan which he was
later to tell about in these words:

. . . . the author . . . . , wishing to show the ridiculous position of the legislature in its true light, and also, by something out of the common track of newspaper writing, to give increased interest and popularity to his little daily paper, bethought himself of the plan to bring a green, unsophisticated lad from the country into town with a load of axe-handles, hoop-poles, and other notions for sale, and while waiting the movements of a rather dull market, let him blunder into the halls of the legislature, and after witnessing for some days their strange doings, sit down and write an account of them to his friends at home in his own plain language.

The first Down East letter and the others that followed it during a period of several years were such a hit that the wolf which had been growling on the doorstep of the *Courier* office slunk away unfed. New England readers enjoyed the sharp digs at both parties in the legislature, because, like Smith, they had enough humor to see funny aspects of the situation. Also they knew their Yankees, and they saw that these pieces were the real thing. Old Preacher Ezra Ripley in Concord, Massachusetts, went so far as to believe that Jack was a real flesh-and-blood man who told the gospel truth. His wise son-in-law, Ralph Waldo Emerson, tried to argue him out of the idea but had no luck at all.

The editor who saved his paper in this way had been lucky in his background—an earlier life which had given him better than average training for writing Yankee stuff. He had been born and brought up among the rustics of New England, hearing their racy speech whenever he listened to talk. He had known the Yankees inside as well as outside, because he had been one of them. Then he had gone to a New England college, he had traveled away down South into the slave states—and he had gained the insight into Yankee character that came from looking at his neighbors from a distance.

So when Smith sat down to write the letters he had planned, he had a good idea of the way a Yankee's brain would work and the way he would express himself. In the back of Smith's mind were vivid memories of the little town of Turner, Maine, where he had lived in boyhood—how it rested in a green valley with rugged hills to the east and west and Sandybottom Pond to the south, how the schoolhouse, the cobbler's shop, the tavern, and the blacksmith-shop stood along the tree-shaded main street. It was easy, therefore, for him to imagine how Jack Downing, a young man from a village just like that one, Downingville, would write to the folks back home.

The Downing skits showed what a writer of talent could do to improve on the shadowy rustics of the almanacs or even on the lopsided pictures political reporters had drawn of Crockett. Jack wore shoes covered with the mud of Downingville, and references to places and people of that village kept cropping up in the thoughts he expressed. His kinsfolk, some of whom wrote letters to Jack which came out in the *Courier*, had individual quirks that made them recognizable human beings. Nobody had any difficulty about believing in Grandpa Downing, who limped around telling everyone who would listen how he had won the Revolution. Jack's soft-spoken, hard-working father was just as convincing. So was Uncle Joshua, "a clear shirk," who "never would work if he could help it" but who read the papers and "knew more about politics than any other man in Downingville." Violent-tempered Cousin Nabby and Mother Downing, who, right after the honeymoon, went "snooping" at the homes of new brides to see how they kept house, were equally believable, as were dozens of others in the letters.

Because he had such a solid background and because he was a member of such a human family, even though he was imaginary, Jack seemed more real than the less definitely attached Davy Crockett.

He seemed more real, too, because he was not so much of a cartoon figure as Davy had been in the newspaper stories which prejudiced journalists had written. In those stories, if they were written by Davy's enemies, Davy had been ignorant and therefore a fool; if they were written by Davy's friends, he had been self-educated and therefore blessed with more mother-wit than a man was who had been "spiled by book larnin." Morally, depending on the purpose of the newspaperman who wrote about him, Davy had been either jet-black or pure white, a lying rascal or a good honest man. Smith was neither for nor against Jack Downing: he merely used him because the hayseed had a mind which would emphasize funny details in happenings when he told about them. So Jack, in the letters, sometimes showed himself up as a fool, but sometimes, thanks to his shrewdness, he cut through piffle to the heart of truth. And, like most men, he was neither an angel nor a devil but a mixture of both, quaint and human and lovable.

All this made Jack appealing. He was interesting, too, because Smith finally made him get into a series of adventures more comic than those Davy managed to have in politics. Jack had the jump on the Coonskin Congressman, because the amusing things that could happen to him were limited only by Smith's imagination, and Smith had a lively fancy.

That fancy really got going when Jack, having said all he could about the Maine legislature, heard that there were

SEBA SMITH'S JACK DOWNING SITS AND TALKS FAMILIARLY WITH
JACKSON IN THE WHITE HOUSE

some juicy political jobs in Washington and decided to try for one. "I see Gineral Jackson was getting into trouble," was the way he unselfishly put it, "and I footed it to Washington to give him a lift." The trip across country took so long that when travel-tattered Jack reached the Capitol the jobs were all gone. But the Yankee was able to write home that Old Hickory and he hit it off with each other from the start and were as close as two peas in a pod. Soon Downing was in a better place than Davy Crockett ever had been to "tell the low-down" on high life in Washington. With Kendall, Lewis, Hill, and Little Van, he was in the Kitchen Cabinet.

The President was embroiled in the battle against the National Bank, and Jack pitched in to help, telling everything the "Gineral" had to say about the rumpus. South Carolina got sulky and threatened to pull out of the Union. In a summary of his heroic career, Jack told how he helped:

I brought my old company of Downingville militia to Washington, under the command of Cousin Sargent Joel, and kept 'em there, with their guns all loaded, till the danger was over. And I used to go up top of the Congress House every day, and keep watch, and listen off toward South Carolina, so as to be ready, the first moment nullification bust up there, to order Sargent Joel to march and fire. The Gineral always said the spunk I showed was what cowed nullification down so quick, and he always felt very grateful to me for it.

Naturally—if you believed what Downing said in his letters—the President loved his Yankee pal even more after such bravery in battle; and naturally when he started a grand tour around the country in 1832, he had to have Downing with him. Jack, always helpful, was particularly so in Philadelphia. Though poor old Jackson had been trotting around to see the sights, wining and dining at every stop, shaking thousands of hands, as soon as he got to the Quaker City, the wobbly-legged executive, Downing said, was pulled into a hall "as big as a meeting-house," with a great mob of people lined up to shake his hand:

The President shook hands with all his might . . . . till he got so tired he couldn't hardly stand it. I took hold and shook for him once in a while to help him along, but at last he got so tired he had to lay down on a soft bench covered with cloth and shake as well as he could, and when he couldn't shake he'd nod to 'em as they come along. Then I kind of stood behind him and reached my arm round under his, and shook for him about a half an hour as tight as I could spring. Then we concluded it was best to adjourn for to-day.

When Harvard planned to give the President an honorary degree and the "Gineral" wondered what he ought to do if professors spouted Latin at him, he consulted his friend and got good advice.

I told him my way, when anybody talked to me in a lingo that I didn't understand, was jest to say nothing, but look as knowing as any of 'em. At that the Gineral fetched me a slap on my shoulder, and haw-hawed right out. Says he, Major Downing, you are the boy for me; I don't know how I should get along in this world if it wasn't for you.

And when the party went back to Washington, Jack kept on helping the President.

The letters told about these things, and they also gave shirt-sleeved pictures of men clustered around Old Andy. Lewis and Kendall, for example, were shown getting peeved when someone told the President to shake hands with Federalists. They "hop right up as mad as march hairs, and tell him if he shakes hands with a single federalist . . . . the democratic party will be ruined." Or Jack told how Van Buren became jealous when Downing got more cheers on the tour than he did—how he turned "as red as a blaze of fire" and snorted that "it was a fine time of day if a raw jockey from an obscure village away down east, jest because he had a Major commission, was going to throw [him,] the Vice President of the United States . . . . into the back ground." Jack told how he got back on the Magician:

At this my dander began to rise, and I stood right up to him; and says I, Mr. Van Buren . . . . if you'll go to Downingville and stand up before my company with Sergeant Joel at their head, and call Downingville an obscure village, I'll let you use my head for a football as long as you live afterwards. For if they don't blow you into a thousand atoms, I'll never guess again.

III

It is hard today to realize what a thrill such breezy pieces gave people in the 1830's, because the trick has since been repeated too often. It was a time when the presidency still had an odor of sanctity about it—something like kingship—when most writing about politics was couched in a high-toned, fancy style, as if they were by editorialists hell-bent on squeezing every common phrase out of their elephantine sentences. In Smith's papers the President was a man with his boots off, who smoked a corncob pipe and shook with rage or laughter. The Chief Executive and Jack put their stockinged feet on the same White House table, while the Down East man talked as freely as he would to a farmer fishing for pickerel with him. The style of the pieces was as homely—and as snappy—as a cold mug of hard cider. Readers delighted in the audacity, the unconventionality, of it.

Jackson proved that his sense of humor was that of the people by laughing at the pieces even as he lay on his sick-bed in a Boston hotel. When an aide read aloud Jack's story of the way he had shaken hands for Andy in Philadelphia, the President cackled and credited the Little Magician with its writing. "Depend upon it," he said gleefully, "Jack Downing is only Van Buren in masquerade."

It was astonishing how many times people paid tribute to Downing by nominating him for office or voting for him in real elections. Some Maine state legislators cast their good votes to make him speaker pro tem and major general. Some of the people of Portland gave him votes for mayor. Ballots for him were counted all over New Hampshire when the state elected a governor, and one town went unanimously for him. Newspapers were always saying he was the man for some office or other—some put him up for governor and quite a few came out for him as president. More than one considered that a ticket with him for president and Crockett for vice-president would be hard to beat. And newspapers everywhere in the East were glad to reprint Downing letters. Sometimes, instead of shouting the news, newsboys would yell that their sheet had a new Downing piece that day.

Quite often, newspapers would put out items about the man as if he were not an imagined but a real character. "APPOINTMENT BY THE PRESIDENT" was a headline over one story that said Jack had just been promoted from the rank of major to that of colonel in the army. Another headline read "MARRIAGE EXTRAORDINARY"; it was above a piece saying that Jack had done something handsome for the President. He explained that "on his eastern tour the President requested him to *sleep* for him, to save time, and following the hint, he had now got *married for him*." Or there was a story in the *Boston Transcript* which sounded pretty much as if the writer had taken hints from the tall yarns about Davy Crockett then going the rounds:

MAJOR DOWNING

We understand that Major Jack Downing arrived in this city, on Friday morning, and took lodgings at the Exchange Coffee House. He called for three beds, four warmingpans, and two boot-jacks.

He has been visited by several distinguished strangers, now in the city. Among the number we observe the Marquis of Snooks, Col. Pluck, &c. The Major is very abstemious in his eating. He diets on green turtle soup, beefsteak, oyster sauce, broiled chickens, currant jelly, plum puddings, pies, and "such like."

He says, he has been troubled with a sort of Nullification in his digestive system, and is obliged to lessen the number of mint juleps before breakfast, stick more to gin cock-tails, as the weather is pesky sight colder here than in Washington. He intends leaving Boston for Downingville tomorrow, in three carriages, to prepare for the reception of the President, who has kindly accepted his invitation to remain a few days with him, at his residence, on his visit to the eastward.

Smith would every now and then make Jack, like any public man, deny untrue news stories about himself. But such stories, as a matter of fact, were good evidence that Jack was still a first-rate meal ticket. Plays about the Major on the New York stage and a Jack Downing songbook also showed his popularity.

IV

There was one result of the Major's popularity, however, that Smith did not like so well. As his articles were reprinted everywhere throughout the country, several people who enjoyed them decided to have a try at writing Downing letters themselves. They would recall whatever Yankee phrases they knew and use them in letters about local or national politics, sometimes getting weird results. But, whether the results were weird or not, the proud authors would sign Jack's name or the name of a kinsman to them and send them off to be printed. Scores of these fake letters Smith came upon in exchange copies of newspapers.

Though such hit-and-miss imitations were irritating, Smith held his peace about them. But when in June, 1833, the *New York Daily Advertiser* started to use a whole series of letters which Smith had not fathered, the original Jack Downing began to growl about rascally "fellers . . . . worse than the pickpockets . . . . that's got to writing letters and putting my name to 'em, and sending of 'em to the printers." He quoted Shakespeare to the effect that "he that steals my name ought to have his head broke."

But the New York man went on pouring out his imitation letters. Over the name of Downing he claimed that *he* was the Downing who had been put up for president, that *he* was the author of the original papers, and that he was now doing better stuff for an intelligent New York audience. He sent a contemptuous letter to the editor of the *Courier* saying that writing "juvenile productions" for that paper was all right for a starter, but he had moved up in the world and was through with puny little Portland: "It was jest like go into market—you know what suits Portland won't suit New York; hogs' lard will do for one, but the other won't take nothing but fresh butter to fry their fish with." To top it all, he hinted that he might get his letters (and Smith's) out in book form before Smith could, pocketing all the royalties. Smith hurried to get a book of his stuff published, winning out over his sassy rival by about three months.

In the days when two sets of Downing letters were coming out, many readers had no idea that each set was by a different man. The New York pirate had stolen not only the name of the farmer-author but also the village of Downingville and all the folks there: he kept referring back to "his" early letters in the *Courier*. He signed his pieces "J. Downing, Major" instead of "Jack Downing," but, naturally, few noticed the difference. Newspapers, as quick to use the counterfeits as they were the originals, featured "J." or "Jack" indiscriminately.

Who was this high-handed thief? Smith learned his name in time, but he probably never learned the worst about him. He was Charles Augustus Davis, a man who was as near to being a Yankee as a swan is to being a goose. He had been born not in New England but in New Jersey, so his knowledge of Down Easters was probably quite theoretical. Any acquaintance he had with a hayfield must have been a passing one; he had taken up with commerce in New York City as a partner in the firm of Davis and Brooks, shipping and commission merchants. Possibly he had never been at a quilting bee or a cornhusking—a ball at Saratoga Springs or at the home of Mrs. Breevort or a banquet with rich Philip Hone or Merchant-Prince Aspinwall was much more his style.

Before the 1830's his interests in literature had been those of a dabbler who enjoyed the charming company of the choicer spirits who wrote. A member of exclusive literary clubs which specialized in wining, dining, and bright talk, he was fond of writers like traveled Washington Irving and polished Fitz-Greene Halleck. If his taste in books was the same as his taste in authors, he avoided low, homespun stuff and enjoyed poems or essays which had grace, gentility, and an English flavor.

How did this elegant gentleman happen to stoop to writing slapstick letters in the language (as near as he could learn it by his reading) of a sweat-stained hay-pitcher? If Smith had known all the answers to this question, he might have put Davis on a very uncomfortable spot.

The New York businessman was a staunch conservative, down on Old Hickory and his plebeian party. In 1831 he took a prominent part in a convention which met in New York to pulverize Jackson's tariff policy. John Quincy Adams, who, on being replaced by Andy in the presidency, had showed bitter anger by sulking like a spoiled child, was Davis' close acquaintance. But, what was more important, Davis was hand in glove with Nicholas Biddle, and that fact, if he had known it, could have provided Smith with some flashing and noisy fireworks. For, even in the 1830's, when no one in America was very suspicious of capitalists, pro-Jackson newspapers had an easy time drawing Biddle as a villain and getting people to hiss at "Czar Nicholas," as they called him.

The son of an old Philadelphia family, Biddle had been a precocious child, admitted to a university at ten, ready to graduate by the time he was thirteen. Not only was he book-learned enough to floor dons in Cambridge university in an argument about philology; in addition he was widely traveled and well trained in diplomacy and law. As a writer, he was versatile enough to write essays for a literary magazine, a memoir, an account of the Lewis and Clark expedition, and a heavy tome on international exchange. In the Pennsylvania legislature at twenty-four, he began immediately to outtalk older men in political arguments. At thirty-seven, he was the head of the most important financial concern in the country, the United States Bank, the government's fiscal agent and a chartered monopoly—the cock of the American financial walk.

Like many people handicapped by a precocious child-hood, Biddle, a curly-haired young man with a round boy-like face, liked to have his own way. When he was crossed, he lost his temper—even when the man who crossed him was Andy Jackson, who had a flaring temper of his own. In 1831 these two stubborn men got into a fierce battle, which shook the whole country and, before it was finished, started a financial panic. Davis and his J. Downing papers were part of Biddle's campaign against Jackson's bank policy.

Jackson acted against the United States Bank because he did not like banks in general, because—like many an inde-pendent Westerner—he hated a monopoly such as the bank had, and because his opponents defied him to fight them. He vetoed a bill to recharter the United States Bank and wrote a strong message explaining his act—a message which went straight to the heart of the people, voicing, among other things, the great American belief that every man had enough gumption to make his own decisions: "Each officer who takes an oath to support the Constitution swears that he will support it as he understands it, and not as it is under-stood by others." Biddle liked the old man's fighting talk. He wrote:

As to the veto message, I am delighted with it. It has all the fury of the unchained panther, biting the bars of his cage. It is really a manifesto of anarchy, such as Marat and Robespierre might have issued to the mob . . . . ; and my hope is that it will contribute to relieve the country from the domination of these miserable people [the Jacksonites].

With all his might and much of his money, Biddle fought Jackson on the issue of the bank when the old warrior ran for re-election in 1832. The bank man was quick to help needy politicians who might be useful on his side, and he was glad to give hard cash to newspapers which would help spread what he called "the facts" about the bank. But Kendall and others in the Kitchen Cabinet, political Big Berthas who made the Biddle crowd sound like popguns, shot out propaganda aimed squarely at the rank and file, scoring hit after hit. Great political meetings whipped mobs into storms of hate against Czar Nick and his "Soul-less Corporation." When the returns came in, Jackson was the winner, hands down. He set his lean jaw and started to make plans to cripple the bank by withdrawing government money from it for deposit elsewhere.

It was at this point that Davis, probably with the blessing and perhaps with the advice of Biddle, started to make humble Major Downing a mouthpiece for the financier. The head of the bank evidently had little to do with the exact form the pieces took, though every now and then Davis wrote a letter about what he was doing, and now and then Biddle made it plain that he was pleased. These letters, in the Biddle papers, hint how things were between the banker and his apologist.

The best proof Biddle gave of liking Davis' work was the coy mention, in a letter of December 4, 1833, that "our mutual friend Major Downing . . . . will have to take a seat at the Board [of the New York branch of the United States Bank] on Saturday next. . . . . I wish you to communicate it to him—but to no one else." Davis, in other words, was appointed to a job with a handsome salary—and the letter telling about the appointment referred to "our mutual friend Major Downing," so proper credit might be assigned. Davis, in a letter of January 29, 1834, reported what he had done when a false rumor was started that the New York branch had called in its loans. "I hastily prepared an article," he said, "which appears . . . . this morning. I wrote it as mean as I could in old Downing's style, and the effect of it is so evident that I don't regret now the report got out."

V

Written for a different purpose, Davis' *J.* Downing letters naturally were different in their tricks from Smith's *Jack* Downing letters. Both J. and Jack were uneducated, were from Downingville, and were friendly with the President. But more important than these resemblances were the differences between them.

Of course, with his low-comedy idea of country dialect, Davis could not hope to write Yankee talk as lifelike as Smith's. Knowing little of Down East life, he could not put Downingville background into his letters as his Maine rival had. Finally, he could not make J. as rich a mixture of simplicity and wisdom as Jack was because that would not have helped Biddle's cause enough.

Jack, as Smith let him show his mind, was often naïve. Sometimes he was credulous enough to believe at one time two statements which contradicted each other, as he did when he said: "But both parties say they've got the constitution on their side, so I think it likely they'll both beat." When, hiking to Washington to strike Andy for a job, he told several newspaper editors that he was a Republican, one of them took it that this meant that he was for Henry Clay, another that he was for Calhoun, a third that he was for Jackson or Van Buren. This did not cause Jack to see that the Republican badge was pinned on three opposed attitudes. Nor was Jack any good at covering up his real motives by claiming he had others, as when he said he wanted a cabinet job because he thought it was "the duty of all true republicans to have the good of the country at heart, to take hold and help the President along in these trying difficulties," but it was clear that the chief attraction of the job was the six-thousand-dollar salary.

But often Jack, as Smith said, was far "from being an awkward . . . . boor"; he was "on the contrary singularly wise, penetrating and observant." Laws and learning with which he had no truck might confuse him, but never human nature. When men's ways were back of happenings, his experience gave him shrewd insights. What he said about newspapers is still worth recalling. Once, he said, he had thought newspapers were like smoke:

> But I'm thinking after all they are more like *rum* than smoke. You know rum will sometimes set quite peacable folks together by the ears, and make them *quarrel* like mad dogs—so do the newspapers. Rum makes folks act very silly—so do the newspapers. Rum makes folks see double—so do the newspapers. Sometimes rum gets folks so they can't see at all—so do the newspapers. . . . . Remember that, uncle, and dont believe anything you see in the papers this summer, unless you see it in the Daily Courier [for which I'm writing]. . . . .

Time after time, Jack's mother-wit made it possible for him to say keen things about national problems.

Davis' J. Downing was more naïve than Jack—quite stupid about all sorts of political matters. But he was pictured as being even closer to the President than Smith's character—sleeping with him, practically running the government for him. Since J. was so ignorant, this closeness to Old Hickory, of course, showed up Jackson. But ignorant though he was, J. could see some obvious things such as the folly of action against Biddle's bank. If he stuck by his chief on the financial issue, it was not from conviction so much as childlike loyalty. One part of a letter which told how J. came back to Washington from a trip to New York after the President had issued his bank proclamation is typical. Said J.:

It was nigh upon midnight when I got to the White House, and the Gineral was abed; and as I knew he wanted to see me dreadfully, I went up into his room and woke him up. "Why," says he, "Major, is that raly you? . . . . I'm glad you are back agin, for things are gittin pretty stormy here; So you come to bed, and we'll talk about it." As soon as I got alongside the Gineral—"There now," says he, "Major, I don't care for all the rest of the Government, except Mr. Van Buren; and if we three ain't a match for all creation, I'm mistaken." Says he, "Major, hain't you seen my Proclamation agin Biddle?" "Yes," says I, "Gineral, you know I tell'd you I'd stick to you thro' thick and thin, and I'm to be depended on."

In J. Downing's letters all the best horse sense was doled out to the men on Biddle's side. J. wrote of Biddle in such a way that the supercilious financier became a lovable man, kind, tolerant, just filled with common sense. "Squire" Biddle, as he was called in the letters, patiently explained banking by using homely illustrations, making clear the value of the Bank, say, by telling a little story about marketing Downingville potatoes. Or Zekel Bigelow, the smartest old "coot" in J.'s home town, after looking over the financial setup in New York, made childishly simple the exchange problem (as Davis and his friend Biddle saw it) by taking his watch to pieces, as a concrete example.

Davis' best stunt, however, was to put into story form little scenes which were very much like telling cartoons. Political cartoons were beginning to prove their value in campaigns, and, whether he knew it or not, Davis often used words which were similarly useful. One good example ap-

peared in a few sentences which vividly made the point that
Little Van was so slick a politician that he could wriggle out
of even the most awkward situation. When the Magician
was tossed from the back of his horse, said J.,

> . . . . Deacon Willoby saw the hull on it, and he says Mr. Van Buren
> hung on like a lamper-eel, till he was kinder jerked up like a trounced
> toad, and he came down on the horse's rump jest as he kicked up behind,
> and that set him clean over the fence into the Deacon's potato-patch.
> He turned over so fast in the air you could not tell one end from tother;
> but his feet struck first, and he stood there, the Deacon says, and made as
> handsome a bow to the folks as if nothing on earth had happened to him.

This could be drawn with lines, lights, and shadows to have
much the same meaning in picture form as it has in words.
Similar word-cartoons, full of fancy in their details but getting sharply at political points, came often in the letters.

There can be no doubt that Davis' J. Downing attracted
a host of readers. Several pieces he wrote came out in as
many as a hundred newspapers. Biddle wrote Davis in January, 1834:

> You continue to be delight of the town and country. I learn from the
> West that I am known in that quarter almost exclusively by the name of
> the Squire, and I have just seen a drawing which is to accompany an
> edition of your manifesto in German, wherein I figure with a tremendous
> whip on the wheel horse of a Conestoga . . . . driving six horses, while
> sundry small vehicles are upsetting or upset around us.

Historians see that he had more to do with the popular
idea of what Jackson was like than anyone else—including
Jackson. Public men as well as private citizens remembered
and quoted him. Crockett told John Quincy Adams in front
of the Capitol one day that J. was "the only person in whom
he had any confidence for information of what the government was doing." A member of the Kitchen Cabinet wrote

Jackson that he thought Van would come out of a political fight "in the same dextrous way" as he came out of his spill from the horse in the J. Downing letter. There is good evidence that Davis' imitation became more famous than the original Jack. Many historians mention Davis but not Smith as Downing's creator.

VI

Davis used his Yankee at the time of the bank fight and then discarded him. Smith found his Jack Downing useful for a much longer time, yelling, whenever he got the chance, that Davis had stolen from him. In 1836, evidently sick of being robbed, he killed his hero and had Cousin Nabby and Uncle Joshua compose accounts of his handsome funeral. "Major Jack Downing, we see it announced," said the snippy *New-Yorker*, "has departed this life. High time." But in 1840, Smith evidently thinking that Jack could be made useful again, announced that he had been miraculously brought back to life with some of the pills manufactured by a certain Dr. Solomon Wise. Jack plunged back into governmental affairs and worked off and on for Smith from then on until 1859, commenting on public men and measures through administrations beginning with Jackson and ending shortly before the election of Abraham Lincoln.

Amusingly, though Smith howled loudly about the way Davis had stolen from him, he in his turn evidently took not a few things from his imitator. Very soon after Davis started operating, Jack's letters lost their tolerant way of being funny about both parties and began to stand for one side, just as Davis' did. For example, instead of showing Van Buren in a friendly light, as they had before, they whacked sharply at him and began to show a strong liking for Webster. About two weeks after Davis began making word-cartoons, Smith's Jack took over this trick in his talk about nullification, putting the whole dispute in terms of a story about some youngsters on a raft on Sebago Pond. And the word-cartoon was often useful to Smith from then on. In time some characters that Davis had invented and a ship he had given to J. Downing turned up in letters from Jack. A result of this copying was that the Jack Downing letters, though they lost some of their art, became much more effective as political weapons.

In 1834, Henry Clay wrote Smith a letter approving his satire against the party of Old Hickory: "I am happy to tell you that the Jackson party has been completely annihilated at our elections in Kentucky. . . . . It remains to be seen whether Maine, New York, Pennsylvania, and Ohio will continue to inflict the curse on us."

Smith died in 1868, when Jack Downing was almost forgotten, though his literary offspring were writing humor in every corner of the country. A remark of the *New York Daily Tribune* in its obituary of Davis supplied a fitting end to the story of Biddle's staunchest supporter and his plagiarist: "Many of the 'Downing' letters," it declared, "were directed *against* the United States Bank and the financial policy of Nicholas Biddle." Nothing could have been more in harmony with the ironic writings of Davis than this ironic mistake in the notice of his death.

CHAPTER IV

A Brahmin Dons Homespun

Fust come the blackbirds clatt'rin' in tall trees,
An' settlin' things in windy Congresses,—
Queer politicians, though, for I'll be skinned
Ef all on 'em don't head aginst the wind.

—HOSEA BIGLOW, JAALAM, MASSACHUSETTS

The one [dialect poem] I sent you is better [than another], though not so well
adapted to the ears of the groundlings.

—JAMES RUSSELL LOWELL, CAMBRIDGE, MASSACHUSETTS

I

HOMESPUN oracles were moving up in the world. One named Davy Crockett had got into the United States Congress. Another named Jack Downing had joined the circle of the President's best friends. In 1840, however, one of these common-sense heroes climbed even higher. Though he was just as much of an imagined creation as mythical Davy or fictional Jack, this man was elected to the presidency of the United States—or at least many of his backers thought he was.

The invention of this log-cabin leader was something of an accident. The Whig party, split to slivers after losing thousands of votes in the election of 1839, in December of

77

that year met in a bickering convention. The delegates, after much bitter battling, nominated a mediocrity named
William Henry Harrison to run for president. For months
thereafter his prospects looked very bad. Whigs in many
parts of the country, when they heard about his nomination, frankly said that they were disgusted. A typical comment was the crack of a peevish southern senator that "*avail-
ability was the only ability sought by the Whigs*" when they
made their choice.

Then the opposition party—the Democrats—made a mistake which gave the Whigs the idea of inventing a brand-
new vote-getting personality for their candidate. Old General Harrison, a descendant of one of the first families of
Virginia, had a handsome manor on an estate spread over
two thousand acres along the banks of the Ohio River. He
had, as incomes went then, a fine income of six thousand
dollars a year. He was fairly well educated, having done
some work in college. But the Democrats made the mistake
of claiming that he was poor, lazy, and ignorant.

"Give him a barrel of hard cider," one of their newspapers sneered, "and settle a pension of two thousand a year
on him, and my word for it, he will sit the remainder of his
days in a log cabin by the side of a 'sea coal' fire. . . . ."
The *New York Post* printed a dispatch from a Washington
correspondent, saying that Harrison's poverty had "awak-
ened the sympathy of the ladies of the District" and that
they were taking up a collection to buy him a suit of clothes.
"If you have any old shoes, old boots, old hats, or old stock-
ings," it added, "send them on and they will be forwarded."

Instead of nailing these whole-cloth lies about their candidate, the Whigs gleefully took them up and used them as the
basis for their whole campaign. A nation-wide political ma-

chine, in slick working order, made the log cabin and the cider jug symbols of its democracy, used with endless repetition at political rallies throughout the whole of the country. As one history says:

There were log-cabin badges and log-cabin songs, a *Log Cabin* newspaper and log-cabin clubs, big log cabins where the thirsty were regaled with hard cider that the jealous Democrats alleged to be spiked with whisky; little log cabins borne on floats in procession, with latch-string out, cider barrel . . . . by the door, coon-skin nailed up beside, and real smoke coming out of the chimney. . . . .

It was, in some ways, a fraud. In much of the eastern part of the country the real backers of the Whigs were largely the propertied and educated people—manufacturers, merchants, and bankers in the North, and planters and die-hard conservatives in the South. The tactics used in handling the doddering candidate were so like those which had been suggested by the sinister Nicholas Biddle of the United States Bank a few years before that it seems likely that he had a finger in the foxy campaign. To a fellow-Whig, Biddle had written:

Let him [Harrison] say not a single word about his principles, or his creed—let him say nothing—promise nothing. Let no committee, no convention—no town meeting ever extract from him a single word, about what he thinks now, or what he will do hereafter. Let the use of pen and ink be wholly forbidden as if he were a mad poet in Bedlam.

Old Harrison's literary output was cut off almost as thoroughly as Biddle had said it should be. One satirist claimed that the chimneys of the aged man's fireplace were carefully scraped so that he would be unable to make ink out of soot, that all the fowl at his North Bend farm went around shiveringly naked of feathers, plucked clean so that the nominee would be unable to get any quills to use for pens.

Such a blanketing of Harrison's real attitudes, of course, made it possible to build up his political personality without being bothered by facts. For the most part, during the campaign old "Tippecanoe" Harrison kept his mouth shut beautifully. There was, as a matter of fact, no need for him to say much at the meetings he attended: his mere appearance was enough to make cider-filled partisans howl their heads off for him. By then, newspaper stories about people like Downing and Crockett evidently had made a fairly large number of people believe that a man who lived in a log cabin had to think right.

The opponents of the Whigs got nowhere by nicknaming the antique soldier "General Mum" or by pointing out (as they did) that a mix-up had attached the symbol of the log cabin to the wrong party. The Whigs were far ahead of the Democrats at concocting "plain folks" slogans like "Harrison, two dollars a day, and roast beef." They dusted off a pamphlet, published under Davy Crockett's name in 1835, which had libelously claimed that the Democratic candidate, Van Buren, dressed like a dandy, "strutted and swaggered like a crow in a gutter," and "laced up in corsets, such as women in town wear, and, if possible, tighter than the best of them." They embroidered these charges by saying that Van Buren perfumed his whiskers, dined off dishes costly beyond even the dreams of the common man, and did what he could to turn the White House into a gilded palace. Part of the propaganda was that an aristocrat like this could not think right on political problems.

As these lies spread, ignorant voters everywhere came to hate the invented Van Buren as thoroughly as they came to love the fictional Harrison. In one backwoods section of

Alabama, for example, lived an old shrew so ignorant that when a census taker went to interview her she suspiciously avoided giving him data about her family. But illiterate though she was, she knew enough about the propagandists' version of little Van to want to kill him. "I'd cut his head off," she stormed. "A pretty fellow to be eating his vittils out'n gold spoons that poor people's taxed for, and raisin' an army to get him made king of Ameriky—the oudacious, nasty, stinking old scamp!"

Democratic rebuttals might as well have been shouted into an empty cider barrel for all the good they did. They were completely drowned as backers of Tippecanoe howled one of their many catchy campaign songs:

> Let Van from his coolers of silver drink wine,
> And lounge on his cushioned settee.
> Our man on his buckeye bench can recline,
> Content with hard cider is he,
> The iron-hearted soldier, the true-hearted soldier,
> The gallant old soldier of Tippecanoe.

And when the people went to the polls, though they thought they were settling the hash of one flesh-and-blood man and honoring another, they really were paying a beautiful tribute to a melodrama which had been built up for their delusion. Van Buren and Harrison, at the polls, were simply the names of two invented characters: people voted against an imaginary silken dude and for a mythical homespun oracle.

Not long afterward, poor Daniel Webster had the job of revising the inaugural address the supposedly uneducated Harrison had written. It was full of references to historical figures about whom the President-elect had learned from

Plutarch. When Webster arrived at a dinner after the ordeal, he looked so bedraggled that his worried hostess asked if anything had happened. "Madam," said Webster fiercely, "you would think something had happened, if you knew what I have done. I have killed seventeen Roman proconsuls as dead as smelts!"

II

No one, it would seem, could have been farther from the emotional flimflam of the log-cabin campaign of 1840 than one of the aristocrats of cultured Cambridge, Massachusetts —rosy-cheeked Jamie Lowell, later to be famous as James Russell Lowell. Twenty-two in 1841, when Harrison's censored inaugural was delivered, Jamie, scion of *the* Lowell family, was much less interested in its contents than he was in reviews of his first little book of poems, a small edition of which had appeared about two months before the President took office.

The remoteness of young Lowell from worldly affairs was suggested by the fact that he had published the book at all. He was trying to get started as a lawyer, and publishing poems was as good a way as most to scare off clients. His remoteness from the hurly-burly of practical affairs was also suggested by the names of typical poems in the thin, brown-backed volume—"With a Pressed Flower," "Irene," "Ianthe," "A Love-Dream," and "On Reading Spenser Again"—all sweet names for delicate ditties.

Looking at the ivory-tower liltings in this fragile volume, no one but a first-class prophet would have been able to guess that, five years later, to battle for a red-hot political cause, Lowell—not unlike the victorious Whigs—would be donning homespun and talking Yankee dialect through his

nose. And if the first-class prophet knew much about the
young man's background, even he might be slow about
making his prediction. It was a background the young man
had to leave far behind if he was to be either a radical or the
writer of farmyard arguments.

Jamie was a member of the most exclusive caste in New
England—the group in time called, with almost religious
awe, the "Brahmins." Brahmins were members of the old,
old New England families who had been haughtily ruling
the section ever since their ancestors had come over on the
Mayflower or some almost equally ancient ship. They were
learned, well to do, and (of course) conservative. And on
any list of Brahmin families the Lowells were sure to come
near the top. Eventually some poet was to make immortal
their position

> In the beautiful city of Boston,
>   The home of the bean and the cod,
> Where the Lowells speak only to Cabots,
>   And the Cabots speak only to God.

Lowell's birthplace as well as his class had done everything possible to make him stodgy and genteel. He was born
in 1819 in a huge pre-Revolutionary mansion, "Elmwood,"
in the old town of Cambridge. The great house with its tall
pilasters was the last edifice on Tory Row—on aristocratic
Brattle Street. Later he was to warn a friend about the effect of living on such an estate. "It will make a frightful
Conservative of you before you know it," he said; "it was
born a Tory and will die so."

Whether the house deserved the blame or not, most of
Lowell's older relatives had joined the standpat forces early
and had not deserted them. James's grandfather until the

day he died had been a hard-working member of the most conservative party America had produced—the Federalists. His father, even in 1844, was lovingly talking about "the old Federal Party with Washington at its head" and ferociously scolding that upstart Jefferson, then, you would imagine, rather harmless, since he had been dead eighteen years. His Uncle John was "a capable lawyer-politician, one of the directing minds of the Federalist machine, earnestly engaged in defending Massachusetts against the wicked Republicans." Another uncle was a big man in manufacturing—one of the founders of the industrial city of Lowell.

Carefully trained exactly as other upper-class New England boys were—at dame's school, at an exclusive preparatory school, at Harvard—Jamie, when he got his Bachelor's degree, seemed safely headed for respectability. There was a small blot on his college record: the day he was elected class poet, he took too much wine and stood up at chapel service to bow, rather unsteadily but with great solemnity, first right and then left, to his giggling classmates. But nobody was much disturbed by this *faux pas;* it was blamed on youthful high spirits. And in the near-by town of Concord, where he was shortly sent to repent his sins, he wrote a class poem which must have cheered up any worried member of his Tory family.

The poem—a fierce attack upon what Jamie believed was the cant of the day—was a pretty good index of the things which then made New England aristocrats purple and apoplectic. On behalf of respectable Unitarians, Lowell soundly spanked two dangerous preachers of the left-wing Transcendental religion—Carlyle and Emerson. On behalf of lovers of vintage wine (including himself), he fumed at advocates of temperance. But he made his most vigorous stabs at the abolitionists—the fanatics who wanted to abolish slavery—and at the women who (Jamie thought) proved their immodesty by helping them.

Even his most violent prejudices were typical Brahmin attitudes in the 1830's. The abolitionists were attacking property rights of southern planters—and property rights were sacred. More serious, they were embittering the producers who sent raw materials to northern textile mills. It seemed best to the prosperous New Englanders, therefore, for people to keep their mouths shut about the dangerous subject of slavery. And if the people were women—"females," as they were called then—it was best for them to keep their pretty little mouths shut about any political subject whatever.

Those were the ideas expressed, in polished old-fashioned couplets, by young Jamie Lowell. "Oh abolitionists," he said sternly,

> Oh abolitionists, both men and maids,
> Who leave your desks, your parlors, and your trades,
> To wander restless through the land and shout—
> But few of you can tell us what about!

Get along with you, he said, and preach your nonsense in the South, where your talk will really be dangerous. Then he tacked on a bitter footnote about "those fanatics who try to get up an excitement and especially the females . . . . who go around ranting, when they ought to be at home educating their children. . . . ."

The boy was "sound," evidently, on political and social matters. Even tendencies of his which propertied Yankees might call "unsound" were not tendencies toward radi-

calism. What seemed a real danger was indicated by Lowell, Sr., when he heard that his offspring was to be class
poet. "Oh dear!" he fretted. "James promised me that he
would quit writing and would go to work!" Poetry seemed
more of a menace to Lowell respectability than radicalism.
Just out of college, the starry-eyed young man grew a Shake-
spearean beard and glossy, auburn locks which almost
touched his shoulders. He dressed in a dark-brown jacket
and a lace collar, and went around cornering any victims he
could, so that he might read to them, in a thin crooning
voice, Shakespeare's sonnets. Stuck into a law office, he
wrote a poem which was a melodramatic cry of youthful
agony:

> They tell me I must study law.
> They say that I have dreamed, and dreamed too long;
> > That I must rouse and seek for fame and gold;
> That I must scorn this idle gift of song,
> > And mingle with the vain and proud and cold.
> > > Is, then, this petty strife
> > > The end and aim of life,
> All that is worth the living for below?
> *O God! then call me hence, for I would gladly go!*

It seems a little extreme to prefer dying to giving up poetry
for law study.

III

But, even when he wrote this woebegone complaint,
young Lowell was beginning to change his mind about reform and the nature of poetry. Before long he was to pepper
his pages with hot talk about all sorts of social changes.

The first hint of the change is puzzling. A few short
months after the class poem was written, Lowell suddenly
mentioned in a letter to a friend that he was "fast becoming

ultra-democratic" and that "the Abolitionists are the only ones with whom I sympathize" among present-day parties. Just what brought this beginning of the shift is hard to guess. But the reason for the rest of the change—the reason for the whole change as he remembered it later—is much easier to learn. An attentive reader of the letters he wrote will find, back of the shift, a pleasant bit of comedy.

Near the end of 1839, Jamie went with a former college chum, W. A. White, to the White home in Watertown to spend a week end. A letter told of his meeting White's sister, "a very pleasant and pleasing young lady." He was impressed by her knowledge of poetry, though he was somewhat pained because she knew the modern poets but not the ancient ones—"the pure wellsprings of English poesy," as he called them.

But Maria White, with her delicate features, transparent skin, pale-blue eyes, and light-brown hair, had the ethereal kind of beauty then very fashionable. (She was to die a few years later.) She sang old English ballads sweetly in candle-lit parlors or on moonlit seashores. After seeing her a few more times, Lowell forgot her ignorance of Chaucer and Spenser and described her as "beautiful—so pure and spirit-like." "On the mantel," he wrote a friend, "is a moss-rose which she gave me and which when it withers I shall enshrine in my Homer."

Maria was beautiful; he had fallen in love with her. The complication was that the delicate girl somehow had developed a mind of her own, a very good mind, and she just happened to believe in all the things Jamie had damned so ferociously in his class poem—Transcendentalism, temperance, abolition, and feminism. This was a complication, though, which did not prove very serious. Before long, Jamie was toying with Transcendental philosophy and was advocating temperance, feminism, and abolition. His revised attitudes toward temperance and women in politics come comically to light in a letter describing a very damp occasion:

Last Friday Maria presented a banner to the Watertown Washington Total Abstinence Society in the name of the women of Watertown. There were more than a thousand persons present. The meeting was held on a beautifully wooded hill. . . . . The day was as fine as could have been wished. Maria looked—I never saw any woman look as grand. She was dressed in snowy white, with a wreath of oak-leaves and water-lilies around her head, and a water-lily in her bosom. There were a great many tears in a great many eyes when she presented the banner.

And soon, too, he was writing abolitionist articles for the *Pennsylvania Freeman* and the *National Anti-slavery Standard*.

The articles, as weapons for the cause, were pretty dull. Lowell was fresh out of college and busy in the library, and he could not resist parading his book learning. Big words clogged long sentences, which meandered down soporific pages. If, for example, his idea was "You shouldn't judge a man by the blackness or the whiteness of his hide," what he was likely to say was:

An aristocracy of intellect may claim some leniency of judgment from the reason, and there are certain physiological arguments to bolster up an aristocracy of birth; but a patent of nobility founded on no better distinction than an accidental difference in the secreting vessels of the skin would seem ridiculous even to a German count who had earned his title by the more valid consideration of thirty-six dollars.

Historical and literary allusions, ink-horn phrases, poetic quotations, and now and then snippets of Latin made his writings sound more like bits from textbooks than like arguments written to sway public opinion. Whether his reasoning was sound or not, his pieces were woefully weak attempts to reach a big audience.

He was not only too bookish to sparkle as a propagandist, he was also too arty. The long poem, "A Legend of Brittany," which filled the opening pages of his second volume of poetry, carefully followed the footprints of the unworldly John Keats. His blunt friend, Charles F. Briggs, gruffly told him that the thing had a hothouse quality about it that made a man uneasy. "It is," said Briggs, "too warm, rich, and full of sweet sounds and sights; the incense overpowers me. . . . . I am too much a clod of earth to mingle well in such elements. I feel while reading it as if I were on a bed of down with a canopy of rose-colored silk above me. . . . ."

Even when he gave poems in the book the job of preaching, Lowell failed to cut them loose from bookish influences. "Prometheus," which he thought was fine, was a windy harangue in blank verse by a hero out of Greek myth—so highfalutin that only book-learned readers could be expected to keep reading until they had found the sermon staggering through its maze of words. The sermon in "Columbus" took the form of a monologue which anyone who had not gone to college (and many who had) would have had to read several times to dig out a meaning. And in a prose volume called *Conversations on Some of the Old Poets* the young highbrow tried to get readers to listen to social preachments buried—of all places—in drawn-out dialogues about Chaucer and the Elizabethan dramatists.

Lowell had a problem. He had, by the grace of Maria White, a message, and he thought his poetry ought to tell it to the world. But his message was so muffled by learning and "artiness" that ordinary readers could neither listen nor understand. One of the poems of the time—"An Incident in a Railroad Car"—neatly contrasts the sort of thing another poet—Robert Burns—had done, with what he himself had been able to do. On the coach, says the poet, he heard a fellow-passenger talk about Burns to some workmen and then read aloud some of the Scottish poet's verse. Because Burns's heart, said Lowell, using a rather bad metaphor, was "made of manly, simple stuff as homespun as their own," the listeners welcomed his poetry. Lowell thought, he said in the poem, that speaking out in that direct way to "the untaught poor" put into shadow the "lore of classic Greece and Rome"—that it was more glorious than writing poetry for two or three high souls. What he wanted was

> To write some earnest verse or line,
> Which, seeking not the praise of art,
> Shall make a clearer faith and manhood shine
> In the untutored heart.

Lowell had a fine grasp of the theory of the thing. But when he tried to preach in the poem immediately after this one in his book, he produced "Rhoecus," an unrhymed version of a Greek myth much too complicated to make an untutored heart skip a single beat.

This looked fairly hopeless, but there were some signs that the poet might do better in future. In the prose articles, for all his big words, now and then he jolted a nodding reader awake by inserting a witty paragraph or so. The poem about Burns, after all, and some other poems in the 1843 volume which contained it were in forms not too difficult for the general reader. In 1844 there were two good omens: He had a try at a Franklin-like satire, sending to a New York editor some letters supposedly from a homespun politician named Matthew Trueman. Also, he wrote a poem called "The Present Crisis," which swung along like something by Kipling and which in time was going to furnish many a preacher with lines to quote in his sermons. As 1846 approached, other poems now and then—some of them in the style of Whittier—suggested that some day, with good luck, Lowell might learn to write for people who were uneasy in a library. But no poem before 1846 hinted at the exact way he was going to reach a really large audience.

IV

In the spring of 1846 the United States started a war so questionable that many patriotic people nowadays are not sorry to forget it. Chivalrously loading all the blame on puny little Mexico, Congress solemnly declared that a state of war existed between that country and the United States. Since it was going to extend slave territory, the war was unpopular with abolitionists, though the "our-country-right-or-wrong" crowd managed to work up some tolerance for it in the north. President Polk called for volunteers, and flashily dressed sergeants strutted the streets of various cities, trying to get young men to enlist.

Lowell was in a lawyer's office in Court Square, Boston, one June day when the music of a fife and drum floated through the window. Looking out, the men in the office saw a recruiting sergeant, feathers in his hat, brass buttons on his bulging chest, marching along the sidewalk ahead of a fifer and a drummer. Anger kindled in Lowell's eyes, and he gritted out harsh criticisms of this trick to get Yankees to fight in what he thought was an unjust war.

Perhaps the spark of rage was what he needed to get him going. At any rate, this incident started him off, a few days later, on the writing of pieces which were to make him more popular than all his learned arguments and elegant poems had made him. On June 17, 1846, the *Boston Courier* printed a letter and a poem about a recruiting sergeant. They were written by Lowell, but the letter was signed Ezekiel Biglow and the poem was attributed to old Ezekiel's son, Hosea.

Father Biglow, writing from his farm near Jalaam in the broadest Yankee dialect, told how his son had been inspired by a corn-fed Muse. The boy had gone to Boston, said Zeke, and had seen a "cruetin Sarjunt a struttin round as popler as a hen with 1 chicking." He had "com home considerabal riled," and that night his parents had heard him thrashing around in his bedroom "like a short-tailed Bull in fli-time." Though Mrs. Biglow had been afraid that the poor fellow was "took" with cholera, it turned out that he had simply been writing a poem, which Zeke inclosed.

The poem, likewise in rustic dialect, was a series of jeers at the pouter-pigeon sergeant and his musicians which told what a Yankee farmer thought of the war. "Rattle your drums all you want," said Hosea, in his prancing verse; "blow your fife until you're yeller. But I won't jine up with you. The Bible says war is murder, an' this war's jest makin' catspaws o' Yankees to help the slave states. Besides—my Nancy,

> She wants me for home consumption,
>   Let alone the hay's to mow,—
> Ef you're after folks o' gumption,
>   You've a darned long row to hoe."

What the author had done, he himself has said quite plainly:

Thinking the Mexican war . . . . a national crime committed in behoof of Slavery . . . . and wishing to put the feeling of those who thought as I did in a way that would tell, I imagined to myself . . . . an up-country man . . . . capable of district school English, but always instinctively falling back into the natural stronghold of his homely dialect when heated to the point of self-forgetfulness.

This Yankee characterization of "common-sense vivified and heated by conscience" was made a mouthpiece for the witty scarification of things his creator hated. Evidently Lowell deliberately had assumed a role he knew would have a wide appeal. About the time he wrote the poem he told a friend:

We have got now to that pitch when uneducated men (self-educated they are called) are all the rage, and the only learned animals that continue to be popular are pigs. The public will rush after a paper which they are told is edited by a practical printer. . . . . [Did he mean Franklin?] We shall ere long see advertised "easy lessons in Latin by a gentleman who can testify that he knows no more of the language than Mr. Senator Webster. . . . ."

In spite of the fact that he was sure that he was writing what the public wanted, Lowell was bowled over by the reception his dialect verse got. Even this first poem made a stir. "If I may judge from the number of persons who have asked me if I wrote it," he said, "I have struck the old hulk of the Public between wind and water." As other pieces followed the first, he said years later:

The success of my experiment soon began not only to astonish me, but to make me feel the responsibility of knowing that I held in my hand a weapon instead of the mere fencing-stick I had supposed. Very far from being a popular author under my own name, so far, indeed, as to be almost unread, I found the verses . . . . copied everywhere; I saw them pinned up in workshops; I heard them quoted and their authorship debated. . . . .

Eastern newspapers tucked the popular poems into corners not needed for news, and soon the Yankees to whom Lowell had given tongues were better known than their anonymous creator. A man who happened to have the same name as a character mentioned in the verse sent a letter to say that as a result of this accident his name would soon be better known than he himself had been able to make it during a lifetime. In Washington, D.C., the night before a president was inaugurated in 1848, a fellow told the crowd in a tavern that he had uncovered a great Yankee poet, though he did not know the author's name. Reading one of the Biglow poems from a newspaper clipping, he was cheered by a batch of appreciative politicians.

V

Anyone who knows the ways of straw-hat philosophers before Lowell will meet old friends with new names in the verses. Here was Hosea, a naïve countryman like a character in Davis' articles, who had the same name as his father did (Zeke Biglow), spouting his ideas about the political squabbles of the day. Because he was plumb-full of gumption, Hosea could tear into the arena of politics and knock down foolishness and hypocrisy. Like Poor Richard, he was a horse-sense character.

Some of the others who spoke up in the poems showed themselves to be, not horse-sense characters, but fool characters of the established sort. In one letter, for instance, Hosea turned into rhyme a speech purported to be made by one Increase D. O'Phace to a crowd on State Street in Boston. The speech showed that Increase had a name well suited to his politics, since a "doughface" in the language of the day was one who wanted to give the South whatever it asked. Instead of the gumption of Biglow, this fellow had the low cunning of a rascal: he spluttered angrily about a Congressman who had riled the South and thus lost the party some votes. A politician, he claimed, ought to hew to the party line, let his principles fall where they may. It was the well-worn trick of having a despicable character favor policies his creator wanted discredited.

Two stand-bys of common-sense writers, in other words, turned up in these pieces. But Lowell cleverly added some other elements. For one thing, the dialect of real Yankees was echoed in the verse with almost scientific accuracy. Better even than Seba Smith, the clever young man who wrote the poems caught the exact ways of New England speech. For another thing, this series was written in verse. Though Poor Richard had been able to put some of his wisdom into snappy couplets without scaring readers away, most smart caterers to popular taste had avoided poetry for their homespun preachments as if it were the plague. When some prospective readers saw Lowell's long passages in rhythm and rhyme no doubt they bolted. But much of the verse was of a kind that even unliterary men might like, verse that jiggled like a nursery rhyme, sticking pleasantly in the memory—like that in "What Mr. Robinson Thinks":

> We were gittin' on nicely up here to our village,
>   With good old idees o' wut's right an' wut ain't,
> We kind o' thought Christ went agin war an' pillage,
>   An' thet eppyletts worn't the best mark of a saint;
>   But John P.
>   Robinson he
>   Sez this kind o' thing's an exploded idee.

It is noticeable—to mention a third element of novelty—
that religion loomed larger than it had in earlier hayfield
discourses. Hosea was a Down East churchgoer, and he
could hardly utter a sentence without showing it. Not only
in the John P. Robinson poem but elsewhere also he talked
dogmatically about God's "idees." For example, "As for
war, I call it murder," he said flatly in another composition.
"I don't have to go no further than my Testyment fer that.
That's what God said it was—plumb and fairly. And you've
got to get up early if you want to take in God." This pawky
farm hand, close to the puritan Deity since infancy, knew
Him well enough to talk about Him as if He were following
a plough in the next field. What is more, creating God in
his own image, Hosea paid the great Being the finest compliment he could: he allowed He had first-class Horse Sense.
Biglow's God, like the wise bird, was an Early Riser. He
watched His bargains and collected His just debts.

This childlike religious belief made the farmer oracle
lovable and helped make pious northern rural readers sympathize with his opinions. When a contrary opinion, however, was to be stated, Lowell often put it into the mouth of a
sanctimonious hypocrite. "The Pious Editor's Creed," for
example, lists the things the editor believes in. Usually the
editor spreads around what Huck Finn called "soul butter"
to make his beliefs sound pious. To cite one instance, he
says smugly that he believes in "special ways of praying and
converting." That sounds fine only until he gives away the
sense in which he uses the religious words:

> I mean [I believe] in preyin' till one busts
>   On wut the party chooses,
> An' in convartin' public trusts
>   To very privit uses.

In drawing both good characters and bad ones, Lowell thus took advantage of the piety of his readers.

A final novelty in these papers was a kind of character which appears only two or three times in American humor. Most characters in our humor—or that of any country—are exactly the same when their story ends as they are when it begins. But in the *Biglow Papers* a fellow named Birdofredum Sawin, a boyhood friend who every now and then sends Hosea a letter, is a changing, a developing, character. Sawin was a poor but well-meaning country hick who became so excited when he heard fife and drum music that he signed on the dotted line for the recruiting sergeant. After enlisting to go to Mexico, he was "some punkins" for a while—bussed by all the girls, pointed to with pride by all the screeching orators, cheered when he paraded. But down in Mexico, he found things were different. Mosquitoes there were so big that they stuck their nippers clear through his legs; scorpions were unco-operative, and so were vermin. Mexicans, failing to understand America's high motives, were so impolite as to shoot at the invaders. Army officers who had been pals in Boston were, south of the border, bullies who made life unbearable.

Thus Mexico started the job of Birdofredum's disillusionment. The battlefield finished up the job nicely, and almost finished Sawin to boot. About to be mustered out, the youngster took stock of his losses—an eye, a leg, and—

Where's my left hand? O, darn it, yes, I recollect wut's come on't.
I hain't no left arm but my right, and that's got just a thumb on't;
It ain't so hendy ez it wuz to calculate a sum on't.

But the physical banging-up was even less thorough than the moral breakdown the poor man had undergone. No longer believing in anything, battered, bedraggled, and addicted to drink, the cynical Sawin made plans to prey, by hook and crook, on the society that had defrauded him. Later reports showed him sinking deeper and deeper into rascality.

VI

Several people who had read Lowell's earlier stuff sneered at the rumor that the bumpkin doggerel of the *Biglow Papers* was written, of all people, by him. One night, in pauses between numbers at a concert, the poet listened gleefully to a neighbor who proved beyond doubt that Lowell could not possibly have done the hayseed monologues. When, finally, his authorship was established, many must have wondered how this arty and cultivated young man had managed to sound so much like a collection of earthy and ignorant Down Easters. Some years later, Lowell himself, reading over the papers, asked in wonder, "Are those yours? How did you make them?"

Really the answer is fairly simple. For one thing, he had, over the years, heard a good deal of Yankee talk. In his childhood, Cambridge had been more of a country village than a city: "I was born and bred," he said, "in the country, and the dialect was homely to me." As a boy, in winter he had worked with countrymen cutting ice on Fresh Pond. In summer, in the Elmwood hayfields, he had heard, at noonings, "the talk of Sam and Job over their jug of blackstrap under the shadow of the ashtree." He had heard farmers boast at cattle shows, had seen them drill at militia musters.

As a man, he had continued to hear the old chimney-corner English. Ancient men and women in Cambridge still used it in daily talk. Country folk who came to town for the carnival fun of Commencement at Harvard could still be heard chaffing one another in broad Yankee. On lecture tours he talked to farmers or heard them make salty speeches at antislavery meetings. He had a good memory for turns of phrase because he was a brilliant scholar of linguistics. The rural speech which he overheard had made him a master of the dialect. *102796*

Further, what he could not learn from hearing Yankees, this bookish young man (whose writings always were full of echoes) could learn by reading. He could—and evidently did—read Jack Downing and such followers of his as the less memorable Enoch Timbertoes and Sam Slick, both of whom were quoted in contemporary newspapers. He could, and did, read a novel, *Margaret*, published a short time before he began writing dialect verse. From a character in this book whom he greatly admired, he got several hints useful to him when he created Hosea.

These facts show, I think, that—though he may not have realized it—Lowell was almost as artful as the Whigs of 1840 when he started to write barnyard English. For though he could sound very much like a Yankee, it is doubtful whether he felt or thought like one—even whether he was capable of sympathetic understanding of common men. His blood was Brahmin; his home was Harvard and Elmwood on Tory Row; and his head had more than his heart to do with his democracy.

There are several proofs of this. Note the painstaking care with which more than once he traces American expressions back to their use in old England, as if ancient mother-country ancestry made them more respectable. Hear him advising a friend to settle in cultured Boston because "it is always disagreeable for a man of education to be pitched into the midst of barbarians." Catch the tone of condescension as he characterizes Yeoman Joe Bird as "a great brown-faced, hard-handed giant of a farmer" and adds, "I could have hugged the great brawny, honest-hearted fellow." Consider whether, if a Brahmin had deteriorated as Farmer Sawin did, Lowell would not have considered the change less amusing than tragic.

Finally, note what happened to the first series of Biglow Papers when he put them into a book. Now and then, as the series came out in newspapers, Hosea mentioned the preacher at Jalaam, one Parson Homer Wilbur, who had helped him with his versifying. Once, when Hosea was attacked in the *Boston Post*, Lowell, in the character of this invented parson, sent a letter signed "Homer Wilbur" to the *Boston Courier* defending Biglow. As Lowell himself saw, this preacher was in several ways the opposite of Hosea. Notably, he was learned and pedantic instead of uneducated and pawky. It occurred to Lowell that if he put into the book a number of bits in Wilbur's highfalutin style alongside pieces of Hosea's homely writing, there would be an amusing contrast.

Moreover, when the Brahmin propagandist collected his pieces for publication between book covers in 1848 and reconsidered the writings of earthy Hosea and rascally Sawin, he was dissatisfied with them. "I feared," he said, "the risk of seeming to vulgarize a deep and sacred conviction." He needed "on occasion to rise above the level of mere *patois*." He wanted to glance at things "beyond the horizon" of humble Hosea and Birdofredum. In other words, he doubted whether American common sense and *mere* American talk were really enough to reveal all the truth.

What he did, therefore, was build up Wilbur. Wilbur was given the job of editing the book—of writing a "Note to the Title-Page," a windy "Introduction," some "Notices of an Independent Press," several pages of limping Latin, and long, dull notes on the various poems. Whatever was his value as a humorous character for book-learned readers, the parson was a hard pill for common readers to swallow. It was as if the Lowell who had loved mouthing big words and parading his education in his antislavery prose had been jealous of Hosea's popularity and had sneaked into a book with him, disguised as Homer Wilbur.

The result was that the book called *The Biglow Papers* had much less popular appeal than the original papers had had. And never again was Lowell to get so close to the group he contemptuously called the "groundlings" and the "paddies." When, in the days of the Civil War and reconstruction, he struggled to get back to the Biglow style, though he did some fine things artistically, he fell far short of his earlier success as a preacher to the populace. And the rest of his works had a great deal of the aroma of a stuffy library.

The whole story reminds one of an experience Jamie and Maria had when, in the early days of their marriage, they were trying hard to be democratic. A friend tells how "the old family servants were bidden to the table of the master and mistress, but this was soon felt to be an inconvenience, and the custom did not long continue." Similarly, Lowell could don homespun for a while, but the plebeian cloth was soon felt to be an inconvenience, and the costume was discarded.

CHAPTER V
Horse Sense, Southern Style

There is no telling which way luck or a half-broke steer will run.
—SIMON SUGGS, CAPTAIN OF THE TALLAPOOSA (ALA.) VOLUNTEERS

Well, to tell you the truth, I like the opera well enough, all but the singin. If operas didn't come from Paris, whar all the fashionable bonnets and every thing else comes from, and it wasn't considered unfashionable not to admire 'em, I don't believe there's many people in this country that would be willin to pay a half a dollar a night to hear sich a everlastin caterwaulin as they do make.

—MAJOR JOSEPH JONES, PINEVILLE, GEORGIA

I

ONE evening in the late 1830's, Simon Suggs, walking along the street in Tuskaloosa, Alabama, stopped to stare into the window of a bookstore. Simon was no beauty: he had a big head, a hawk nose, watery little eyes, and a thin mouth; his neck was long and skinny, and his body was the same. His shabby old clothes were cheap and rather threadbare.

The sight of the shelves and shelves of books made Simon talk to himself, putting into clear words a basic idea of the school of Homespun Philosophy. He mumbled:

Hell and scissors! Whoever seed the like of the books! Ain't there a pile? . . . . Well, mother-wit kin beat book-larnin, at *any* game. . . . . Human natur and the human family is *my* books, and I've never seed many but what I could hold my own with. . . . . Books ain't fittin for nothin but jist to give to children goin to school, to keep 'em outen mischief. As old Jeddiah used to say, booklarnin spoils a man if he's got mother-wit, and if he ain't got that, it don't do him no good. . . . .

Simon Suggs was an imagined character in a series of stories by Johnson J. Hooper which came out between book covers in 1846 as *Simon Suggs' Adventures, Late of the Tallapoosa Volunteers.* This southern book by a southern author, about a man who had very little money but who lived by his wits, contrasts interestingly with northern and western books of the same period.

A hard-bitten wanderer in sparsely settled parts of Alabama, Simon was an out-and-out rogue, who boiled down his whole notion about getting along into the brief motto, "It is good to be shifty in a new country." Putting the motto into practice, as a youngster, he swindled his pious old father out of a horse, thus starting a career as shifty as it was shiftless, which included crooked land speculations, thievery at a camp meeting, the blackmailing of a widow, gambling, and any other bits of skullduggery that might yield a few dishonest dollars. When luck was good, he was quick to make the most of it; when it was not so good, he connived to get bigger takings.

Hooper, Simon's creator, an Alabaman of good family, made his book about Suggs an ironic parody of a campaign biography. In the first chapter he pointed out that, though writers usually wait until a man dies before they praise him, the authors of campaign biographies are not so slow about dishing out compliments:

Thus Jackson, Van Buren, Clay, and Polk have each had a biography published while they live . . . . and in the front of each "Life" there is found . . . . a "counterfeit presentment" of the subject of the pages which follow. And so . . . . an attempt is made to create an idea of his physique. By this means . . . . future generations of naughty children . . . . will be frightened to their cribs by the lithograph of "Major General Andrew Jackson," which their mammas will declare to be . . . . the Evil One—an atrocious slander, by the bye, on the potent, and comparatively well-favored, prince of the infernal world.

Simon was a politician set to run for office. So here was his campaign biography, using for its frontispiece a picture of the dour old rascal astride a hammer-headed, bedraggled nag. And the book ended with a plea to the voters:

Men of Tallapoosa, we have done! Suggs is before you! We have endeavored to give the prominent events of his life with accuracy and impartiality. If you deem that he has "done the state some service," remember that he seeks the Sheriffalty of your county. He waxes old. He needs an office. . . . . His military service, his numerous family, and his long residence among you, his gray hairs—all plead for him! Remember him at the polls.

Between the start of the biography and the appeal for votes was story after story of Simon taking in people who had money but not enough shrewdness to hang on to their rolls.

When this book, which came out of the South, is compared with contemporary works from the West or from New England, it suggests an interesting difference between the South and other parts of the country. Davy Crockett, the Westerner, in the book he claimed to have written, had depended on the prejudice many people had in favor of mother-wit to help him get across the idea that he was not only a keen man but also a fine fellow. Jack Downing, the Yankee, had a touch of sinfulness and foolishness in him, but, to win the sympathies of his readers, he always professed, like Crockett, respect and liking for poor men blessed with gumption. Hooper, the Southerner, however, sneered not only at his hero Suggs's shifty ways but also at his belief that mother-wit was better than anything out of books. He obviously assumed that his readers would sneer with him.

Southern writers of the day show that Hooper had good reason for this assumption. When the great Charleston novelist of the day, William Gilmore Simms, wanted a villain for a story, he would often make use of a man very much like Suggs. When southern humorists showed men of the same class in some of the best humorous stories ever written in this country, they would take care to make it plain that, on a hunt or by a campfire, men of Simon's class were great fun. The finest pre-war pieces produced in the South were written reports of the talk of yarn-spinners who sat in firelight letting their words reveal strange characters or their minds invent tall stories about strange doings. But often the writer was likely to take pains to show that, when matters of importance—like politics—were concerned, he took no stock in the insight into such matters of a poor man.

The attitude probably was due to conditions peculiar to the South. In that part of America, at the time, classes of whites tended to be rather more definitely stratified than they were elsewhere—with the rich planter on a fine estate run by many slaves at the top, then, in the middle, the smaller landowners with a few slaves, and at the bottom the poor whites, with little land and no slaves. Other white men —and even some slaves, contemptuous of the group at the bottom of the lowest strata—called them "white trash," "pineywoods tackies," "clay-eaters," or other contemptuous names. It is true, as several students have recently shown, that there were gradations between the classes—siftings up and down from one stratum to another. And the line was not always easy to draw between, say, a man at the top of the poor-white group and a man lowest in the stratum above the poor whites. But down at the bottom there was a group very little admired. As W. J. Cash says, in *The Mind of the South:*

Not a few of the more abject among them were addicted to "dirt-eating," but the habit was by no means so universal as has sometimes been claimed. . . . . The houses of the run of them were mere cabins or hovels, with shutters for windows, and with chinks wide open to the wind and rain. . . . . The men might plow a little, hunt a little, but mainly passed their time on their backsides in the shade of a tree, communing with their hounds and a jug of . . . . "bust-head." And finally, as the very hall-mark of the type, the whole pack of them exhibited, in varying measure, a distinctive physical character—a striking lankness of frame and slackness of muscle . . . . a boniness and misshapliness of head and feature, a peculiar sallow swartness, or alternatively a not less sallow faded-out colorlessness of skin and hair.

In the West or Down East, in other words, a poor ignorant man might well be a respectable person on his way to the top, but in the South he might be—like Simon Suggs—a member of a class apart, so no-account and ignorant that nobody cared about his ideas.

The men who did a large share of the thinking and much of the writing for some groups and some sections south of the Mason-Dixon line were plantation-owners or—like Simms—men who wanted planters to do something for them. The high-stepping plantation gentlemen, some of them living in splendor almost as sumptuous as that shown in plantation sets of moving pictures like *Gone with the Wind*, were likely to think that wealth and culture and training such as they had and others did not have were what anybody needed if he was to be a proper leader. Naturally, the arrogant planter in his top hat and fine, imported clothes was not likely to pay much heed to what an ignorant squatter in a tattered wool hat and faded jeans had to say about important problems. So at a time when, in some parts of the country, a man could win friends and influence people by showing he had horse sense, in quite a few parts of the South a man probably would be asked whether he came of a good family and whether he had training and culture before he could get a hearing as a prophet.

II

But Major Joseph Jones of Pineville, Georgia, a character in two books by W. T. Thompson, at first glance looks like an exception to this. Though the Major was so uneducated that he was lucky to get three words in a row spelled right, though his grammar was bad enough to make a fussy school-teacher scream, and though his family was not much to talk about, he wrote horse-sense letters that delighted many Southerners. His *Major Jones's Courtship* (1843) and *Major Jones's Sketches of Travel* (1848) at first glance appear to be the work of a sort of southernized Davy Crockett. Though Joseph was naïve about some things, he was sound on many questions—a good man who knew many of the answers. As Marse Henry Watterson points out: "The Major is a simple, yet shrewd, straightforward Georgia lad . . . . he knows a thing or two, albeit his education in 'grammar' and 'retorick' has been neglected. His character, like his diction, is homespun." But the Major Jones sketches boomed sales in the South of the periodicals which printed them, and, collected in books, they brought Thompson a great deal of popularity in his part of the country.

How did a homespun philosopher like the Major get along so well in the South? Several things explain his unusual success. In the first place, he was well above the level of the poor whites—considerably above the ordinary run of Down Easterners in lands and money: Jack Downing would have called a man as propertied as Jones was, a Squire. In other words, though Jones was not one of the rich planter class, he was in the stratum just below the top one; he had a plantation with several slaves to work it—perhaps a place of three hundred acres or so, in cotton. Further, though he was a butcher of the king's English, he had picked up enough education somewhere to quote Shakespeare or Swift or a sentence of Latin every now and then—accomplishments sure to impress quality folk. Then, again, it is worth noticing that the Major did not start out as a man with ideas to spread: the first book about him was not much more than a series of amusing little yarns about his courtship and marriage, with a few ideas sneaked in. It was only in his second book, after he had won many friends, that he began to have his say on big subjects. Most important, Joseph was the one character in southern humor who had been made to order for the largest class of people in the section.

William Tappan Thompson, author of the Jones letters, had been born in Ohio, the son of an Irish mother and a Virginia father. He had started life as a printer's devil, then had gone South with a lawyer and studied law. After working on an Augusta newspaper for a while and fighting in the Seminole War, he had started a literary magazine called the *Augusta Mirror*. This magazine he had tried to save from bankruptcy by combining it with the Macon *Family Companion*—but after the combination, he had been forced to leave the magazine. Before he left, however, he had printed Major Jones's first letter. When he was looking for a way to get a fledgling newspaper, the *Southern Miscellany*, out of the red, he recalled the reception of this piece. The *Southern Miscellany* was published in Madison. Madison, compared with some other towns or cities of the South, was a good place for such material to originate. As it happened, it was surrounded by a country in which there were few big plantations, but many small ones. Said Thompson:

Having written and published anonymously a letter by Jos. Jones in the *Companion* which proved very popular, greatly to my surprise, I determined to continue the letters in the *Miscellany* with a view to adapt the paper to a local country circulation. I had originally no plot or plan for the letters which finally grew into a sort of narrative. . . . . Many of the points . . . . were suggested by local incidents, and when I revised the copy for publication in book form I struck out many things of a purely local character. . . . .

Because, then, Thompson adapted the Jones letters very well to "a local country circulation"—to readers who were less likely to be bothered by class consciousness than some other southern groups—he quickly picked up a good following. And there is no blinking the fact that, eventually, some of his opinions were of a sort the big planters were very glad to have spread by a popular author.

III

Major Jones, in the first book about him, was a character bound to please the particular group of farm folk for whom his stories had been written. He kept telling about his part in happenings in the district in which they were interested, like commencement exercises and militia musters and local political campaigns. Further, in that period, when middle-class people somehow had a great fear of letting females read books which raised what was called "the blush of shame" on their cheeks—and when many rough male humorists put stuff into their writings which threatened to turn feminine cheeks red forever—Jones and the people in his letters were as pure as the driven snow.

If blushing easily and often was a sign of virtue—and in nineteenth-century writings it often was—the girls in the Major's sketches proved to country readers that they were crimson-cheeked angels. Look at the passage (in which I have italicized the blushes) which tells what happened when Joseph, one Christmas eve, called on his sweetheart, Mary:

Crismus eve I put on my new suit, and shaved my face as slick as a smoothin iron, and after tea went over to old Missus Stallins's. As soon as I went into the parler whar they was all settin round the fire, Miss Carline and Miss Kesiah both laughed right out.

"There! there!" says they, "I told you so! I know'd it would be Joseph."

"What's I done, Miss Carline?" says I.

"You come under my little sister's chicken bone, and I do believe she know'd you was comin when she put it over the door."

"No, I didn't—I didn't no such thing, now," says Miss Mary, and *her face blushed red all over.*

"Oh, you needn't deny it," says Miss Kesiah, "you belong to Joseph now, jest as sure as ther's any charm in chicken bones."

I know'd that was a first rate chance to say something, but the dear little creeter looked so sorry and *kep blushin so,* I couldn't say nothin zactly to the pint! So I tuck a chair and reached up and tuck down the bone and put it in my pocket.

"What are you gwine to do with that old chicken bone now, Majer?" says Miss Mary.

"I'm gwine to keep it as long as I live," says I, "as a Crismus present from the handsomest gal in Georgia."

When I said that, *she blushed worse and worse.*

"Ain't you shamed, Majer?" says she.

"Now you ought to give her a Crismus gift, Joseph, to keep all her life," said Miss Carline.

"Ah," says old Missus Stallins, "when I was a gal we used to hang up our stockins—"

"Why, mother!" says all of 'em, "to say stockins right before—"

Then I felt a little streaked too, cause *they was all blushin as hard as they could*.

The last sentence shows that Jones, militia major though he was, was himself a rather delicate fellow. His maiden-like shyness, as a matter of fact, was what got him into his best-remembered adventure. Too shy to pop the question to blushing Mary Stallins, Joseph got the girl to promise that she would keep whatever he gave her for Christmas forever, and then had her hang a large bag on the front porch. Mary knew what was up, probably, but Jones did not know that she did—and the dear girl evidently was very glad to give her tongue-tied swain what help she could in solving his problem.

At midnight Joseph sneaked over to the Stallins house and found the empty meal bag hanging from a joist on the porch. To get into the thing was monstrous unhandy, but Joseph set his jaw, stacked some chairs on the bench, climbed shakily on top of the stack, and flipped into the bag. The sack swung and banged Joseph against the furniture. The furniture toppled to the porch, making enough racket to wake an old cur dog, who sniffed and barked and whined around the porch all the rest of the night. As the long dark hours dragged by, a cold wind swung the bag around until Joseph got sea sick. He was cramped and racked with pain and as cold as an iceberg when the roosters began to crow at dawn and Mary came out to find him. Of course, "she blushed as beautiful as a morning-glory, and said she'd stick to her word."

Thus, in the Major's letters, romance joined chaste sentiment in appealing to farm readers. Since most of these readers were religious, Jones's trips to church each Sunday helped him win the love of people of their piety. And Thompson, who enjoyed dipping his nose into a julep as well as the next man, made his hero a member of the Washingtonian Temperance Society so that the liking his readers had for that movement might be satisfied.

In the first set of letters political passages were rather scarce. Jones came nearest to political comment when he repeated two speeches, each by a candidate for the legislature, which were given before the Major's battalion of militia. Both the speeches were by fool characters—perhaps from the Suggs stratum of society. "If I's elected," shouted one, in a typical part of his talk, "I shall go for makin the banks redeem their bills in silver and gold, or put every devil of 'em in the penitentiary to makin nigger shoes. I's a hard money man and in favor of the vetos. I goes for the poor man agin the rich, and if you elect me that's what I mean to do." But Jones made no remarks about the things the two silly candidates said, and he did not, therefore, get very deep into political disputes. It is noteworthy, though, that these fool characters were satirically, and therefore contemptuously, drawn. And they evidently were on the same social level as Simon Suggs. Jones—or his creator, rather—evidently looked down on them, thought very little of their intelligence and their virtue. In Thompson's thinking, as in Hooper's, a man had to be well above the level of the poor white to find the path to wisdom. One had to be, it appears, on at least the level of Major Jones.

IV

In the second series of Jones's letters the Major began by painting a picture of domestic bliss which must have charmed many a farm wife who took the paper for which he wrote. Mary and Joseph, having acquired a lovely baby named Henry Clay Jones, were living in complete happiness together on their plantation near Pineville. The Major was as unblemished as ever in his talk: in his Preface he boasted that anyone could read his book with "little damage to his morals."

Before long, though, after a tearful goodbye to his wife and the slaves, the Major was out of Pineville, traveling northward and sending home reports of what he saw and did in the big cities. He kept striking the domestic note by remarking, time after time, how lonesome he felt for Mary and little Henry Clay. There were still the same old signs of simplicity in what he wrote. He might let a tiny youngster cheat him; he might stand in the street in New York a long time, waiting for the crowd to pass; like any yokel, in a hotel he might jerk a bell cord, believing he was lowering a curtain. And no matter where he was, he would still show himself a rustic Georgian by the way he talked. For him the streets of Boston were not "much wider than the space between the rows of a pea patch"; the Hudson River was "sleepin still and dark as a nigger baby in a shuck-pen"; and, standing by Niagara Falls, he felt "no bigger than a seed-tick in Scriven county."

Major Jones Bidding an Old Slave Goodbye before Leaving
for His Tour of the United States

But the Major had taken on new duties. Though he said firmly in his Preface that "this little sketch of my perry grinations among the big cities . . . . was writ with no higher aim than to amuse the idle hours of my friends, and if it fails to do that, its a spilt job," he had some axes to grind. Every now and then the unlettered Georgia farmer stopped his talk about travel to speak a piece about important matters, and thanks to the unerring way he used the mind God had given him, he said bright things.

It is very possible Thompson had decided that his country would like the Major better if a few morals were tacked on to his discourses. Or maybe Thompson, wanting to say certain things himself, thought the funny Georgian could do well as a mouthpiece. These new letters had been written to appear in the *Western Continent* of Baltimore, of which Thompson was editor. This newspaper was an active "exponent," as he put it, "of Southern views" and "interests"— "not in hostility to the North, but in justice to the South." His description of the policy of the paper fits the travel letters to a *T*. However it was, Jones turned into a first-class homespun philosopher. When the illustrator of his book pictured him, it was as a sort of Georgia Jack Downing, and the illustrator was Darley, one of the best in the business at the time.

The traveling Southerner was a Whig. When the doorman at the White House talked of admiring old President Harrison, the Major's face was all smiles, and he insisted on shaking the man's hand. Looking at Jackson's coat in the National Institute, Jones had a time of it forgetting that he "never voted for General Jackson, because he thought his politics was wrong"—long enough to work up a proper feeling of reverence for the hero of New Orleans. And when, on coming back from Canada, Major Jones was annoyed by custom-house officers, he cooled down as soon as he was reminded: "It's only the tariff bisness what you whigs voted for at the last election . . . . and I'm sure you're too good a whig to make a rumpus about it."

But, boosting the Whig party was no more than a part-time job for a man who could think great thoughts on far more complicated subjects than the Whigs. For example, this wanderer—no doubt to the delight of his housewifely readers (though perhaps to his discredit as a fond husband) —kept a very busy eye peeled for data about women wherever he stopped. In Baltimore he made perhaps his most illuminating remarks on this favorite kind of scenery:

You may suppose I seed a heap of butiful wimmin in Baltimore street. Well, so I did; but, to tell you the truth, I seed some bominable ugly ones too. The fact is . . . . wimmin's wimmin, all over the world; and the old sayin, that "fine feathers makes fine birds," is jest as true here as it is in Georgia.

Tucked into the Pineville man's letters from various towns and cities were bits of chatter about subjects just as hard to handle as womankind, and he stepped up to them and had his say with all the confidence of a man who knew he had been born with a hard head and keen eyes for facts.

No one with sense could travel all the way from Pineville, Georgia, to Quebec, Canada, in the 1840's without wondering at man's mechanical achievements. So Jones marveled about railroads, inventions, progress. "If there ever was a thing what deserves a vote of thanks from all the pullin generation of animals," he said, "I think it's the locomotive engine. Jest to think, the amount of horse flesh it has saved

sense it took to carryin the mails." In Lowell, Massachusetts, he saw a machine that "went a little ahead of any
thing I ever heard or dreamed of." This great thought came
to him, and he wrote it down: "The man that invented that
machine could invent one to eat shad without swallerin the
bones, or one that could pick a man's pocket when he was
wide awake, without gettin found out." Near the end of his
"perry grinations," the Major had a very big thought on the
subject of progress:

This is a go-ahead country, to be shore. I couldn't help but think . . . .
how the old codgers what lived three or four thousand years before the
Fourth of July would be tuck a-back if their ghosts was to cum on a
jurney to the United States now—how their old notions would have to
stand out of the way before the march of human knowledge which they
would see displayed in evry thing around 'em. What, for instance, would
old Mr. Abraham think, to see more'n a thousand people, with bag and
baggage—more'n all the jack-asses and camels in his kingdom could
carry—travelin at the rate of fifteen miles a ower, all of 'em as comfortable and snug as if they was settin in their own parlors? . . . .

I used to think that the people of the old times had a monstrous sight
the advantage of us, livin as they did to be five and six hundred years old;
but, when I come to consider, I don't know as they was much better off
than we is. . . . . If we can git up a bigger nation in half a century than
they did in five times as long—if our boys know more about science and
other matters at ten years old, than their's did at a hundred—if we can
travel farther and see more of the world in a week than they could in five
years—if we can make the lightnin carry our mails from one end of the
yeath to the other in the twinklin of a eye— . . . . then what's the use of
our livin as long as they did?

Jones had ideas about the advantages of wealth, the need
for manufacturing in Augusta, noise in the cities, statuary
(the naughty fellow liked a nude female statue more than
any other), education, the "buties" of nature, and a score of

other things that gave his busy mind powerful, hard shoves. But if there was any sort of thinking he put in more time on than another (that about women excepted), it was thinking of a patriotic kind.

He went for America in a big way. Even when he talked about operas, the Major could not help remembering that the foreigners who enjoyed such things—the French, Germans, and Italians—"ain't good for much else but music." Up in Canada he grew very angry at "the monarchial institutions that makes slaves of white men, trains 'em to be contented in their servile conditions, and teaches 'em to glory in the shallow glitter of a crown that is upheld by their own sweat and blood." And every now and then he would take a crack at a critical English travel-book writer, like Dickens or Marryat, who had journeyed through the country "jest to make a book for a people who is so blinded with prejudice that they can't see any thing but faults." But the author's patriotism really soared like an eagle when he visited Washington's grave at Mount Vernon, or the national Capitol, or Bunker Hill. Of the Bunker Hill Monument, "the Sinai of American Freedom," as he called it, he wrote:

If there is a man in the nation what don't like the Union and don't feel willin to shed his blood to preserve it, he ought to make a pilgrimage to this consecrated spot. If, standin on this majestic pile and looking down on the ground that received the fust red baptism of Liberty, while he breathes the air that received the breath of so many martyred heroes, and looks upon the sky that witnessed their heroic valor, he does not feel his bosom glow with patriotic emotion, and imbibe a love of country above all sectional prejudices or interests, then he may be sure he was born on the wrong side of the Atlantic.

V

When he was at Bunker Hill, perhaps Jones could be against sectionalism. At most other times, nevertheless, he was sure that the South was the best part of America and Georgia the best part of the South. If anything made him distrust mechanical progress, it was the fact that Yankees had had so much to do with it. As he looked at the women of New York, it appears that he amended his claim that the creatures were the same everywhere by adding the phrase, "except in the North":

The fact is, I find the further North I go the more fine clothes and the less handsum faces I see. It would take enuff money to buy a plantation to dress one of these Broadway bells as they call 'em, and after all a man of taste couldn't see much in 'em to fall in love with. . . . . And even if you do now and then cum across a handsum face there's sumthing wrong about 'em, that I can't exactly understand. Sumhow there ain't enuff difference between the expression of the countenances of the wimmin and the men. . . . . There's the same difference between the eyes of the Northern wimmen and the eyes of our gals at home as there is between a lookin-glass and a deep pool of pure, crystal water.

Perhaps the cleverest thing in the book is the way it stands up for slavery, which was even then beginning to drive a wedge between the North and the South. At the beginning and at the end, the proslavery touches come in naturally, as part of the account of how Joseph went away and returned. There are pathetic scenes of farewell from the devoted Negroes, and the Major talks very lovingly of the slaves after he gets home. A nice touch makes it impossible for Mary and the baby to go with him on the trip, for fear the abolitionists will steal away Prissy, Henry Clay's nurse. Mary would not think of letting a plaguy, trifling, free Negress take care of her dear baby, and as for a white nurse—"I never," said she, "could bear to see a white gal toatin my child about, and waitin on me like a nigger. It would hurt my conscience to keep anybody 'bout me in that condition, who was as white and as good as me."

Wandering alone through the North, Mary's spouse harped many times on the theme of slavery. In Philadelphia he was touched by the sight of "such butiful, rosy-cheeked white gals, doin work that is only fit for niggers." "Slewers or whatever they is," he said angrily, "they is my own color, and a few dollars would make 'em as good as their mistresses." In Philadelphia, too, he had a whack at the Quakers, "monstrous good people only they will meddle with what don't consarn 'em, and keep all the time botherin the Southern people 'bout their niggers." He made the point that, as nonresisters and lovers of freedom of conscience, the folk of the sect should not fight about allowing "the people of the South liberty of conscience" to judge "their own domestic institutions."

The free Negroes of the North were worth a good many paragraphs. Their plight in the Quaker City was pitiful. "Gracious knows," wrote Jones, "if anybody wants to get their sympathies excited for the poor nigger, all they have got to do is to go to . . . . Filladelfy. I've been on the big rice plantashuns in Georgia, and I've seed large gangs of niggers that had the meanest kind of masters, but I never seed any poor creaters in sich a state of wretchedness in all my life. I couldn't help but feel sorry for 'em, and if I was able, I'd be willing to paid the passage of the whole generation of 'em to Georgia." He could not help guessing that the abolitionists who wanted Negroes to live that way were either hypocritical scoundrels or ignoramuses, who did not know anything about the fine conditions of the "happy black people of the South." Then followed a fine bit of philosophy:

For whar social equality cannot possibly exist, the black people are miserable jest in the degree that they approach to equality in wealth and edication with the whites, and are enabled to understand their degraded position. What's the use to talk about equallity when no such thing exists? . . . . The races is, naturally, social antagonists, and it is only in the relation of master and servant that they can exist peaceably together.

On other occasions when he talked about free Negroes, the traveling observer's indignation was roused by the uppish ways they had taken on since they had come into their liberty.

When he deals with such matters as patriotism and slavery, you feel that the Major is not really the one doing the talking. His pen is on the paper all right, spelling words wrong, but back of him stands Thompson, dictating what he is to tell the world. For the time being, Jones is no more than a name signed at the end of a screed: his comic simplicity, the rustic way he usually expresses himself, the good-natured attitude he has, are all gone—and the character of the man disappears. It may be this happened because Thompson felt that his readers would not tolerate jokes about such serious subjects, or it may be that he himself got so wrought up about them that he forgot and lowered the mask of Major Jones he had been wearing.

The Major was back in the picture, though, when the book ended. His Georgia drawl, his ignorance, his shrewd horse sense were in the summary of his findings, with only a few bits stuck in to please Thompson:

I've travelled more'n four thousand miles—I've seed sum fourteen states, and more'n five hundred cities and towns—I've seed the northern people . . . . and though I've got a good deal better opinion of 'em . . . . than I had afore, still I say, give me old Georgia yet. We hain't got so many cities, nor sich fine ones—we hain't got so much public improvements . . . . but we've got a plenty of evry thing that is necessary to make us independent and happy. We've got as fine a soil, a finer climate, as smart men, and handsumer women than any other country in the world, and nothin can hinder us from bein one of the greatest states in the Union, if we go to work as we ought to, and develop our own resources.

I believe a jurney to the North is calculated to do a southern man a grate deal of good, if he goes thar in the rite spirit . . . . and though . . . . the Northerners is very different from us in a grate many things, the majority is actuated by the same impulses, and is strivin for power like all the rest of the world. There's a good deal of ignorance and prejudice at the North, to be shore, specially about matters what don't consarn their own interests; but it is to be hoped that whar there is so much patriotism and intelligence, they will some day larn to mind their own bisness.

This last letter he signed as he did all the rest, with a greeting that was half old fashioned, half naïve—"Your frend til deth, Jos. Jones."

CHAPTER VI
Abe Lincoln

Mr. Chairman, this work is exclusively the work of politicians; a set of men who have interests aside from the interests of the people, and who, to say the most of them, are, taken as a mass, at least one step removed from honest men. I say this with the greater freedom because, being a politician myself, none can regard it as personal.

—ABE LINCOLN, SANGAMON COUNTY, ILLINOIS

God must love the common people, He's made so many of them.

—ABRAHAM LINCOLN, WASHINGTON, D.C.

I

IN THE summer of 1832 young Abe Lincoln took part in a political meeting held in the little town of Pappville, Illinois, where some red-necked farmers had got together to bid at a stock auction and to hear some talks about the August election of state legislators. Abe, stumping for his election to the state legislature, was in various ways like the Davy Crockett of a few years earlier; his audience resembled the crowds Crockett had won early in his career. Like Davy of the canebrakes, Lincoln was a man towering over six feet, with some strength to him; he had the tanned face of a rough but shrewd frontiersman. His own story of his meager schooling almost matches Crockett's similar story. In only six months, altogether, or less, he had done all his schoolwork with teachers who had proved they could hold their jobs by showing they could do a little reading, writing, and ciphering. "Of course," he was to say of himself later, "when I came of age I did not know much. Still, somehow, I could read, write, and cipher to the·rule of three; but that was all. I have not been to school since."

But Lincoln's listeners, like Davy's, took stock in other matters than "book larnin." Frontiersmen, without education themselves, they hoped they were strong, as one of them said, in "the culture that comes of observation, experience, and reason." If you noticed how sharply these men saw things, how living and broad their experience was, and how they could reason "about men, commerce, laws, institutions, human nature, and the world and its affairs generally," the old-timer said, no doubt you would join him when he concluded, "I have never seen such people . . . . for good horse sense." When the time to vote came, these settlers were likely to go for a man they thought had the same kind of gumption that they had, whether he knew much about the inside of books or not.

Lantern-jawed Abe stood awkwardly on a box, ready to talk to this crowd. He had on tow-linen and flax pantaloons that did not get all the way down his long legs to his rawhide boots; he had on a jean coat with short tails and inadequate sleeves; and he had just taken off an old straw hat. Maybe a city tailor would not have liked the costume much, but it suited the crowd all right—showed Abe was of the people, not above them.

Just as he was getting ready to start, the speaker's deep-set eyes caught sight of a rumpus on the edge of the crowd. Some of the boys in his audience, perhaps because they had

had too much chain-lightning whisky, perhaps because they were having an honest little disagreement, were flipping fists at one another's faces. One of the men in the squabble, a friend of the candidate, appeared to be in trouble. So Abe hopped down from the box top, walked over to the fighters, stuck his long arms into the whirl, and jerked out the man who was whacking his friend. Lincoln's bony hands gripped the man by the collar and the seat of the pants, Lincoln's big muscles heaved, and the man sprawled on the ground ten feet away. Abe made his way back to the box, climbed up, and delivered his brief talk.

"Gentlemen and fellow-citizens," he said, "I presume you all know who I am. I am humble Abraham Lincoln. I have been solicited by many friends to become a candidate for the legislature. My politics are short and sweet, like the old woman's dance. I am in favor of a national bank. I am in favor of the internal improvements system and a high protective tariff. These are my sentiments and political principles. If elected, I shall be thankful; if not, it will be all the same."

If the scene and the speech were to turn up in some fictional biography of Davy Crockett, a reader would feel they were highly appropriate. The straight-from-the-shoulder talk of the backwoods strong man to voters, his funny turns of phrase, the wry way he spoke about himself, were all quite Crockett-like. But of course, though Lincoln started his political life *à la* Crockett, he developed in time into a much bigger man. In all that people knew or said about Davy, a very simple character was shown. There was a complexity in Lincoln's character which made even his closest friends aware of depths of mystery in the man which they could not plumb. It would be irrelevant to treat all the facets of his character here; but, though he was a fine horse-sense humorist, it would be wrong even to imply that he was nothing more.

II

The Abe Lincoln who made himself known to the voters of Illinois in his young manhood showed his log-cabin rearing in the way he talked. He pronounced words as people said them in the Kentucky wilderness of his boyhood— "idea" became "idee," for example, and he drawled out "really" so that it sounded like "ra-a-ly." Figures of speech of exactly the sort settlers used when they sat by firesides came often from his lips. He said once, for example, that a political rival's argument was as thin as "soup made by boiling the shadow of a pigeon that had starved to death." Again, he claimed that the outcome of an election was "as plain as adding up the weight of three small hogs." Or a stupid judge made him angry, and he said, "If you were to point your finger and a darning needle at the same time, he would never know which was the sharper."

As the years passed and honors came with them, Lincoln did not slough off the use of such homely comparisons. The President of the United States, in the White House, he compared a northern army and a southern army, both wary, to "two dogs that get less eager to fight the nearer they come to each other." He complained that two generals were "so slow that molasses in the coldest days of winter is a race-horse compared to them." Or someone asked him whether he found the trying days of wartime were hard on him, and he said simply, "Yes, it's a heavy hog to hold." Talk of this sort came from country experiences like watching a dog fight in the square on market day, up-ending a molasses jug in the shed some biting January morning, and holding up a dead hog at butchering time while someone sluiced scalding water over its hide.

Similar comparisons were the stock-in-trade of whole batches of nineteenth-century humorists, who put on paper comic versions of the talk of American farmers and woodsmen like Jack Downing, Major Jones, and Davy Crockett. And Lincoln's utterances showed that this was not his only borrowing from American humor. A reader of our native humorists from his youth, he often won laughter by cracking jokes like those of the unofficial jesters of his countrymen.

When he turned his hand to it, Lincoln himself could write letters, much like those of Downing, which convulsed readers in every part of the country. It was 1842, and the future President did not like the way a strutting politician, James Shields, was running the office of state auditor of accounts. Lincoln sat down and wrote a letter, signed "Rebecca"—a letter in the style of a simple countrywoman who was saying her say about this Shields. The letter, published in the *Sangamo Journal*, set forth that the politician was a fool and a liar—what's more, an inferior liar: "As for getting a good, bright, passable lie out of him, you might as well try to strike fire from a piece of tallow." The letter went on to picture Shields carrying on at a charity bazaar during the previous winter:

. . . . I looked in at the window, and there was this same fellow Shields floatin' about on the air, without heft or earthly substances, just like a lock of cat fur where cats had been fighting.

He was paying his money to this one, and that one, and t'other one . . . . ; and the sweet distress he seemed to be in,—his very features in the ecstatic agony of his soul, spoke audibly and distinctly, "Dear girls, it is distressing, but I cannot marry you all. Too well I know how much you suffer; but do, do remember, it is not my fault that I am so handsome and so interesting."

As this last was expressed by a most exquisite contortion of his face, he seized hold of one of her hands, and squeezed and held onto it about a quarter of an hour.

Rebecca not only showed Shields acting like a fool; in addition, she puzzled her silly head about Shields's politics, telling about her perplexity in such a way that Shields was shown up as a very inconsistent sort of person.

Perhaps because the letter almost led to a duel—led, in fact, to an accepted challenge and the edge of an encounter with broadswords—Lincoln, who disliked duels, wrote no more notes signed "Rebecca." However, in his political arguments he frequently used irony similar to that in his pseudonymous dialect letter and other humorous pieces of the day. As this study has made dear, a typical method of many a humorist was to take on the guise of a dolt whose stumbling mind led him to very stupid conclusions. The dolt's name—Birdofredum Sawin, say—would be signed to the letter, but any bright reader would catch on to the fact that back of the dolt was his creator, a man of intelligence who disagreed with him. A good share of the fun, no doubt, arose from the fact that there was a laughable contrast between the fool and the bright fellow who for the moment was acting his part. In speech-making, it was possible for a humorist to get pretty much the same effect by pretending he was a fool—saying patently senseless things in the manner of a numskull, though the audience knew all the time that the speaker held exactly opposite views.

Ungainly, countrified, Lincoln could, if he chose, play the part of the bumpkin to perfection. In the spring of 1849

From a cartoon in "Vanity Fair"

ABRAHAM LINCOLN CONGRATULATED BY ARTEMUS WARD
ON HIS ELECTION

two Hoosiers—Thomas H. Nelson and Judge Abram Hammond of Terre Haute—found this out when they took an all-day trip by stagecoach from their home town to Indianapolis. Stepping aboard the stage at daybreak, the two men found that the whole back seat, as Nelson later told it, "was occupied by a long, lank individual, whose head seemed to protrude from one end of the coach and his feet from the other." "He was the sole occupant," Nelson went on, "and was sleeping soundly. Hammond slapped him familiarly on the shoulder. . . . ." The tall man woke up.

"Have you chartered the stage for the day?" asked Hammond.

The stranger said, "Certainly not." He unbent his long legs and eased into the front seat where he would have to ride backward, giving up to the newcomers the more comfortable place.

The interlopers looked him over. They saw, so Nelson said, "a queer, odd-looking fellow . . . . dressed in a well-worn and ill-fitting suit of bombazine, without vest or cravat, and with a twenty-five cent palm hat on the back of his head." The gentlemen from Terre Haute decided it would be fun to crack some jokes at the expense of this hick, who sat there without any expression brightening up his big features. So they ragged him a bit, and he joined in several laughs at his own expense. At noon, when the passengers stopped at a wayside tavern for dinner, the new member of the party gave them some more laughs. Invited to sit at the table with his fellow-passengers, he sidled up to his place as if he thought they had conferred a great honor on him. The little chair was big enough to hold only about half of him, and, as if he were afraid someone would steal his two-bit hat, he tenderly held the thing under his arm during the meal.

The joke Nelson remembered best came during the afternoon part of the trip, when talk turned to a subject scientists were saying a great deal about at the time—a comet. Greatly interested in this subject, the stranger asked many questions and made several suggestions so absurdly silly that they were startling. Sure that their acquaintance would swallow anything they said on this subject, no matter how idiotic, the two Hoosiers had a grand time, mouthing all the long, thunderous words they could remember, and tying them up with the discussion. They enjoyed the look on their listener's face, which, they thought, showed he was more dazzled and bewildered every minute.

"What," the stranger asked, finally, "is going to be the upshot of this comet business?"

Nelson, looking important, said: "I'm not certain. In fact, I differ from most scientists and philosophers. I'm inclined to the opinion that the world will follow the darned thing off!"

Pleased as Punch about the way they had taken in the gullible oaf on the stage, the humorists lost sight of him when they got to Indianapolis. It was late that evening that Nelson caught sight of him, asked who he was, and found out he was Abraham Lincoln, a member of the United States Congress. Nelson and Hammond sneaked out by a back door so that they would miss seeing the man who, by acting the fool so well, had taken them in.

In his comic speech against Cass in the House of Representatives, the Illinois Congressman whacked at the presidential candidate of the rival party, who was being held up

as a military hero, by acting the fool and comparing his own
record in war with Cass's record.

> By the way, Mr. Speaker [he said], did you know I was a military hero?
> Yes, sir; in the days of the Black Hawk war I fought, bled, and came away.
> Speaking of General Cass's career reminds me of my own. I was not at
> Stillman's defeat, but I was about as near it as I was to Hull's surrender;
> and, like him, I saw the place very soon afterward. It is quite certain I
> did not break my sword, for I had none to break; but I bent a musket
> very badly on one occasion. If Cass broke his sword, the idea is he broke
> it in desperation; I beat the musket by accident. If General Cass went in
> advance of me in picking huckleberries, I guess I surpassed him in
> charges upon the wild onions. If he saw any live, fighting Indians, it was
> more than I did; but I had a good many bloody struggles with the mos-
> quitoes, and although I never fainted from the loss of blood, I can truly
> say that I was often very hungry.

Again, when Lincoln was debating with Douglas, the
latter, much more famous then than Lincoln and much
more successful, showed in almost everything he said that he
thought himself a long way above his opponent. But the
great orator tried to cover his condescension by saying Lincoln was a "kind, amiable, and intelligent gentleman."
Lincoln, sensing the real feeling behind the pat on the head,
knew that the compliment was not of much value and that
he would get no really first-rate boosts from the Little Giant.
He resented Judge Douglas' taking for granted that a crumb
of praise like that would be prized as a tidbit. He did not
want to show resentment too clearly by attacking directly,
but he wanted to show up the absurdity of such obvious
insincerity. So he compared himself with a fool character
who got joy out of half a bite of comfort. He said:

> . . . . as the judge had complimented me with these pleasant titles (I
> must confess to my weakness), I was a little "taken," for it came from a
> great man. I was not very much accustomed to flattery, and it came the

sweeter to me. I was rather like the Hoosier with the gingerbread, when he said he reckoned he loved it better than any other man, and got less of it.

There was the same sort of assumed simplicity, with intelligence peeping out from behind it, in Lincoln's kind words about a rival candidate who had given him a lift to a political meeting: "I am too poor to own a carriage, but my friend has generously invited me to ride with him. I want you to vote for me if you will; but, if not, then vote for my opponent, for he is a fine man."

III

The humor of the fool character, however, was only a sideline with Lincoln. If what people in his day said about him, and what they still say about him, is true, his specialty was telling good jokes. Everywhere he went in his youth and early manhood, it seems, he got into a crowd of fine story-tellers—at Anderson Creek ferry, in the little store where he clerked in New Salem, on a raft drifting downriver to the South, in the taverns where lawyers swinging around the circuit foregathered at night after hard days in court, in his law office at Springfield, in the state legislature, in the United States Congress.

Taking part in these sessions himself, he early became famous as a teller of good stories. Bill Green, who worked in the store with him and sometimes slept with him, told some friends: "He kin make a cat laugh. I've seen the whole neighborhood turn out to hear him tell stories. . . . . He's a great big feller, with a big mouth, and he kinder acts it all out, smilin' and laffin'. I never seed a real clown, but he'd make one." When he got into Congress, after only a few months word got around that a new champion yarn-spinner had invaded Washington. A newspaperman set forth admiringly that he "never told a story twice, but appeared to have an endless repertoire ready, like the successive charges of a magazine gun."

The picture of Abe the jester was repeated many times in newspapers and talk when he got to the White House. His friends showed the chief executive of a great nation swapping stories with humble people who came to see him, or melting the ice of formal gatherings by cracking jokes. His enemies tried to use the picture against him by showing him hearing about a great slaughter on the battlefield, then saying, like a simpleton, "That reminds me of a little story," and telling a crude joke which, in the circumstances, was ghastly in its bad taste. They were likely to call him a "low buffoon" or "the Nero who cracked jokes while Rome was burning."

The picture of Lincoln the jokester came down to modern times, when it has been repeated tenderly by biographers, fiction-writers, and poets. Thus Stephen Vincent Benét, in his epic poem about the Civil War, *John Brown's Body*, wrote of the tall American hero—

> The lank man, knotty and tough as a hickory rail,
> Whose hands were always too big for white-kid gloves,
> Whose wit was a coonskin sack of dry, tall tales. . . . .

There is no doubt that this part of the lasting legend about Lincoln is true—that he loved comic stories, told them often, told them well. Further, there is no doubt that the stories he told were useful as appeals to people who had a great liking for gumption. For one thing, as Carl Sandburg says, the many jokes ascribed to the President, the many references to him as a story-teller, made Americans think of him as one of them—"a plain, neighborly, somewhat droll man, nobody's fool, at home to common folks and even simpletons or charlatans who might step into the White House for a look at him." For another thing, they offered a humorous manner of stating a point so that the horse sense about it was emphasized.

His typical use of humor, in other words, was not in the role of a fool character—the indirect way—but in the role of a man strong on horse sense—the direct way. More often he was like Hosea Biglow rather than Birdofredum Sawin. When Lincoln told a joke in a fireside group, his face lost its usual dull, melancholy mask, his eyes sparkled, his whole countenance lit up. At the end of his yarn he would break into raucous laughter which one intimate of his said was no less undisguised and hearty than the neigh of a wild horse on his native prairie: he would howl with laughter, slapping his bony knees with his hands. When he was on a platform and a joke came into his head, people in the audience could tell it was on the way by noticing how his eyes began to sparkle and how they wrinkled at the corners. Such an appreciation for humor showed that there was no pretense of naïveté when Lincoln told one of his comic yarns.

The stories he told were packed with mother-wit. As Bill Green said: "His stories ain't all jest the kind fer women to listen to, but there's always a pint to 'em." Fables of a sort, they often served to give (as his law partner put it) "the coloring, shape, and weight of his ideas," to argue in behalf of his ideas by showing that some past happening threw light on human nature in such a way as to help solve a present problem.

Early in the war, when General Phelps took possession of

Ship Island, not far from New Orleans, the General published a proclamation, full of big words and elegant phrases, declaring that the slaves thereby and forthwith were free. Since Phelps had no right to do this, everybody expected the President to denounce this pronouncement, but no word about the paper came out of the White House. After this silence had lasted a long time, a friend asked Lincoln why he had not taken steps to deny that the proclamation was legal. It is easy to say what Lincoln's attitude toward this matter was because he made it quite clear. He was not taking the flashy proclamation with any seriousness, but being tolerant about it; and he was being tolerant, because it had made possible something that might be illogical but something very necessary to any human being—blowing off steam. The attitude, to his way of thinking, was justified because it was in line with an understandable experience—maybe his own experience with shrewish Mary Todd Lincoln, maybe the experience of a man with gumption whom he had known back in New Salem or Springfield. Those were his feelings and his reasons for them, but he did not put them into as dull and general a form as that. Instead, he told a story which conveyed his tolerance and put the whole argument in a nutshell.

"Well," he drawled, "I feel about that a good deal as a man I will call 'Jones,' whom I once knew, did about his wife. He was one of your meek men, ... badly henpecked. At last, one day his wife was seen switching him out of the house. A day or two afterward a friend met him in the street, and said, 'Jones, I have always stood up for you, as you know; but I am not going to do it any longer. Any man who will stand quietly and take a switching from his wife, deserves to be horsewhipped.' 'Jones' looked up with a wink, patting his friend on the back. 'Now *don't*,' said he: 'why, it didn't *hurt me* any; and you've no idea the *power of good* it did Sarah Ann!' "

Again, an officer who had been disgraced and defeated in one of the battles of the war, sent in a report that slickly slid over the fact that he had been soundly beaten. Uncle Abe's keen gray eyes saw right into the heart of the fraud, and he made known what he saw simply by telling a story that came to his mind. A young fellow, he said, came up to a farmer, out in the field, plowing.

"I want your daughter!" yelled the young man.

The farmer went on plowing as if the interruption was not worth stopping his work to take care of. All he did was shout over his shoulder, "Take her."

The young man stood there on the edge of the field, looking puzzled, scratching his head, and saying dubiously, "Too easy, too durned easy!"

Here and elsewhere, it was better to show an attitude in a story than it was to come right out and put it into words. A blunt statement like "the officer is a liar" would not have been nearly so tactful and good-natured, and at the same time so pointed, as the yarn about the farmer. Another story Lincoln told made it possible to give General Sherman some ticklish instructions without putting them into so many words. Hotheads in the North were yelping that Davis, the president of the Confederacy, ought to be captured and hanged. Lincoln, eager to heal the nation's wounds as soon as possible, saw good reasons for refusing the request. But it was not politic for him to let it be known that he had come right out and said what he wanted. The General told how the President handled the matter:

I asked Mr. Lincoln explicitly, when we were at City Point, whether he wanted me to capture Jeff Davis or let him escape, and in reply he told me a story. "I'll tell you, General," Mr. Lincoln began, "what I think of taking Jeff Davis. Out in Sangamon County there was an old temperance lecturer who was very strict in the doctrine and practice of total abstinence. One day, after a long ride in the hot sun, he stopped at the house of a friend, who proposed making him a lemonade. As the mild beverage was being mixed the friend insinuatingly asked if he wouldn't like to have a drop of something stronger to brace up his nerves after the exhausting heat and exercise. 'No,' replied the lecturer, 'I couldn't think of it; I'm opposed to it on principle; but,' he added with a longing glance at the black bottle that stood conveniently at hand, 'if you could manage to put in a drop unbeknownst to me, I guess it wouldn't hurt me much.' Now, General," Mr. Lincoln concluded, "I am bound to oppose the escape of Jeff Davis; but if you could manage to let him slip out unbeknownstlike, I guess it wouldn't hurt me much."

All these typical stories had other things than humor in common. They came pat for the situation in which they were used. They put Lincoln's policies in a good light because they seemed to back them up by showing people acting in a true way, thus taking their roots deep in human nature. Finally, they had about them a rural or village flavor. As a friend of his, Joseph Gillespie, said, the President based his most amusing yarns on "incidents in his boyish days amongst his country playfellows." Gillespie went on to say: "He always maintained stoutly that the best stories originated with country boys in the rural districts." And the reason for this liking, Joe hinted, was this: "He had great faith in the strong sense of country people and he gave them credit for greater intelligence than most men do."

IV

Out of Lincoln's love for country lore came a habit of his frequently to hark back to some of the wise saying, that farm people had garnered from the days of their lives and had thought good enough to keep in mind. "My old father," he wrote to a friend in 1842, "used to have a saying, 'If you make a bad bargain, hug it all the tighter.'" Another pro- verbial expression of his father which he treasured was, "Every man must skin his own skunk." He told a boy who was about to start work as a West Point cadet: "Now, boy, on your march, don't you go and forget the old maxim that 'one drop of honey catches more flies than a half-gallon of gall.' Load your musket with this maxim, and smoke it in your pipe."

Americans were to remember many sayings of Lincoln that had the style and content typical of cornfield proverbs. Here, rather than in the stories he told, the great man was an originator. When it came to stories, "I never did invent anything original," he said. "I am only a retail dealer." But he could coin better original aphorisms than any other man who ever sat in the White House. Late in summer, meeting a man on a Springfield sidewalk, he could say off- hand something worth treasuring—"The rain makes the corn laugh." Up for re-election, he could get off a good saying about how bad it was to switch horses while crossing a stream. Or, in a speech at Clinton, Illinois, he could make up a saying that people still quote often: "You can fool all the people part of the time and part of the people all the time, but you can't fool all the people all the time."

Usually, in looking at a horse-sense humorist, one has to be satisfied with certain earmarks of gumption, such as his playing the fool or using fables, folk sayings, and home-made aphorisms to get his ideas across, because no more data can be collected about the working of the man's mind. In the case of Lincoln, however, the study can go further than usual, because men who were close to him pondered about the matter and many letters and speeches which show his mind at work are available for study. As a result, Lincoln offers as good an example of the common-sense way of thinking as any man in American history.

Joe Gillespie, after years of knowing Lincoln, kept feeling that, to him, the most remarkable thing about the great man's mind was that it was such an ordinary sort of mind.

I never could discover anything in Mr. Lincoln's mental composition remarkably singular [he said]. His qualities were those ordinarily given to mankind, but he had them in a remarkable degree. . . . . He had passed through all the grades of society when he reached the Presidency, and he had found common sense a sure reliance and he put it into practice. He acted all through his career upon just such principles as every man of good common sense would approve. . . . . If I may be allowed the expression, Mr. Lincoln was a great common man.

How the "great common man" arrived at truth he himself put into a few words in a speech he made at Columbus, Ohio, in 1859. "There are two ways of establishing a proposition," he said. "One is by trying to demonstrate it upon reason, and the other is, to show that great men in former times have thought so and so, and thus to pass it by weight of authority."

Usually, Lincoln used the first way. But when he showed a line of thinking was reasonable, he did it in a horse-sense fashion which was very different from a book-learned fashion. Where the educated man might begin with a generalization, an abstraction, Lincoln, if he possibly could, would carefully avoid such a thing. Again and again he took digs at people who got started on a train of thought by dusting off what he called a "glittering generality." To the end of his life, he held to an attitude he showed clearly in a speech in 1848, when he said: "An honest laborer digs coal at about seventy cents a day, while the President digs abstractions at about seventy dollars a day. The coal is clearly worth more than the abstractions."

When a man started to mull over a problem he should not, as a rule, be concerned at first with a general law about it. Instead, he should dig into the problem until he found the essential fact. This fact should be sorted out: Lincoln had about as much scorn for a man who could not see what was vital, as he did for a person who went for windy general laws. It was the wonder of Leonard Swett, a fellow-lawyer during Abe's circuit days, how he gave away point after point in most of his lawsuits but saved the basic one and triumphed: "By giving away six points and carrying the seventh he carried his case, ... the whole case hanging on the seventh. . . . ."

How did he find his essential fact? Actually, by following a principle—but the principle was so simple that any man with a good head probably would grant that it was an undeniable part of horse sense to take that principle for granted. What that common concept was, his old law part- ner, Herndon, set forth clearly when he told of the talk the two of them had after a trip to Niagara Falls. Herndon, who sort of fancied himself as a literary man, admitted that, as he himself talked about the Falls, he became excited and poetical—"indulged in a great deal of imagery." Then he paused and asked a question.

"What," I inquired, "made the deepest impression on you when you stood in the presence of the great natural wonder?" I shall never forget his answer, because it in a very characteristic way illustrates how he looked at everything. "The thing that struck me most forcibly when I saw the Falls," he responded, "was, where in the world did all that water come from?" He had no eye for the magnificence and grandeur of the scene, for the rapids, the mist, the angry waters, and the roar of the whirlpool, but his mind, working in its accustomed channel, heedless of beauty or awe, followed irresistibly back to the first cause. It was in this light that he viewed every question. However great the verbal foliage that concealed the nakedness of a good idea Lincoln stripped it all down till he could see clear the way between cause and effect. If there was any secret in his power this surely was it.

Cause-and-effect relationships were the ones Lincoln constantly watched for. "Lincoln's whole life," Swett claimed, "was a calculation of the law of forces and ultimate results. The world to him was a question of cause and effect. He believed the results to which certain causes tended would be sure to follow."

These cause-effect ties were not, however, found by following abstract rules. A man hit on them by paying close attention to the peculiar circumstances involved, and each problem differed from almost every other one, because the circumstances were different. When, in a lecture on "Discoveries, Inventions, and Improvements," Lincoln wanted to make clear how mankind moved onward and upward, he pictured the great inventor of a steam engine "observing, reflecting, and experimenting" until he found a cause-effect connection. "This," said he, "is not the actual history in detail, but the general principle." Probably part of his dislike for abstractions arose from the fact that they did not take any account of factors peculiar to a problem, and he thought the whole practical solution of any puzzle depended entirely on taking account of its unique features. James

Russell Lowell noted that Father Abraham, "the incarnate common-sense of the people," as he called him, "seems to have had but one rule of conduct . . . . to let himself be guided by *events*. . . . ."

Looking at the circumstances before him, he first sought to discover their essential nature. Then what he had learned by experience became useful. Looking back, he could find a set of circumstances in essential ways like the present set. Knowing what the outcome of the past set had been—how the chain of events following them had turned out—he could see the import of present circumstances. If the causes were basically alike, the effects had to be alike. That was all a man needed to know to find the solution of a problem.

Such were the things Lincoln brought out when he used his first way of establishing a proposition—"trying to demonstrate it upon reason." Sometimes—notably in some of his law cases and the Cooper Union speech—he used the second way, establishing it "by weight of authority." A paragraph in the Cooper Union address harked back to the stand taken by the founding fathers on a phase of the question, "How should slavery be handled?" Said Lincoln:

The sum of the whole is that of our thirty-nine fathers who framed the original Constitution, twenty-one—a clear majority of the whole—certainly understood that no proper division of local from Federal authority, nor any part of the Constitution, forbade the Federal Government to control slavery in the Federal Territories; while all the rest had probably the same understanding. Such, unquestionably, was the understanding of our fathers who framed the original Constitution. . . . .

The use of this kind of proof in a speech tremendously important to Lincoln shows he thought well of it. It was not unreasonable for him to take such authority as proof, because here his notion was that great men of gumption, using exactly the way of finding the right answer he would use himself, had hit on the truth. "Law," he told Herndon, "is nothing else but the best reason of wise men applied for ages to the transactions and business of mankind."

But even here, every care had to be taken to make sure that any unique qualities in the situation did not throw out the old findings. Talking about law, he said: "Judicial decisions are of greater or less authority according to the circumstances. That this should be so accords both with common sense and the customary understanding of the legal profession." And in his Cooper Union speech, though he argued against slavery by showing how the founding fathers had felt about it, he made quite clear that "to follow implicitly in whatever our fathers did" would be "to discard all the lights of current experience."

When he talked to an American audience, Lincoln could be sure that either of these ways of arguing would be a good way, because the audience itself would be chock-full of horse sense. He trusted the people to have good eyes for seeing the truth when it was put before them. David Ross Locke, himself a man capable of horse-sense humor, got an insight into this notion of Lincoln when he heard him debate with Douglas at Quincy. Said Locke:

He admitted frankly all the weak points in the position of his party in the most open way, and that simple honesty carried conviction with it . . . . [and] strengthened his position on points where he was strong. He knew that the people had intelligence enough to strike the average correctly. His great strength was in trusting the people instead of considering them as babes in arms. He did not profess to know everything. He said wonderfully witty things, but never from a desire to be witty. He never cared how he made a point, so he made it.

Such a belief in the good gumption of his listeners probably had much to do with the strange style, for the times, that Lincoln used when he spoke. In his day very few public men could climb onto a platform and speak, as the saying of the time put it, without making the eagle scream. It was an age of rhetorical flourishes and welkin-shivering sentences. But, as many have noticed, Lincoln evidently had little taste for the highfalutin style. Lord Charnwood, a great English biographer, noticed that Lincoln, in his speeches, did not work up to a climax, that, instead, he "just used up the last few minutes in clearing up some unimportant point which he wanted to explain only if there was time for it." Charnwood went on to note:

We associate our older parliamentary oratory with an art which keeps the hearer pleasedly expectant rather than dangerously attentive, through an argument which if dwelt upon might prove unsubstantial, secure that all leads in the end to some great cadence of noble sound. But in Lincoln's argumentative speeches the employment of beautiful words is least sparing at the beginning or where he passes on to a new subject. It seems as if he deliberately used up his rhetorical effects at the outset to put his audience in the temper in which they could earnestly follow him and to challenge their full attention to reasoning which was to satisfy their calmer judgment. He put himself in a position in which, if his argument were not sound, nothing could save his speech from failure as a speech.

The gist of the whole matter was this: that, since Lincoln trusted his hearers to think rightly if they saw clearly, he concluded that the only thing he had to do was make them see clearly. Probably he was more interested in clarity in his speeches than he was in anything else. His old schoolteacher, Mentor Graham, said that he had known the man for fifty years and from childhood up to the time he lived in the White House, he always had one trait in character and style: "He studies to see the subject matter clearly and to express it tersely and strongly. I have known him down here in Menard study for hours the best way of any of three to express an idea. . . . ." Swett said: "His mode and force of argument was in stating how he had reasoned upon the subject and how he had reached his conclusions rather than in original reasoning to the hearer; and as the mind of the listener followed in the groove of his mind, his conclusions were adopted."

Lincoln added a word about the matter. He told a man interviewing him:

I can say this, that among my earliest recollections, I remember how, when a mere child, I used to get irritated when anybody talked to me in a way I could not understand. I don't think I ever got angry at anything else in my life. . . . . I can remember going to my little bedroom, after hearing the neighbors talk of an evening with my father, and spending no small part of the night walking up and down, trying to make out what was the exact meaning of their—to me—dark sayings. I could not sleep . . . . until I had put it in language plain enough, as I thought, for any boy to comprehend. . . . . I am never easy now, when I am handling a thought, till I have bounded it North, and bounded it South, and bounded it East, and bounded it West.

A good argument in favor of the American pride in the common sense of common men is that this way of arguing was beautifully, inspiringly successful. "I don't keer fur them great orators," said an Illinois farmer in 1854. "I want to hear jist a plain feller like the rest of us, that I kin foller an' know where he's drivin. Abe Linkern fills the bill." Colonel Finch, a leading Whig politician in Knox County, told a young man: "I've seen Abe Lincoln go into a caucus or a convention, and jist git up and talk kind of honest-like, with no fuss, but jist plain sense, windin' up with a story square to the point, and carry the whole outfit, bag and baggage, along with him." And in the White House, according to Carl Schurz:

There never has been a President in such constant and active contact with the public opinion of the country, as there never has been a President who, while at the head of the government, remained as near to the people. Beyond the circle of those who had long known him, the feeling steadily grew that the man in the White House was "honest Abe Lincoln" still, and that every citizen might approach him with complaint, expostulation, or advice, without danger of meeting rebuff. . . . . The conversations he had and the correspondence he carried on about matters of public interest, not only with men in official position, but with private citizens, were almost unceasing, and in a large number of public letters, written ostensibly to meetings, or committees, or persons of importance, he addressed himself directly to the popular mind. . . . . Thus he presented the singular spectacle of a President who, in the midst of a great civil war, with unprecedented duties weighing upon him, was constantly in person debating the great features of his policy with the people.

While in this manner he exercised an ever-increasing influence upon the popular understanding, his sympathetic nature endeared him more and more to the popular heart. In vain did journals and speakers of the opposition represent him as a light-minded trifler, who amused himself with frivolous story-telling and coarse jokes, while the blood of the people was flowing in streams. The people . . . . looked at him as one who was with them and wept with them; and as his heart was theirs, so their heart turned to him. . . . . To Abraham Lincoln the people became bound by a genuine attachment.

It was the most natural thing in the world that a man like this should become what so many people took him to be—a great common man who had a habit of telling jokes to show how he felt about a subject. A story to the point offered, to his way of thinking, the best of arguments about any matter in hand. When he told such a story, he showed that he had used his favorite path to get to his conclusion. He had studied the problem to see just what was basic in it. Then, in his mind, he had ranged through memories, not of abstractions, but of situations that had worked out in the past. He had reasoned from a particular instance to another particular instance essentially like it. Cutting through great differences, he had seen the real resemblances, as he did when he saw how a general's wartime proclamation was really like a shrewish wife switching her husband. Such a story carried his idea straight to an audience who went for a line of reasoning like that because they themselves had plenty of horse sense.

CHAPTER VII

Civil War Humor—Fools for Propaganda

Every critter what has ever seed me, if they has sense enough to hide from a coming calamity . . . . jist knows five great facts in my case. . . . . Firstly, that I hain't got nary a soul, nothing but a whisky-proof gizzard. . . . . Secondly, that I's too durned a fool to come under military law. Thirdly, that I has the longest pair of legs ever hung to any carcus, excepting only of a grandaddy spider. . . . . Fourthly, that I can chamber more corkscrew, kill-devil whisky, and stay on end, than anything excepting only a broad-bottomed churn. Fivety, and lastly, kin get into more durned misfortunate skeery scrapes, than anybody, and then run outen them faster, by golly, nor anybody.

—Sut Lovingood, The Knobs, Tennessee

Mr. Lincoln, Sir, our people get more stubborn every day. They go mighty nigh naked, and say they are saving their Sunday clothes to wear after we have whipped you. They just glory in living on half rashuns and stewing salt out of smoke house dirt. . . . . I feel very gloomy, Mr. Lincoln, about this destructive war. . . . . As General Byron said, at the Battle of Waterloo, "I ain't now what I used to was, and my spirits are flutterin, faint and low."

—Bill Arp, Georgia

I denounce this war as unholy, unconstitutional, unrighteous and unmitigated.

—Petroleum V. Nasby, Wingert's Corners, Ohio

I

SOME details about Lincoln's journey to Washington for his inaugural that never have been put into a biography were published in a Nashville newspaper, the *Union and American*, between February 28 and March 5, 1861. There a series of sketches, signed with the name of

149

Sut Lovingood, told how young Sut, a lanky Tennessee mountaineer, had helped the new President get safely to the White House.

Sut said in the first of his articles that, shortly after he hit Baltimore early in 1861, he came upon a fellow who was sitting on a barrel and filing the lock of a Revolutionary War pistol. When asked if he was going to war, the man said, "Yes, I'm gwine to bore old Abe's ears for him as he comes along." After walking a little farther, Sut saw a fat man with a monstrous knife—and the man said he planned to use the knife to execute the executive-elect. A little later, the Tennesseean came upon a man shining up a cannon as big as a pump log. This fellow, too, was getting ready to welcome the man from Illinois. He planned, he told Sut, "to take Old Abe in the place what first touches a hoss, and damn if he don't light beyond Washington, hit'll be that this here powder ain't good."

These subtle hints having given him the idea that maybe Baltimore would be an unhealthy place for the victorious candidate, Sut hurried along and joined Lincoln at Harrisburg. When Abe heard what was in store for him, said Lovingood,

. . . . his eyes sort of bulged and sort of spread, and his mouth swelled out, and says he, "I hain't perpared to die, Sutty, my Son"—he calls me Sutty when he wants help, and Mister Lovingood when he's got his dignity on . . . . and he feels good and safe—"I has done the things I hadn't oughter, and left undone the things I had oughter. . . . . Sutty, what had I best do in this awful emergency? The party can't spare me now. Besides, I ain't fit to die, and my whiskers have jest begun to grow, and I want to try the vittles in Washington City. Hit won't do to let me be made a sifter by these seseachun bullets just at this time. Will it, Sutty, my son?"

Seeing how abject Lincoln's terror was, Sut said, to help the poor man get to Washington he followed a strange plan:

I had a tailor . . . . measure a tobacco hogshead for the body, and a pare of telegraph poles for the legs, and make a jacket and a pair of britches, out of cross-barred truck . . . . and bring along a pot of red paint and a small bale of hay. Well, he did hit, and I ran the old Winding Blades into the britches, and tied a string round the ankles; then stuck in . . . . [the] hay. I did likewise with the jacket, and produced the biggest cross-barred man you ever seed. To judge by sight, he weighed seven hundred pounds, [and] his head didn't look bigger nor an apple. I painted the yellow off his face with the red truck . . . . and I swear, when I were done with him he looked like he'd been on a big drunk for three weeks.

Thus disguised, Lincoln, according to the mountaineer, climbed aboard the train and rode unrecognized to Baltimore. At that city, as the two made their way through a crowd of people with clubs and guns, Lincoln, so terribly frightened that the ashy pallor of his face showed through the red paint, made his trembling way to the train. The rest of Sut's account told how, after much more trouble with his fear-stricken companion, he finally managed to land him, safe and sound but shaken, at the Willard Tavern in Washington.

All this was never put into any biography for the best reason in the world: there is no truth in it. Sut Lovingood was an imagined character, and his whole account was put together as a humorous attack on the new executive. It was, according to most modern standards, a rather queer type of humor, though it is not without modern parallels, of a sort. Charlie Chaplin's picture, *The Dictator*, is a roughly parallel twentieth-century effort—a mixture of burlesque with fact, the end of which is the expression of hate. The product, like

Chaplin's piece, of bitter times, the Lovingood stories will introduce the pattern used by the humorists, northern and southern, who did very well during the Civil War.

The history of Sut Lovingood before he wrote these pieces of his shows how not a little American comic writing changed about this time. The man who created Sut was George Washington Harris of Tennessee, one of the most interesting humorous writers America has produced—interesting as a man and also as a writer.

Harris, born in Allegheny City, Pennsylvania, in 1814, was carried southward by his pioneering parents before he was six. In Knoxville, Tennessee, where the Harris migration ended, he had perhaps eighteen months, altogether, of schooling, before he was apprenticed to his half-brother in a jewelry shop. That was the beginning of a career that had a great deal of variety in it. Not only did he become a skilled worker in metals, who advertised that he could make a whole list of things, ranging all the way from dentists' instruments to racing cups from the latest English models, but in addition, at one time or another, he was a political pamphleteer, a steamboat captain, an inventor, a professional humorist, a postmaster, a surveyor, and a railroad superintendent.

In Knoxville the male citizenry knew Harris as a short and wiry man who did a grand job of telling humorous stories. One of his fellow-townsmen wrote to a newspaper a letter which pictured George charging down the street to find a good listener for a cock-and-bull story about a steamboat explosion—a yarn which was very good, especially when Harris told it. Something of the art which made his yarns so attractive came in handy when the Knoxville man turned writer and, in the fifties, won a reputation that was more than local by telling Sut Lovingood's yarns.

Sut Lovingood, as Harris showed him, was constantly riding into town on his bow-necked horse and stopping off at Pat Nash's popular saloon to yarn by the hour to the crowd of mountaineers gathered there. "Sut," said Harris, in the story which introduced the young man, "was 'queer looking' "—and the details he added proved the claim. Sut was "long-legged, short-bodied, small-headed, white-haired, [and] hog-eyed." But as this youth lolled around the bar and told stories about his escapades, his listeners howled with laughter. And though today women who read Lovingood's tales as Harris put them into print sometimes are puzzled to understand why horrid men think the things are funny, robust males still agree that they are choice humorous pieces. A book of the stories, *Sut Lovingood's Yarns*, which came out in 1867, has been kept constantly in print all the years since its appearance to supply a host of masculine readers with copies.

Sut offers more proof for the claim made a few chapters back that the typical humorist of the South was apt to season his liking for the low-class fellows he found amusing with a sprinkling of contempt. Sut was a member of the lowest class—except the slave class only—in the Knobs of Tennessee, shiftless if work of any kind was in sight, living only for whatever frolicking, forty-rod corn whiskey, and hell-raising he could horn in on. He took great pride in his reputation "for raisin of the devil personally, and promiskusly discomforting the women very powerful, and skeering of folks ginerally a heap." Parson Bullen, the preacher in the little church near his family's cabin, thought Sut was "a living proof of the hell-desarvin nature of man," and maybe the parson was right.

Lovingood, with his low-class background and work-shirking ways, was many cuts below George Harris on the social and moral scale. But Harris pictured him as a fellow of infinite mirth and had him speak most of the words in the pieces about him. His yarns made clear that he was one of the greatest oral story-tellers that either life or invention in America has produced. His drawled tales about people who got into all sorts of painful fixes—scrambles with bulls on a rampage or with quarts of angry hornets and the like— were told in racy language so full of comic touches that phrase after phrase, after all these years, still seems powerful-ly funny.

But though Harris gave Sut a great deal of credit for tell-ing yarns which were things of beauty, he did not often give the boy much heed when—and if—Sut made any comments of a significant sort. The boy knew human nature, yes, knew enough about its weaknesses to take advantage of it when he played his tricks—knew enough about it to bring out its con-tradictions, its incongruities. But aside from some cracks at frailties such as hypocrisy, stinginess, and love, one does not often find Sut saying much that has any wisdom in it. His frequent talk about himself as "a natural born durned fool" —as far as knowledge, say, of political matters went—was evidently talk that Harris thought right.

Harris, however, was a violent partisan in politics. His start as a writer was in composing campaign propaganda. When the Civil War came, he was so down on the North that he took his family away from Knoxville, which was largely pro-North, and wandered around from place to place for several years—to Nashville, to Decatur, Alabama, to Trenton, Georgia. It was natural that a man with such interests in politics should want to preach his opinions to other people.

It was natural, too, that he should want his most popular writings—the Lovingood yarns—to spread his doctrines to as large an audience as he could reach. But there was an obvious problem involved in any plan to use the Lovingood writings: how could a character whose understanding of political problems was next to worthless, a character who in all likelihood could not get acquainted with the big man of the day, as Downing had—how could such a character be used to get Harris' attitudes across?

In 1856, Harris hit on one solution to this problem. He wrote an article beginning with a paragraph in which someone said, "Well, Sut, what was your dream? Tell us. If ever you dreamed anything smart your friends ought to know it . . . . , for cuss me if you ever *thought* anything smart awake." Thus bantered, Sut leaned against the bar of the groggery in which he was standing and told his dream. In it he had found himself in a room of a Washington, D.C., tavern, watching three men play a game of cards, and another man watching them. The three men playing were Buchanan, Filmore, and Frémont, presidential candidates; the watcher was Seward. Sut had nothing to say about their political ideas; all he did was to tell how the game was played, how Seward watched it. The details of his dream, though, were symbolical of the political situation of the time. It was an indirect way of getting at the matter, but apparently it was not a bad way, because the article was reprinted in more than one newspaper.

In 1861, however, Harris found another method of show-ing how he felt about the election of Lincoln. He made Sut say he had actually joined Lincoln on the trip to Washing-ton, and then he based the things that supposedly happened during the journey on an actual fact—that there were some threats that the new President would be assassinated on the way to the White House. As the summary at the beginning of this chapter shows, Sut brought out in his parable one of the frailties Southerners liked to think marred Lincoln's character—cowardice. A more complete summary would add that Sut showed him to be, in addition, persecuted by fleas, greatly addicted to drink, and in other ways fairly dis-gusting. Lovingood used a great talent for the grotesque to show how ugly the man was, in his view: "His mouth, his paw and his footses am the principle features, and his strik-ing pint is the way them ar legs of hisn gets inter his body. They goes in at each edge, sorter like the prongs inter a pitchfork. . . . . He looks like a yeller ladder with half the rungs knocked out." The description ended with a nauseat-ing comparison between Lincoln and a defunct frog which had been stretched into a grotesque shape after death—"same shape, same color, same feel (cold as ice) and I'm damned if hit hain't the same smell."

Finally, to slash at what he thought was Lincoln's stupid-ity, Harris made capital of the mountaineer's favorite way of characterizing himself as "a natural born durned fool." How much this was a phrase he used to make his stories comic no one can say; but the effect was to underline the harum-scarum and careless qualities of his character—his lack of gumption. During his tale about helping the Presi-dent-elect, Sut was made to rejoice that Lincoln and one of his associates, General Scott, were both greater idiots than he himself was. After Lincoln got word from Scott exaggerating the dangers waiting in Baltimore and took the General's report seriously. Sut said:

I jumped outen bed and lit afore him and looked him steady in the eye for a minute and I felt that I were a-standing for the fust time afore a man I warn't afraid of, and too, I knew were scarser of sense than I were. And I were glad I had found him, for you know, George, that I thought I were the greatest fool of the world, and always felt 'shamed and under cow about it. . . . . I stood astonished, first of him and then at old Scott, two bigger fools in the world than me, and both on 'em able to read and write and a-holding high places in the nation. Sut's got a chance yet, thought I.

Again Sut persuaded his disguised companion to make a speech which would give people the idea he was crazy. His instructions were: "Give 'em a crazy speech. . . . . It won't cost you much trouble to do that, and it will convince 'em you am addled. Jist talk nateral; that's all you have to do." As the mountain boy heard the talk, "I swear," he said, "natural born durned fool as I knows I is, I felt ashamed, and sorter humbled, and I sorter felt like cuttin' of his throat. . . . ." Thus fierce contempt and hate found their expression in the words Harris gave Sut to say about Lincoln.

II

The formula for North-versus-South humor used by Harris was, in short, to set up a numb-headed and rather vicious character, show how he traitorously sympathized with the wrong side, have him, in an irritating fashion, give his rascally aid to the enemy, and then have him tell his story. A very similar formula was used with much wider success by Charles H. Smith of Georgia and by David Ross Locke of Ohio.

Smith put a good part of his biography into a few words for a newspaper thus:

Born in Gwinnett county, 1826; father a native of Massachusetts, and mother from South Carolina; father came to Savannah when a youth; taught school and wedded his pupil, and never returned North . . . . [I] grew up with all the other town boys, and was about as bad; went to school some and worked some; was brought up a merchant; went to college at Athens, Ga.; studied law and got married, and when the war came commenced writing rebellious letters, and continued to write while in Virginia in the army.

The first "rebellious letter" Smith wrote was concocted in April, 1861, a little while after Lincoln had put out a proclamation urging the southern armies to disperse. On the face of it, this letter, as it came out in a newspaper, was written by an uneducated man down in Georgia who was all for Lincoln, who wanted to do whatever he could to help him, but who was having some troubles. Like Harris, Smith was playing the role of a traitor to the South who was giving stupid help to Lincoln. As he later put it, he was "writing as though I was a good Union man and a law-abiding citizen, and was willing to disperse, if I could, but it was almost impossible, for the boys were mighty hot . . . . but still . . . . if we could possibly disperse in 30 days we would do so. . . . ." The "good Union man" signed the letter with the name Bill Arp.

Naturally, Bill was unpopular with his neighbors. "Mr. Linkhorn, sur," he said respectfully, "I'm afeer'd I'll git in a tight place here among these bloods, and slope out of it, and I would like to have your Scotch cap and cloak that you travelled in to Washington. I suppose you wouldn't be likely to use the same disgize again, when you left, and therefore

I would propose to swap." Bill was a rascal: he was also a fool. Phrases in his letters showed that, though he wanted to disperse, one of his troubles was that he did not know exactly what the word meant. He was having other troubles, too:

Your proclamation says something about taking possession of all the private property at "All Hazards." We can't find no such a place on the map. I thought it must be about Charleston, or Savannah, or Harper's Ferry, but they say it ain't anywhere down South.

As the war stretched on for months, Bill sent Lincoln other screeds full of bad grammar, poorly spelled words, and good wishes. In one written in January, 1862, Bill told how he and some other friendly Southerners had done their best to see the President, but had had no luck. Then, innocently, the Cracker asked "Linkhorn" to drop around for the doings on the first anniversary of Georgia's secession: "Let me know if you and Seward are coming, so we can fix up and swap a lie or two with you. . . . Do you chaw tobakker? We have some that is good." Almost a year later, December 2, 1862, he wrote the President to say how much he longed for the day "when Africa is to be unshackled"—all the slaves free:

What a glorious day that is to be! What a sublime era in history! What a proud culmination and consummation and corruscation of your political hopes! After a few thousand have clasped you in their ebony arms it will be a fitting time, Mr. Lincoln, for you to lay yourself down and die. Human ambition can have no higher monument to climb.

And later in the same month, Bill wrote his last letter to the President, telling how worried he was for fear that the Emancipation Proclamation was not going to have a good effect.

These letters, read by many guffawing Southerners, did much the same thing the Lovingood letters had done but made use of several devices that were novel. For example, Bill might, in his ignorance, ask sympathetic questions which happened to pour vinegar on wounds newly suffered by the Union. When—to cite one instance—the North did not enjoy remembering what had recently happened at Harper's Ferry, Bill blithely asked:

Mr. Linkhorn, sir, have you any late news from Mr. Harper's Ferry? I heerd that Stone W. Jackson kept the payroll for a few days, and that about fourteen thousand crossed over in twenty-four hours. . . . . Do your folks know how to make it pay?

Or he heard a rumor which had rather nasty implications, and, with great sympathy, he asked about its truth: "How are Bill Seward? I heern that a mad dog bit him the other day, and the dog died immediately. Are it a fact?" Now and then he used bad spellings, which, of course, were to be expected from an ignorant man but which happened to be more malicious than the correct spellings would have been. An instance was his saying: "I would like to see you pussonally, Mr. Linkhorn, and hear you talk and tell some of your funny *antydotes*. . . . . I laffed when I read em till the tears fairly rained from my eyelids." Again he made a bad mistake in capitalization, considering that Robert E. Lee was a southern general, when he warned the President that "the *Lee* side of any shore are onhealthy for your population." Another series of mistakes in using capital letters caused him to substitute the names of several southern military leaders for geographical terms, with changed implications:

Mr. Linkhorn, Sir, your generals don't travel the right road to Richmond, nohow. The way they have been trying to come is through a mighty *Longstreet*, over two powerful *Hills*, and across a tremendious *Stonewall*. It would be safer and cheaper for em to go round by the Rocky Mountings, if spending time in military excursions is their chief object.

Each of these passages turned what were supposed to be friendly notes into biting attacks—and they got into the letters because their author, Arp, was an ignoramus. Better than anyone before who had made a fool character his mouthpiece, Smith used the ignorance of his creation to good purpose. Bill's slips in writing made him say—apparently by accident—what southern readers were eager to have him say. Because he was on friendly terms with the enemy, it was almost as pleasant to read his foolishness as it would be if the enemy were entertaining them by making fools of themselves.

III

A few weeks before Bill Arp got his first letter into print, his northern prototype, Petroleum V. Nasby, signed his name to the first of a long series of letters which were to give Northerners many laughs during the hard days of the war.

Nasby's creator was David Ross Locke, born in upstate New York in 1833, brought up by a family interested in abolition, and trained for writing less by schools than by many printshops and newspaper offices in which he earned his bread from the time he was ten years old. After a start as a printer's devil, Locke finished his period of apprenticeship in 1850, then became a tramp printer, wandering westward. In the fifties he got a start as a newspaper editor, setting up a paper in some Ohio town or other, nursing it along for a few years, then selling out at whatever profit he could get, and moving on.

In March, 1861, shortly after Lincoln had taken the oath of office, he was in Findlay, Ohio, editing a sheet called the

Jeffersonian. The first Nasby letters came out in this paper; after 1865, when Locke became editor of the *Toledo Blade,* the later letters were published in its columns. Altogether, Nasby's series of screeds ran about twenty-six years.

The story goes that one night in March, 1861, when Locke went into the drug store in Findlay, he found a man named Levi Flenner going around among the crowd socially gathered there trying to get people to sign a petition. Levi, known to the town as a no-account loafer, had written out an attack on the Negroes of Ohio that he wanted citizens to back up with their names: the idea was that the legislature ought to bar all Negroes from entering Ohio and expel all members of the race who lived in the state. Since Levi was a bum and the few colored people with homes in Findlay were good law-abiding men, most of his audience saw the humor of the situation and refused to sign. (A good many years later, Mark Twain was to put a scene with the same kind of comedy in it into *Huck Finn,* with Huck's trashy pappy storming around against a Negro who clearly was far superior, morally and mentally, to the man who was laying him out.)

Struck by the nonsensical side of Flenner's proclamation —and annoyed by it, too—Locke went to his office and wrote a kind of parody of it. The parody, however, was directed not only at the silly petition but also at a proclamation that South Carolina had recently issued, telling of its secession from the Union. A long list of grievances told why Nasby's town, Wingert's Corners, had followed the "soot" of the southern state.

Enlarging on his model's worthlessness, Locke made his letter-writer the biggest dunce and the most horrible rascal

NASBY'S DREAM OF PERFECT BLISS—AN EASY JOB IN A POST OFFICE

so far invented by an American humorist. He reminds one of Birdofredum Sawin, but Lowell's bad man was comparatively innocent beside the rapscallion from Ohio. Birdofredum had been good once; Petroleum was a scoundrel from the day of his birth. Nasby was a braggart, a liar, a loafer, a drunkard, a coward, a hypocrite, and a bigamist. He was hideously and unreasonably prejudiced against the Negro race. As time passed and the brute gaily recorded his adventures, a tale was unfolded of a thoroughly misspent life.

Nasby, as the story started, was a sympathizer with the South living in Ohio—a Copperhead using puny stratagems against the Union cause. When the draft came along, he managed to think of ten reasons for being exempt, the best being:

1. I'm bald-headed, and have been obliged to wear a wig these 22 years.

2. I have dandruff in what scanty hair still hangs around my venerable temples.

3. I have a chronic catarrh.

4. I have lost, since Stanton's order to draft, the use of one eye entirely, and have chronic inflammation of the other.

5. My teeth is all unsound, my palate ain't exactly rite, and I have had bronchitis 31 years last June. I have a cough, the paroxisms of which is frightful to behold.

Afraid that even such good arguments as these might not keep him out of the army, Nasby climbed aboard a boat in Toledo, along with some other invalids, and rowed to Canada. After he was sure he was safe, he went back home, where, to his horror, he was promptly stuffed into a blue uniform and sent into action. Down South, he deserted to join a Confederate company. But, when he found out how hard it was to help the South, he deserted a second time and went back to his home town. There he started a shoddy church, thus evading the draft and, at the same time, doing his share to help other Copperheads sabotage the northern cause.

A letter of November 1, 1863, which told of an interview Nasby said he had with Lincoln, is as close a parallel as anything he wrote to the wartime letters of Sut Lovingood and Bill Arp. Shortly after C. L. Vallandigham of Ohio, the hero of the Copperheads and the "Saint" worshiped in Nasby's church, had suffered a bad political setback, the rascally Petroleum told how he visited the President:

Introducing myself, I opened upon him delicately, thus: "Lincoln," says I, "as a Democrat, who is prepared to die .... fer the inalienable rite of free speech—knowing also that you are a gorilla, a fiendish ape, a thirster after blood, I speak."

"Speak on," says he.

"I am a Ohio Democrat," says I, "who has repoodiated Valandigum."

"Before or since the election, did you repoodiate him?" says he.

"Since," retorted I.

"I thought so," said he. "I would have done so too, had I been you," continued he with a gorilla-like grin.

"We are now in favor of a vigorous prosecution of the war, and we want you to so alter your policy that we can act with you, cordially. .... We don't want you to change your policy, materially. We air modrit. Anxshus to support you we ask you to adopt the follering trifling changes:

"Restore to us our habis corpusses, as good as new. ....

"Do away with drafts and conscriptions.

"Revoke the Emancipation proclamation, and give bonds that you'll never ishoo another. ....

"Disarm your nigger soljers, and send back the niggers to their owners to conciliate them.

"Offer to assume the war indebtedness of the South, and pledge the Government to remunerate our Southern brethren for the losses they have sustaned in this unnatural war. ...."

"Is that all?" says the gorilla.

"No," says I promptly. "As a garantee of good faith to us, we shall insist that the best half of the offices be given to Democrats who repoodiate Valandigum. Do this, Lincoln, and you throw lard ile on troubled waters. Do this and you rally to your support thousands of noble Democrats . . . . willing to jine the war party reserving to ourselves the poor privilidg of dictating how and on what principples it shall be carried on. Lincoln! Gorilla! Ape! I have done."

The President replied that he would give the matter serious consideration. He would mention the idea of resigning to Seward, Chase and Blair, and would address a circular to the Postmasters et settry, and see how many of em would be willing to resign to accomodait Democrats. He had no doubt several would do it to once. "Is there any little thing I can do for you?"

"Nothing pertikler. I would accept a small post office, if situated within easy range of a distillery. My political daze is well nigh over. Let me but see the old party once more in the assendency—let these old eyes once more behold the Constooshn as it is, the Union as it was, and the Nigger where he ought 2 be, and I will rap the mantel of private life around me, and go in 2 delirium tremens happy. I have no ambishen. I am in the seer and yaller leef. These whitening lox, them sunken cheek, warn me that age and whisky have done their perfeck work, and that I shall soon go hents. Lincoln, scorn not my words. I have said. Adoo."

So saying, I waved my hand impressively and walked away.

PETROLEUM V. NASBY
Paster of sed Church, in charge

It is easy to see, from a sample like this, how Locke got his effects in the Nasby letters. Everything in the piece emphasized the stupidity of its supposed writer. Bad spelling (much more of it than I have reproduced) and horrible grammar made it possible for even unlearned readers to feel superior. When Nasby used the wrong letters and wrote "political daze" and "assendency," instead of what he had in mind, like poor Bill Arp, he hinted by accident at truths he did not want to confess. No one had to study rhetoric to see that by beginning his talk with the fool claim that his hearer was an ape and a thirster for blood, the humble petitioner was getting off to a bad start. Anyone with sense enough to come in out of the rain had no trouble making out that Nasby's request for "trifling changes" in policy was hypocritical, because every demand he made was clearly intended to make a vital wound in wartime policy. Though Petroleum could sense no guile in Lincoln's promises to him, almost any other fool would have guessed that the President was being ironic. And the try the Copperhead from Ohio had at being pathetic when he went into the last lines of his speech was shown up as false oratory by a pseudo-elegance very foreign to a man who could not get two words in a row spelled correctly and also by the tender way he talked about drinking himself into delirium tremens.

The writing in this letter was typical of the Nasby pieces. There was little subtlety in Locke's stuff. Much more than Smith, more, even, than Harris, he hammered out his blunt attacks with a sledge hammer. Letter after letter told of Nasby's villainy—laid bare a heart as black as coal. Phrase after phrase seemed perfectly adapted to show Nasby's shriveled soul, in shivering nakedness, to the world. Hollow rhetoric, smugly religious quotations, or pedantic literary allusions, meant to hide the man's wickedness, only emphasized it.

And, of course, everything he said in letters by the score proclaimed the man a fool as well as a rascal. When he drew his enemies for the world, he made them devils; when he pictured his associates, he gave them wings and haloes—and these characters out of melodrama, as his enemies read about them, stood out as palpably false. Not only did he reason illogically: with sublime faith that no one was as wise as he, he put his arguments in numbered order, perhaps expecting the brieflike forms to impress readers. His pleas for a soft political job, for example, might be put alongside of his reasons for not being drafted.

First, I want a offis
2nd. I need a offis
3rd. a offis wood suit me; therfore
4th. I shood like to hev a offis.

Such was the pattern of the Nasby skits—one after the other putting into bad grammar and worse spelling arguments so feebly supported that only an idiot who had somehow had the same weird aberrations before reading them could possibly find them impressive. Locke, who had a redhot temper, gave it full play in these pieces, creating a gargoyle and exposing its grotesque deformities to arouse scornful laughter.

IV

The writings of Harris, published on the eve of the war, apparently had considerable success. The wartime writings of Smith and Locke, however, had really great popularity. Smith's letters, read and enjoyed by many Confederate soldiers in the field and by civilians at home, gave their author a start on a long career as a prosperous humorist. Locke's papers were even more widely reprinted in the North than Smith's papers were in the South. Week by week, people looked forward to them; and, when they were published, readers clipped them out of the paper and read and reread them until the clippings were worn to pieces.

Lincoln's enthusiasm for the Nasby letters shows how at

least one Northerner with a keen sense of humor cherished them. The President evidently was taken with them from the time they began to appear, scissoring them out of newspapers and stuffing them into his pockets—reading some of them so often that he could recite several whole letters from memory. When a number of them were gathered together in a cheap little pamphlet, he kept the flimsy, yellow-covered book close at hand in a desk drawer, where he could pull it out to read aloud whenever he would collect a listener or two. Visitors to the White House tell how the President, reading Nasby in bed at midnight, now and then came on a bit he liked so well that he just had to share it with someone. So the President of the United States would paddle down the hall in his nightshirt, wake up some White House guest, and read the passage to him.

The crucial presidential campaign of 1864 was ended, the votes had been cast, and Lincoln was tensely waiting to learn whether the people had approved his policy or had arisen against everything he had tried to do in carrying on the war. The bulletins having stopped for a time, he called Charles A. Dana to his side.

"Dana," he said, "have you ever read any of the writings of Petroleum V. Nasby?"

"No sir," Dana answered.

"Well," said Lincoln, "let me read you a specimen." Pulling out a thin yellow pamphlet from his breast pocket, he began to read aloud. "He would read a page or a story," Dana said later, "pause to consider a new election telegram, and then open the book again and go on with a new passage."

Once he told Sumner, "For the genius to write these

things, I would gladly give up my office." Again he said to
some senators, congressmen, and private citizens, "I'm
going to write Petroleum to come down here, and I intend
to tell him if he will communicate his talent to me, I will
swap places with him."

V

Anyone reading this humor today has trouble even in
imagining how such stuff could once have seemed so de-
licious. Even Arp's letters to Lincoln, the mildest of the lot,
seem now rather more violent, more grotesque, than amusing. Lovingood (as a wartime propagandist) and Nasby are
generally dull and sometimes mildly nauseating.

Moreover, the spirit behind the letters was about as play-
ful as a maddened elephant. The letters had a mission—
and, if Charles Sumner is right, the Nasby papers, at least,
carried out their mission very well. Said the member of the
wartime Cabinet:

Beyond the interest in these letters as another instance of a peculiar
literature—illustrated by Major Jack Downing . . . . and . . . . Hosea
Biglow—they have an historic reconstruction. Appearing with a certain
regularity, and enjoying an extensive circulation, they became a constant and welcome ally. Unquestionably they were among the influences
and agencies by which disloyalty in all its forms was exposed, and public
opinion assured on the right side. It is impossible to measure their value.

Clearly the purpose behind these papers was a very serious
one—and the fun in them, understandably enough, is often
weighted down with the heavy intention of Locke.

Why, then, did people once believe this stuff so pricelessly
amusing? I think that the answer has to do with the peculiar
state of mind of the readers. Smith said that he thought the
humor in his wartime letters was entertaining because "it

was pertinent to the occasion that provoked it, and very impertinent to those it held up before the public eye." The pieces, written by men who at the moment were filled with loathing for an enemy, were read by men and women whose normal way of seeing things was equally distorted by war-time hate.

In a life-and-death struggle, people were eager to see even the humorists lash at the other side with ferocious, crushing blows: whether the hits were foul or fair did not greatly matter. Readers were tickled by writers who tied up the utmost in villainy and stupidity with the other side. Even puritanical northern people could enjoy the grossness, the indecency, the impurity of a Nasby if he was enlisted with the forces against which the North was fighting. His creator was not very subtle, but he was sufficiently indirect to make his admirers think the way he showed up their enemies was really funny. Of the three writers treated in this chapter, the two in the South used the peculiar wartime technique only for a short time: Locke alone kept busy with the sort of writing that had made him famous until the late eighties. Down to the end of his career he was enjoyed by the haters for whom he wrote.

CHAPTER VIII

Lost Characters

Some things pay in the short run and for a little while, but honesty and truth and diligence pay in the long run, and that is the run we have to die by.

—BILL ARP, GEORGIA

I have no politics. Nary a one. I'm not in the bizness. . . . . I'm in a far more respectful bizness than what politics is. I wouldn't give two cents to be a Congresser.

—ARTEMUS WARD, TRAVELING SHOWMAN

Little do women realize that all a man needs under the cerulean dome of heaven is love—and board and clothes.

—BILL NYE, LARAMIE, WYOMING

I

AFTER writing four letters to "Abe Linkhorn," Bill Arp stopped corresponding with the President. Before long, however, he began turning out another batch of letters, published in the *Atlanta Constitution*. A typical passage in one of these reads:

Not many days ago the everlasting Yankees (may they live always when the devil gets 'em,) made a valiant assault upon the city of the hills [Rome, Ga.]. . . . . For three days and nights our valiant troops had beat back the foul invader, and saved our pullets from their devouring jaws. . . . . We felt that Rome was safe—because against the world, the flesh and the devil, which last individual is supposed to be that horde of foul invaders who are seeking to flank us out of both bread and existence.

Something curious had happened to Bill Arp. The man who once had been a Union sympathizer, helping the President all he could, was now calling Yankees "foul invaders" and hoping that they would eternally roast in hell. The change in Bill's feeling about the North and the South, of course, had to be the result of one more fundamental, for obviously he could not have come to conclusions which his creator thought were as sound as these without having traded in his feeble brains for a first-rate set. Clearly, Bill Arp, the fool character, had miraculously got some sense into his head.

The new Bill Arp, as Smith conceived him, was—to quote his creator—"an humble man and unlettered in books; never went to school but a month or two in his life, and could neither read nor write; but still he had more than his share of common sense, more than his share of ingenuity, and plan and contrivance, more than his share of good mother-wit and good humor. . . . ." He was a tenant farmer before the war, and when the war started he enlisted with the southern army. "I've seen Bill Arp in battle," said Smith, "and he was a hero. I've seen him when shot and shell rained around him, and he was cool and calm, and the same old smile was upon his features."

It was this unread but right-thinking countryman who, in the days following the war, wrote an illiterate letter to a Northerner whose name he happened to know, tearing into the North for its harsh treatment of the defeated South. "Sum of your folks," he said, "have got to dry up or turn our folks loose."

. . . . talkin the way I see it, a big feller and a little feller, *so called*, got into a fite, and they fout, and fout, and fout a long time, and evry boddy all around a hollerin hands off, but kep a helpin the big feller, till finally the little feller caved in and hollered enuf. He made a bully fite, I tell you, selah. Well, what did the big feller do? Take him by the han and help him up, and bresh the dirt offen his clothes? Nary time! . . . . But he kicked him after he was down and throwed mud on him and drug him about and rubbed sand in his eyes and now hes a gwine about a huntin up his poor little property. Wants to konfiskate it *so called*. Blame my jacket if it ain't enough to make your head swim.

Anyone who reads the letters of Bill Arp through will find that this sudden shift rather blurs the character involved. There is still some consistency: Bill often shows that he is a simple son of Georgia soil, not much touched by culture or the social graces. But, as the reader who has taken for granted this shift in his character reads on in Bill's letters, still more trouble crops up. Not many pages away from the lines about the northern bully, Bill recalled his trip to Rome, Georgia, not long after Sherman had made his ruthless march—a trip, he says, "through a desolate land . . . . where ghostly chimneys stood up like Sherman's sentinels a-guarding the ruins he had made."

This is not the style of a crude Georgia Cracker—it is highfalutin literary talk. And time after time, sentences like this, suggesting a similar background of education, got into the letters alongside of passages much less polished. Literary allusions were sprinkled here and there, allusions which showed Bill had made himself familiar with such classics as *Don Quixote* and the plays of Shakespeare. Or Bill would write a paragraph mysteriously stuffed with historical allusions of a rather obscure sort: "My friends inside had passed the Rubicon, and one by one retired to dream of Botzaris and his Suliote band. Vacant rooms and long corridors echoed with their snores, and they appeared like sleeping heroes in the halls of the Montezumas." It makes no kind of sense to suppose that the author of that sentence was, in Smith's words, "an humble man and unlettered in books." The character of Bill Arp somehow had been mislaid.

II

If Bill Arp were the only comic figure in the decades after 1855 who thus talked by turns like himself and then like somebody else, the inconsistent characterization might be dismissed as a series of slips by his creator and nothing more. But since this sort of thing happened more than once and in the end became a widespread practice, it is clear that he stood for a development in American humor which was becoming general.

Consider the case of Artemus Ward. His creator was Charles Farrar Browne, who had started his career as a journeyman printer, had wandered westward in the fifties, and had finally taken over an editorial desk on the *Cleveland Plain Dealer*. Browne, a man who loved lively talk, hilarious practical jokes, and rambunctious stag parties with plenty of whisky handy, in 1858 started to write a series of letters which put some of his boisterous humor into print.

His creation, Artemus Ward, whose name was signed to these productions, had not turned out many of his little pieces before he became a character well known to everybody who read them. The first letter sketched in details of his makeup quite clearly. Under the headline, "LETTER FROM A SIDE-SHOWMAN," the newspaper said, "Mr. Artemus Ward, proprietor of the well-known sideshow, writes us from Pittsburg as follows." The letter read:

PITSBURG, Jan. 27, 18&58

SIR:

I write to know how about the show bisnes in Cleveland. I have a show consisting in part of a Calforny Bear, two snakes, tame foxies &c, also wax works. My wax works is hard to beat, all say they is life and nateral curiosities. Among my wax works is our Savior, Gen. Taylor and Doctor Webster in the act of killing Parkman. Now mr. Editor scratch off few lines and tell me how is the show bisnes in your good city. I shal have handbills printed at your office. You scratch my back and I will scratch your back. Also git up a great blow in the paper about my show. Don't forget the wax works.

Here was a man who believably combined the poor spelling and horrible grammar of an uneducated man with the child-like faith that others not only shared his back-scratching philosophy but openly admitted they did. He was mildly tinged with rascality, shrewd only to a point where there was no real conflict with his basic ignorance. The details he gave about his little show made clear that it was just the sort of a ridiculous hodgepodge that a man whose mind worked as his did would carry about the countryside.

Later letters, in keeping with this first one, filled in the picture. Swelling with pride because he owned a show which "knocks the socks off from all other shows in the u.s.," the impresario gave more and more details about his attractions. He had a kangaroo, and "it would make you larf to see the little cuss jump and squeal." He had the Lord's Supper done in waxworks—"the prase of all." He would stick by his promise to let the *Plain Dealer* editor do his handbills, "but you must git up a tremendus excitement in yr Paper." Shrewd enough to see that it paid a showman to agree with people, Ward was stupid enough to say—without any shame, "My political sentiments agree with yourn exackly. I know they do, because I never saw a man whose didn't." He was ingenuous enough to take for granted that a newspaper editor would hypocritically connive with him in working on the feelings of subscribers:

Come the moral on 'em strong. If it's a temperance community tell 'em I signed the pledge fifteen minutes arter I's born, but on the contrary if your people take their tods, say Mister Ward is as genial a feller as we ever met, full of conwiviality, and the life and soul of the Social Bored. Take it, don't you?

When such a fence-straddler and nitwit as this bumped up against a political question, one of two things was likely to happen. Because he was eager to keep friendly with the public, he might refuse to show how he felt on the subject. At other times, because he was a fool and a bit of a rascal, he might give out his idiotic opinion. In the latter case, he worked in much the same way Nasby did—and, as a matter of fact, Nasby's creator later was glad to give Browne credit for suggesting his rascally letter-writer.

But in time, Ward—like Arp—began every now and then to write passages much more full of right thinking than anyone who knew the scamp would expect them to be. The man who earlier had been so eager to get along with prospective customers for his show that he always agreed with their ideas found himself in a community of free lovers, in Ohio, amorously pursued by one of the women in the place. He was trying to sell tickets to a performance at the time, and the politic thing would have been for him to be tactful about her advances. Instead, he drove away the crowd by shouting a sermon:

I was very much riled, and fortifyin myself with a spare tent stake, I addressed them as follers: "You pussylanermus critters, go way from me and take this wretched woman with you. I'm a law-abidin' man, and beleeve in good, oldfashioned institutions. . . . . I think your Affinity business is cussed nonsense, besides being outrageously wicked. Why don't you behave decent like other folks? Go to work and earn a honest living and not stay round here in this lazy, shiftless way, pizenin the moral atmosphere with your pestrifrous ideas! . . . ."

The Children in the Wood

Cartoon from "Vanity Fair," May 24, 1862

ARTEMUS WARD AS A PUBLIC LECTURER

The same sort of moralizing talk, as Professor Pattee has pointed out, enters Ward's letters when he "rebukes the . . . . Spiritualists, the Committee from the Woman's Rights Association and the office-seekers about Lincoln, who gives advice to the Prince of Wales and Prince Napoleon, who stands by the flag when the mob destroys his show down among the 'Seshers,' and who later addresses the draft rioters at Baldinsville."

Yet in the very same letter in which he ventured on an opinion, Artemus would often in a moment or so recall that he had no opinions. After he had scolded the office-seekers, for example, in the letter about his visit to Lincoln, he told the President: "Showmen is devoid of politics. They hain't got any principles! They know how to cater to the public." The fool character thus popped in and out of letters written by a horse-sense character who, as Professor Wilt has noticed, constantly "was ridiculing things that most of the people of the country intensely disliked."

From some of the letters, too, even Ward's ailing grammar and limping spelling disappeared. Sloughing off his ignorance for long stretches, like Arp, he could compose passages full of well-chosen words and elegant literary phrasings. His character, like Arp's, eventually evaporated. Whatever laughter he inspired was more at his way of saying things than at the character who said them.

III

It would probably be more tiring than useful to examine many other writings of humorists in this period and note in detail how often something similar happened. It ought to be enough—before guessing about the reasons back of the phenomenon—to notice whether their way of writing was still in use late in the nineteenth century. About the last man in the nineteenth-century humorous school to win great popularity was Edgar Wilson Nye, who wrote under the pen name of Bill Nye. How about him?

Nye differed from Smith and Browne in not starting out by setting up a kind of character such as Bill Arp or Artemus Ward. This Maine man who drifted westward and set up as a humorist in Laramie, Wyoming, on a paper called the *Boomerang*, from the first was a writer who one moment played the role of a fool, the next moment talked straight from the shoulder with only a hint of humorous intention here and there in his phrasing. Nye's first book was *Bill Nye and Boomerang* (1881). His last good book was a comic *History of the United States* (1894). A brief glance at the pages of the latter volume shows the wise man and the fool talking by turn in alternate paragraphs.

Nye, telling of the Revolution, came to the Valley Forge episode. In one paragraph, as the intelligent writer told of the hardships of the soldiers, only the phrase about hiring out, the inadequate word "sad," the words "to rest," and a rather too purple passage at the close hinted that the writer was telling his story humorously:

During the Valley Forge winter (1777–78) Continental currency depreciated in value so that an officer's pay would not buy his clothes. Many, having also spent their private funds for the prosecution of the war, were obliged to resign and hire out in the lumber woods in order to get food for their families. Troops had no blankets, and straw was not to be had. It was extremely sad, but there was no wavering. Officers were approached by the enemy with from one hundred to one thousand pounds if they would accept and use their influence to effect a reconciliation; but, with blazing eye and unfaltering attitude, each stated that he was not for sale, and returned to his frozen mud-hole to rest and dream of food and freedom.

The next two paragraphs, however, were written by a preachy fool who, taking for granted that his readers would follow a dumb suggestion of his, did his silly best to give them a hand:

Those were the untitled nobility from whom we sprung. Let us look over our personal record to see if we are living lives that are worthy of such heroic sires.

Five minutes will now be given the reader to make a personal examination of his personal record.

Nye then ran across the page two rows of asterisks which, presumably, his docile reader would stare at as he pondered the great thought the author had so proudly suggested.

Or Nye came to the time of Lincoln's death and wrote a paragraph which would have been fitting for a serious and formal history:

It is very likely that the assassination of Lincoln was the most unfortunate thing that happened to the Southern states. While he was not a warrior, he was a statesman, and no gentler hand or more willing brain could have entered with enthusiasm into the adjustment of chaotic conditions, than his.

The very next paragraph, however, was written by a man who, it appeared, knew a little French badly, but nevertheless used it to show off—a man who did not let his ignorance about the workings of the Constitution interfere with a guess at its operation which was both brash and idiotic:

The Fourteenth Amendment, a bright little *bon mot*, became a law June 28, 1868, and was written in the minutes of Congress, so that people could go there and refresh their memories regarding it.

Of course, part of the joke was that the fool character, like the wartime Bill Arp, was "accidentally" saying something critical about the Amendment. Actually it *was* in some ways a joke; actually its provisions *were* forgotten. But the cream of the jest was that an unthinking chump, trying to write an impartial but elegant history, should blunder into making such a harsh comment.

Nye's humor at the end of the century, then, like the humor of the final Arp and the final Ward, was writing in which, if a fool character authored one paragraph, a horse-sense character was as likely as not to author the next, and so on to the end of the piece. Sometimes in a single paragraph the two kinds of minds would show up in alternate sentences.

Another thing: from Nye's writings, more even than from the writings of Smith and Browne, the weird spelling and queer grammar had disappeared. This meant that another possible kind of device to distinguish the fool from the intelligent man was no longer helpful. The words and expressions which passed through both kinds of minds were of a similar sort. Even a good many local touches were lost—so it was no longer possible to guess that Ward was from Ohio, Arp from Georgia, and Nye from either Maine or Wyoming.

IV

Connected with these changes in humorous writing as they are seen in Nye's work was another—and an important one—which, like the others, helped to take the characterization out of it. This change will be made clear by a comparison of two pieces—one in the earlier manner, by Nasby, and one in the later manner, by Nye.

The letter of Nasby, dated August 12, 1866, told of a great dream at last come true. After years of conniving for a political job, Nasby had been rewarded. "At last I have it!" he said:

Finally it come! After five weary trips to Washington, after much weary waitin and much travail, I hev got it. I am now Post Master at Confedrit X Roads, and am dooly installed in my new position. If I ever had any doubts as to A. Johnson bein a better man than Paul the Apossle, a look at my commission removes it. . . . . If I doubt his Democrisy, I look at that blessed commission, and am reassured, for a President who cood turn out a wounded Federal soldier, and apoint sich a man ez ME, must be above suspicion.

Nasby went on to tell how he had come into his own: he had recently passed a hard test of his party loyalty by answering a series of questions sent him by the postmaster-general—questions like:

Do you have the most implicit faith in Andrew Johnson, in all that he has done, all that he is doin, and all he may hereafter do?

Do you believe that the Philadelphia Convention will be a convocashen of saints, all actuated by pure motives, and devoted to the salvation of our wunst happy, but now distracted country?

Are you willin to contribute a reasonable per cent. of your salary to a fund to be used for the defeat of objectionable Congrismen in the disloyal states North?

"To all of these inquiries," said Nasby, "I not only answered yes, but went before a Justis of the Peace and took an affidavit to em, forwarded it back, and my commission was forthwith sent to me." The rest of the letter told how Nasby and his low-down political cronies had celebrated the appointment in a parade which crudely stressed all the worst policies of their party and how he had taken his seat in an ideal office—"with but little to do" and with four saloons "within a stone's throw."

Nye's letter accepting a post office in Laramie, Wyoming, is short enough to quote in full:

OFFICE OF DAILY BOOMERANG, LARAMIE CITY, WY.
August 9, 1882.

MY DEAR GENERAL:

I have received by telegraph the news of my nomination by the President and my confirmation by the Senate, as postmaster at Laramie, and wish to extend my thanks for the same.

I have ordered an entirely new set of boxes and postoffice outfit, including new corrugated cuspidors for the lady clerks.

I look upon the appointment as a great triumph of eternal truth over error and wrong. It is one of the epochs, I may say, in the Nation's onward march toward political purity and perfection. I do not know when I have noticed any stride in the affairs of state, which so thoroughly impressed me with its wisdom.

Now that we are co-workers in the same department, I trust that you will not feel shy or backward about consulting me at any time relative to matters concerning postoffice affairs. Be perfectly frank with me, and feel free to bring anything of that kind right to me. Do not feel reluctant because I may at times appear haughty and indifferent, cold or absurd. Perhaps you do not think I know the difference between a general delivery window and a three-em quad, but that is a mistake.

My general information is far beyond my years.

With profoundest regard, and a hearty endorsement of the policy of the President and the Senate, whatever it may be,

I remain, sincerely yours,

BILL NYE, P.M.

Since, as it happens, this is a piece in which the fool role is played consistently by the author, a contrast comes out clearly when the two letters are laid side by side. Nasby's letter, in what it implied about politics, was bitter, nagging, malicious. On the other hand, Nye's letter was as free of harsh partisanship as a piece possibly could be that touched, however lightly, on political affairs.

In the earlier letter much space was given to party issues,

and, further, the issues were put bluntly, in the crudest possible way. From the later letter, party politics had almost entirely disappeared: the satire was not against any party but against practices supposedly of both parties. Nye mentioned nothing so hateful as the handing-over of a percentage of a government salary; Nasby not only mentioned it but made a point of such a corrupt trick's being the usual thing in the gang to which he belonged. Nasby named names; Nye did not. The earlier writer, being a rascal as well as a fool, made the reader suspect that his was a rascally party. Nye, being simply a well-meaning fool, implied nothing so scandalous about the party which had tendered him a job. The joke was on him rather than on his political allies. Thus the bitter partisanship in earlier writings from Crockett right on through several decades had no place in this letter of 1882.

Look elsewhere in Nye's writings, and it will be clear that his whole tendency, as a rule, was to slide away from political subjects. His *History of the United States*, whenever it came near a contemporary question, became skittish and shied away. And his writings as a whole, at least nine-tenths of the time, were concerned with almost everything under the sun except political issues.

There had been preparations for this sidling away from vital governmental issues. Artemus Ward, starting out as a character with no principles, could not, as a rule, even at the outset of his career, say incisive things about political matters when by chance he bumped into an issue. Of the most famous writers of the 1860's, Artemus probably made the fewest bitter assaults on opponents. Later, he touched on politics less and less, and even his mild forays into arguments of the day mostly ceased.

As for Arp, he, in time, left behind his hate-filled assaults on the Yankees and became a commentator on nonpolitical matters: the subtitle of one of his books, "Humor and Philosophy," showed what he had to offer in his last years. A countrywoman had this writer of the later period in mind when she said, "Don't Bill Arp tell things the plainest? I have laughed till I cried over some of his letters; for the same things had happened in our own family, and it seemed that he must have been right there in the house when he wrote it." No doubt she was recalling paragraphs like the following:

> It's a great comfort for me to set in my piazzer these pleasant evenings and look over the farm, and smoke the pipe of peace, and ruminate. Ruminate upon the rise and fall of empires and parties and presidents and preachers. I think that when a man has passed the Rubicon of life and seen his share of trouble, smokin' is allowable, for it kinder reconciles him to live on a while longer, and promotes philosofic reflections. I never knowd a high-tempered man to be fond of it.

Not only most of the bad grammar and spelling but also much of the fire which had flamed in Bill's earlier political letters was missing from this idyllic sketch of a thoughtful old farmer smoking at twilight on the quiet piazza of his home.

A similar omission of many details which might have given them characters of their own kept the dialect, the bad grammar, the bright or simple minds, and the political crotchets out of the writings of dozens of humorists popular in the latter half of the nineteenth century. Thousands of people were delighted with such authors as Robert J. Burdette, known as "the Hawkeye Man" because of his work on a newspaper called the *Hawkeye*, James M. Bailey (the *Danbury News* Man), Charles H. Clark (Max Adeler), George Horatio Derby (Phoenix or—sometimes—Squibob), Stanley Huntley (Spoopendyke), Melville D. Landon (Eli Perkins), C. B. Lewis (M. Quad), Henry Clay Lukens (Erratic Enrique), Robert Henry Newell (Orpheus C. Kerr), George W. Peck, Marcus M. Pomeroy (Brick Pomeroy), Mortimer N. Thomson (Doesticks), and others who wrote pieces from which characterization had disappeared. Clearly such writing became a widespread popular habit.

V

When we try to find what brought about this change of style, it is not easy to put a finger on any single cause. But we can point to some changes in the humorists themselves and in their audience which at least help to explain it. The first of these is that many of the later humorists became known to the public in a new way—as lecturers rather than as writers.

Charles Farrar Browne, it appears, started the great rush of humorists to the lecture platform. In New York in the early 1860's, worried about the future of a magazine he was editing, Browne hit on the plan of tying together some of his most promising jests in a speech and seeing whether he could collect some contracts for a humorous lecture. Serious lecturers were coining money in every part of the country. An English visitor in the entertainment business became quite poetic when he wrote about the size of the audiences lecturers could draw. He wrote:

America is a lecture hall on a very extensive scale. The rostrum extends in a straight line from Boston, through New York and Philadelphia, to Washington. There are raised seats on the first tier in the Alleghanies,

and gallery accommodations on the top of the Rocky Mountains. . . . .
The voice of the lecturer is never silent in the United States.

Browne's hope was that some of these ticket-buyers might be willing to take seats for his speeches.

Once he had started, Browne was a great success in the lecture field. With bureaus and local committees, he lined up dates which took him through much of the East, the Middle West, and, finally, to parts of the West so remote that the customers bought tickets with gold dust. Back from his trip to the mining camps, in 1864, he could draw big audiences to lectures given nightly for two straight months in New York, for two whole weeks in Boston, and also to lectures in other towns and cities in the United States and in Canada. After another big season in 1865, the peak of his fame came in 1866, when he invaded London to become a sensational success in the Egyptian Hall.

Many another humorist, encouraged by Browne's success, took to the lecture platform. Probably a majority of the best funnymen of the day got into the business. Long rides on slow trains, the bad food and lumpy mattresses of hotels, the wearying hospitality of lecture committees, and the stony stares of humorless people who went to the performances tormented them. But they were richly repaid, they felt, for all their suffering, by the fat fees which they received. As a result, many of the comic writers of the time were known not only as writers but also as men who stood up before a crowd and tried to make their listeners laugh.

This meant that people had a chance, time after time, to meet the man back of the humor—to see how wrong it was to identify him with the character whose role he assumed for purposes of amusement. An audience seeing Browne for the first time, for example, probably had the sort of a new insight a New York reporter had when he heard Browne lecture in 1861. Said this writer:

Naturally and justly, those who are acquainted with "Artemus Ward, Showman," through his writings only, pictured him, in fancy, as a burly, middle-aged person in somewhat seedy apparel, and with an address more or less suggestive of the "side-show" type of character. On the contrary, Mr. Browne is a tall, slim, and gentlemanly-looking young man, rather careful in his dress than otherwise. . . . . By the gift of nature, Mr. Brown is a comedian. His delivery is provokingly deliberate, and there is a subdued humor in every expression of his face.

For a man looking like this to play the part of a humorless and coarse showman was impossible—and Browne tried nothing of the kind. His lectures were humor of a sort much better adapted to his real personality—laughable ways of stating things which became more amusing because he looked as humorless as he could, though all the time the glint in his eye showed he had a sense of how ridiculous everything he said was. Bad spelling was, of course, impossible, and bad grammar was largely discarded. What is more, to get the kind of contrast necessary in a humorous lecture—to avoid the surfeit which nothing but humor would produce, at times he would be perfectly serious for as much as a paragraph at a time.

David Ross Locke, when he gave his lectures, similarly adapted his humor to a new medium. He looked more like his character, Nasby, than Browne looked like Artemus Ward. He was on the plumpish side, and his nose was red. But he had more hair than Nasby, and the majesty of an imperial beard and the way he carried himself gave him much more force and dignity than the slimy character he had created could possibly have. On the platform, like Browne, he

BILL NYE

Pictured by MacDougal, cartoonist for the *New York World*. The humorist was delighted by the frequent compliments he received for looking so much like the pictures of him.

did not even try to play the role of his creation. Even more
often than Browne, he would use serious passages which set
off the humorous parts of his talk.

Nye's experience makes clear how needful it was for a
platform humorist to alternate funny passages with serious
ones, though he himself, it appears, could not handle serious
passages very well. With his totally bald head, high brow,
expressionless spectacles, big nose, and lanky figure, he was
built better for mirthful than for serious talk. Probably for
that reason he had little success when he lectured alone. It
was only when he teamed up with someone who could get
more sober effects that he did well. His great success came
when he toured the lecture-circuit with James Whitcomb
Riley, a skilful reader of pathetic poetry. In 1888, a South
Bend poet celebrated their joint triumph in words about
their formula:

> Nye and Riley, Riley and Nye:
> Grin and chuckle, sob and sigh!
> Never had such fun by half,
> Knew not whether to chuckle or laugh.
>
> Jest and joke and preach and sing,
> They can do most anything—
> Make you laugh or make you cry—
> Dear old Riley! Rare Bill Nye!

The point is that lecturing possibly affected the way most
humorists came to write. When he turned out his humor,
Locke evidently was not influenced by his lecturing activity:
he kept grinding out Nasby papers in the same old way.
But a majority of the humorists, I think, did write humor
very much like the kind they found so successful before
audiences. They weakened down assumed characters—

wrote more normally spelled and constructed sentences. They depended more and more on queer ways of putting things for comic effects. More often, they let themselves speak directly and seriously to readers between amusing passages.

These changes in the style of their humor were possibly intensified by others caused by another change in the lives of the humorists—one that had to do with their way of earning a living.

In the careers of nearly all the comic writers before 1855, humor had been a part-time job. Davy Crockett had farmed and knocked down game for food or had drawn a salary from the United States Congress, so his writing had been little more than a side line. Seba Smith had made good money out of Jack Downing, but he had made more by running newspapers and by writing and editing outside of the field of humor. Lowell had been a professor at Harvard, a literary critic, a magazine editor. Thompson not only had drawn money for his Major Jones letters; he also had edited newspapers and had written some plays. And George Washington Harris, as has been said, had had a whole string of trades to supplement whatever income he drew for putting down the talk of Sut Lovingood.

After 1855, on the other hand, a man who had a knack for it could make a very good living grinding out humor and doing nothing else. The three writers considered at the beginning of this chapter, practically all the post-war writers named several paragraphs ago, and scores of others as well drew handsome salaries from newspapers for contributing columns which, in those years, came to be features of many of the papers published in this country. When they clipped their articles, pasted them up, and had a book made out of them, these writers took a very different attitude from that of the average pre-war jester. Before the war a writer would probably be coy about letting his work come out between covers. "My friends have asked me to do this," he would say, or "Some people who liked this have been so flattering as to ask that it be issued in permanent form, because posterity might find it interesting." This new set of humorists was more likely to talk as Nasby did when he wrote in his Preface to a book published in 1868:

Scholars, and men which wasn't scholars, have deprecated the manufakter of so many books. Whether they were justified or not in their strictures, it doesn't become me to say. Probably they would say to me, if I should consult em (which I shall not), "Don't publish this book; there's really no occasion for it!" There isn't? Did the captious adviser see the state of my pants? Did he observe the wrecked condition of my boots? Is he aware that I am in arrears for board? Not publish my book! Can I so far forget my duty to humanity? Nary. Its publication will do at least ONE suffrin man good, and that's more than half of the writers can say. What recks it that that one is ME? What posterity will say I don't know; neither do I care.

Humorists wrote books to sell, and, much to their delight, the volumes coaxed piles of dollars out of American pocketbooks. A few years after he had been struggling along for about twenty dollars a week as a newspaperman, Charles Farrar Browne could make more by publishing a single book than he had made in several years of journalistic work. In 1881 even so unimportant a humorist as Huntley could collect royalties on the sale of three hundred thousand copies of one of his books. Peck, writing of his famous bad boy or drawing together his newspaper articles between covers, could take joy in publishers' reports which showed that his books, most of them, sold in their hundreds of thousands. Nye's history sold well over five hundred thousand copies, and another of his books did almost as well.

It seems likely that the new chance for popularity and the importance of it—the fact that a writer more than ever before was eager to have as many people as possible enjoy his newspaper contributions and buy his books—may have had a great deal to do with the disappearance of violent partisanship from much of the most widely read humor. Though Locke and a few others (most of them, like Locke, part-time humorists) might, evidently, get along by writing vicious attacks, most of the professional funnymen no longer injected party politics into their writings.

Whatever the cause, it is clear that a majority of the comic writers of the time broke away from the old tradition of setting up characters very different from themselves and using them consistently to make people laugh. More and more the literary comedians, stepping into the limelight, pushed their homespun heroes off the stage. The quirks of dialect, of grammar, of intelligence, and the political tie-ups which had in the past given the characters in the writings the breath of life had practically disappeared, and the characters were lost.

CHAPTER IX

Mark Twain, Hank, and Huck

How solemn and beautiful is the thought that the earliest pioneer of civilization, the van-leader of civilization, is never the steamboat, never the railroad, never the newspaper, never the Sunday-school, never the missionary—but always whisky!

—MARK TWAIN

You see my kind of loyalty was loyalty to one's country, not to its institutions or its office-holders. The country is . . . . the thing to watch over, and care for, and be loyal to; institutions are extraneous, they are its mere clothing, and clothing can wear out, become ragged, cease to be comfortable, cease to protect the body from winter, disease and death. To be loyal to rags, to shout for rags, to worship rags, to die for rags—that is a loyalty of unreason . . . . ; it belongs to monarchy, was invented by monarchy; let monarchy keep it.

—HANK, THE YANKEE, HARTFORD, CONN.

Now, one of the worst things about civilization is, that anybody that gits a letter with trouble in it comes and tells you all about it and makes you feel bad, and the newspapers fetches you the troubles of everybody all over the world, and keeps you downhearted and dismal 'most all the time. . . . .

—HUCKLEBERRY FINN, ST. PETERSBURG, MO.

I

DURING a trip Artemus Ward took as a comic lecturer, in 1863–64, he found himself in Virginia City, Nevada, where he was to perform. Virginia City was a town which the Washoe miners had knocked together high on Mount Davidson. Dried by the sun and buffeted by winds which whirled up its eastern and western slopes, the board houses which formed most of the town looked as if, though they had stood a good deal, they were not likely to stand much more. The streets were noisy with the shouts of tough miners on boom-town sprees, and now and then a spatter of revolver shots punctuated the bicker of voices.

Ward, according to the story he later told of his visit, had an interesting welcome:

I had no sooner achieved my room in the garret of the International Hotel than I was called upon by an intoxicated man who said he was an editor. Knowing how rare it was for an editor to be under the blighting influence of either spirituous or malt liquors, I received this statement doubtfully. But I said:

"What name?"

"Wait!" he said. And went out.

I heard him pacing unsteadily up and down the hall outside. In ten minutes he returned and said:

"Pepper!"

Pepper was indeed his name. He had been out to see if he didn't know what town he lived in, ... here was a man so hideously intoxicated that he didn't know what his name was.

I saw him no more, but I heard from him. For he published a notice of my lecture, in which he said I had "a dissipated air."

The welcome, it turned out, set the tone of the lecturer's whole visit. The high points of Browne's stay were furnished by newspapermen on a drinking spree—the rambunctious editors and reporters of the *Virginia City Enterprise*. The journalists were a picturesque crew—Joe Goodman, who had been known to fight a duel at twenty paces with a man who disliked an editorial; Rollin M. Daggett, who was a western Falstaff without a touch of cowardice; bantam-rooster Steve Gillis, who spent his spare time fighting as many men as he could stir up to it; and, finally, Samuel L. Clemens, who wrote humor signed with the name of Mark Twain.

Clemens had as much color in his past as anyone in the diggings. Ex-tramp printer, steamboat pilot, soldier, and prospector, he had roamed widely over the face of the continent, coming to know the ways of men in many parts of it. Then he had started to work for the *Enterprise*, catering to the robust sense of humor of the boisterous miners.

Browne and Clemens hit it off well from the start, for they had many things in common. Both had been wandering printers before they turned humorists. They shared the idea that the basic ingredients for a good party were good fellows and good liquor. Most important, these two funnymen who painted Virginia City red together had written and were writing the sort of humor very fashionable in those days.

II

In much of Clemens' work, at the time he met Browne and for years after he had left Nevada, there was the typical emphasis on saying things queerly, often at the expense of keeping the writing in character. In the years when he was winning fame, like Browne, Clemens usually avoided political controversy. He had discarded touches of dialect and twisted grammar of the kind which had helped many earlier humorists to set up characters—and anyone who saw what kind of a mind lay back of one passage and then looked for the same kind of a mind throughout the rest of a series of letters or a book of his would be bewildered. A constant switching from the fool way of talking to the wise way of seeing and putting things, for example, was characteristic of a whole group of his travel-books, including the Sandwich Island letters in the 1860's, *Innocents Abroad* (1869), *Roughing It* (1872), *A Tramp Abroad* (1879), and *Following the Equator* (1894).

Two of the most famous bits in this humorist's first great success, *Innocents Abroad*, will show how a fool character (who for clarity, may be called Mark Twain) revealed his paltry mind and its workings in one passage and how a man of good sense (who, for contrast, may be called Samuel L. Clemens) spoke out in another.

The fool was at his best as he wrote of a visit to a church in the Holy Land, about which he was told a number of very strange things. He was assured, for instance, that the church had in it a column marking the exact center of the earth. Being a fool, Mark gladly believed what he was told; and being a cocky fool, he put down arguments for his belief. One was:

> The most reliable traditions tell us that this was known to be the earth's centre, ages ago, and that when Christ was upon earth he set all doubts upon the subject forever, by stating with his own lips that the tradition was correct. Remember, He said that that particular column stood upon the centre of the world.

This—if you take it seriously—is a fine example of horrible logic, bolstered up in a way that is downright pathetic. Basing his whole proof on traditions, Twain tried to make his pitiful case better by pointing out that his were "the *most reliable* traditions" and thereby actually underlined the fact that no traditions are any good as historical proof. Then, in the next sentence, after he had admitted his proof was legendary, he stated his conclusion as a fact, vainly hoping that his reader's belief in Christ had made faith in even moss-grown legends about Christ inevitable.

A little later he offered what he thought was a scientific demonstration of his case. "To satisfy himself that this was really the centre of the earth," he said, "a sceptic once paid well for the privilege of ascending to the dome of the church to see if the sun gave him a shadow at noon. He came down perfectly convinced." Anyone who is not suspicious of the scientific impartiality of a man who set out "to satisfy himself" that something was true cannot help noticing that, from the account, the experiment was less of a success than Twain claimed it was—that even he, in the end, seeming to sense its failure, tried to bully his reader into belief by blustering at him:

The day was very cloudy and the sun threw no shadows at all; but the man was satisfied that if the sun had come out and made shadows it could not have made any for him. Proofs like these are not to be set aside by the idle tongues of cavilers. To such as are not bigoted, and are willing to be convinced, they carry a conviction that nothing can shake.

But it appeared that all this was simply preparation for an argument which would batter down any lurking doubts:

If even greater proofs than those I have mentioned are wanted to satisfy the headstrong and the foolish that this is the genuine centre of the earth, they are here. The greatest of them lies in the fact that from under this very column was taken the *dust from which Adam was made*. This can surely be regarded in the light of a settler. It is not likely that the original first man would have been made from any inferior quality of earth when it was entirely convenient to get first quality from the world's centre. This will strike any reflecting mind forcibly. That Adam was formed of dirt procured in this very spot is amply proven by the fact that in six thousand years no man has ever been able to prove that the dirt was *not* procured here whereof he was made.

The clinchers of which Twain was so sure thus turned out to be a batch of insanely illogical assertions.

A paragraph or two later, the idiot who had argued in

such a futile fashion stepped over to the tomb of Adam which, by good chance, had been raised in the same church. Sure that the tomb was that of Adam because, as he said, "it has never yet been proven that that grave is not the grave in which he is buried," Mark pumped up what he felt were proper emotions but what actually were the maunderings of a silly sentimentalist:

The tomb of Adam! How touching it was, here in a land of strangers, far from home, and friends, and all who cared for me, thus to discover the grave of a blood relation. The unerring instinct of nature thrilled its recognition. The fountain of my filial affection was stirred to its profoundest depths, and I gave way to tumultuous emotion. I leaned upon a pillar and burst into tears. I deem it no shame to have wept over the grave of my poor dead relative. Let him who would sneer at my emotion close this volume here, for he will find little to his taste in my journeyings through the Holy Land. Noble old man—he did not live to see me— he did not live to see his child. And I—I alas, did not live to see *him*. Weighed down by sorrow and disappointment, he died before I was born—six thousand brief summers before I was born. But let us try to bear it with fortitude. Let us trust that he is better off, where he is. Let us take comfort in the thought that his loss is our eternal gain.

In such a passage as this—and there were many like it in the book—Mark Twain showed he was as credulous, as featherbrained, and as maudlin as the most idiotic tourist who ever went about abroad, swallowing everything a guide or a guidebook told him and having whatever emotions most wandering fools thought they ought to have when they looked at certain scenes. The fool character, Mark Twain, thus served Samuel L. Clemens very well in satirizing the ways of Americans abroad.

Elsewhere in the book, however—in the famous passage about the Old Masters, for example, Clemens himself spoke directly to the reader. Standing before Leonardo da Vinci's "The Last Supper" were a group of tourists who talked like a crowd of Mark Twains. Said Clemens:

People come here from all parts of the world, and glorify this master-piece. They stand entranced before it with bated breath and parted lips, and when they speak, it is only in the catchy ejaculations of rapture:
"O, wonderful!"
"Such expression!"
"Such grace of attitude!"
"Such dignity!"
"Such faultless drawing!"
"Such matchless coloring!"
"Such feeling!"
"What delicacy of touch!"
"What sublimity of conception!"
"A vision! A vision!"

But Clemens, when he looked at the picture, saw something about which it was silly to exclaim—colors "dimmed with age," faces on the canvas "scaled and marred, and nearly all the expression gone from them. . . . . The hair a dead blur upon the wall . . . . no life in the eyes." And the jabbering of the tourists made Clemens suspect that they were being both fools and hypocrites. Said he:

I only envy these people; I envy them their honest admiration, if it be honest—their delight, if they feel delight. I harbor no animosity toward any of them. But at the same time the thought *will* intrude itself upon me, how can they see what is not visible? What would you think of a man who looked at some decayed, blind, toothless, pock-marked Cleopatra, and said: "What matchless beauty! What soul! What expression!" What would you think of a man who gazed upon a dingy, foggy sunset, and said: "What sublimity! What feeling! What richness of coloring!" What would you think of a man who stared in ecstacy upon a desert of stumps and said: "Oh, my soul, my beating heart, what a noble forest is here!"

You would think that those men had an astonishing talent for seeing things that had already passed away. It was what I thought when I stood before the Last Supper and heard men apostrophizing wonders, and beauties and perfections which had faded out of the picture and gone, a hundred years before they were born.

In a passage like this Clemens spoke in person to his reader, expressing his own opinions in the best language he could find for making them known.

III

But Clemens was reared in the old Southwest, where, as a thin-legged, tow-headed youngster, he heard many oral tales and read others which had been turned into print in the humorous columns of newspapers. Out on the coast he heard other fireside yarns—and his first successful sketch, "The Notorious Jumping Frog of Calaveras County," was a tale he had set down on paper after he had heard it told to a crowd of miners in a California tavern. Furthermore, he leaped to prominence as a humorist at a time when fictionists in every section of the United States were beginning to invade the field many humorists were deserting—the field of local color. Local-color writing was a late nineteenth-century adaptation of old-fashioned humor, sobered down and sentimentalized, with the political stings removed and the characters expanded but with the same old emphasis on provincial flavorings and with something like the same old tie-up with the oral tale.

When Clemens turned to the writing of fiction, he did most of his work as a local-colorist. He did not, of course, stop being a humorist: his fiction usually was humorous. And at his best, using the method of pre-war humorists, he was likely to put himself into the part of a homespun character whose talk told the story. Because he was full of strong prejudices, every now and then he would use such a character to voice an idea. Two highly successful story-tellers of this sort, the Connecticut Yankee and Huckleberry Finn, showed what he could do when he wanted to use such figures in fiction to speak for him.

When Clemens got the idea of writing *A Connecticut Yankee in King Arthur's Court*, he had been having a fine time reading an old book to which he had been introduced by a companion on a lecture trip—the quaint story of King Arthur and his court as it had been told by Thomas Malory in the fifteenth century. He might also have seen—but apparently did not—a book which was the runaway best seller of the day—Edward Bellamy's *Looking Backward*. This popular book was a novel telling how a young Bostonian who fell into a hypnotic sleep in 1887 awoke to find himself in the world of the year 2000. His fascinating story was largely about what he had found in the society of that distant future. Internal evidence suggests that the two books together gave Twain the idea that it would be fun to write about a character who had had a similar experience, but external evidence proves that he did not read Bellamy's novel until after he had finished his own. By sheer coincidence Clemens, too, made a New Englander fall sleep and awaken to find himself in another era. Twain's Yankee, however, instead of shifting his life into the future, was transported to the past—back to the time of King Arthur in the year 528.

The humorist wrote the story of how Hank, the Yankee superintendent in the Colt factory in Connecticut, after being knocked out by a worker with a crowbar, awoke in a field near Camelot. The slangy talk of a nineteenth-century

Yankee alongside the stately language of the Middle Ages was amusing, and his exposition of what a man of the industrial age thought of a feudal society was also comical. And when the Yankee, thanks to his predicting an eclipse, became a dictator and put into practice all sorts of new-fangled plans, incongruities leaped up everywhere—knights in armor and plug hats, knights playing baseball, the news of chivalry written up in a country newspaper, Simon Stylites, attached to a sewing-machine, turning around on his pillar. The book was full of such broad fun.

But, like Bellamy's book, Clemens' story was more than a contrast between civilizations. Because, in the world of 2000, he had found a utopia with many advantages over the society of 1887, Bellamy had made his book a social criticism. Urged on by the fact that he, like his contemporary, had many strongly held notions of his own, Mark Twain also used his book to set forth his ideas about things in general and in particular. Ideas came out through the talk and through the adventures of Hank—so many ideas that many pages of the novel were cluttered up with them.

Hank was a common American, "an ignoramus"—as Mark said he was—in many ways. Looking at the fine tapestries on medieval walls, he kept remembering the hideous pictures on his wall at home in nineteenth-century America and longing for a sight of them.

Not a chromo [he moaned]. I had been used to chromos for years, and I saw now that without my suspecting it a passion for art had got into the fabric of my being, and was become a part of me. It made me homesick to look around over this proud and gaudy but heartless barrenness and remember that in our home in East Hartford, all unpretending as it was, you couldn't go into a room but you would find an insurance-chromo, or at least a three-color God-Bless-Our-Home over the door; and in the parlor we had nine.

Or the Yankee noticed the way the aristocracy observed the forms of religion and was not keen-eyed enough to notice how little these forms meant:

I will say this much for the nobility: that, tyrannical, murderous, rapacious, and morally rotten as they were, they were deeply and enthusiastically religious. Nothing could divert them from the regular and faithful performance of the pieties enjoined by the Church. More than once I have seen a noble who had gotten his enemy at a disadvantage, stop to pray before cutting his throat; more than once I had seen a noble, after ambushing and despatching his enemy, retire to the nearest wayside shrine and humbly give thanks, without even waiting to rob the body. . . . . All the nobles of Britain, with their families, attended divine service morning and night daily, in their private chapels, and even the worst of them had family worship five or six times a day besides.

The naïve visitor seemed bowled over by such piety. Many of the other notions which Hank cherished and made known were just as stupid as this—the half-baked judgments of an uneducated man.

But, though Hank shared the stupidities of ordinary Americans, he was a good man, he had been brought up in a country where people in general had the right view of things, and usually, when he pondered important matters, he made good use of his horse sense. It was as easy as pie, for example, for him to see what a horrible thing the aristocratic form of government was for the people in the land where it was in operation:

And the people! They were the quaintest and simplest and trustingest race; why, they were nothing but rabbits. It was pitiful for a person born in a wholesome free atmosphere to listen to their humble and hearty outpourings of loyalty toward their king and Church and nobility; as if they had any more occasion to love and honor the king and church and noble than a slave has to love and honor the lash . . . .! Why, dear me, *any* kind of royalty, howsoever modified, *any* kind of aristocracy, however pruned, is rightly an insult; but if you are born and brought up under that sort of

arrangement you probably never find it out for yourself, and don't believe
it when somebody else tells you.

That was doctrine which could be preached in America
without much danger. It—and much of the other preaching
in the book—seemed to apply entirely to other countries.
But Clemens was not satisfied with social criticism which hit
countries across the sea but did not hit America. In the tradition of Jack Downing, Hosea Biglow, and other humorous
commentators in homespun, the Yankee tore into the
United States as well as other lands.

The book was written and published at a time when
Americans in increasing numbers were beginning to see that
their system could do with a good deal of tinkering. In the
years since the Civil War, the tie-up between big business
and government had reached such impudent heights that
many had begun to voice their disgust. Bellamy's book had
been only one in a great flood of similar books calling attention to a need for changes of a vital sort. In 1884, after
many years of Republican rule, the dissatisfied faction had
managed at last to cast enough votes to defeat Blaine and to
put Grover Cleveland into office. Cleveland was a stuffy fellow and a poor hand at politics, but he had a better notion
than any successful American political leader between
Abraham Lincoln and Theodore Roosevelt of what was
wrong with the country, and he had enough courage to try
to do things. He tried to reform the civil service, tried to cut
down graft, tried to get the tariff whittled down to a reasonable size. But one after another of his sensible reforms
bumped up against a stone wall of resistance.

Clemens, who had been a vigorous supporter of Cleveland's candidacy, made his book speak in favor of the Presi-

dent. Along with the low comedy and the snaps at England in the *Yankee* were passages which one way and another backed up Cleveland's most important policies—the policies repudiated by the electorate in 1888 when Cleveland, running for a second term, was defeated.

A fable about military examinations in Arthur's kingdom had to do with spoils-system appointments. The Yankee told how he had introduced, among other innovations in the country, a West Point, where army officers were carefully taught all the complexities of warfare. When, however, an examination was held, though the West Pointers knew answers to all questions asked, the commissions were all given to chuckleheads who knew nothing about military matters. The reason was that the West Point students were commoners, while the numskulls were nobles. For readers engaged in the red-hot arguments of the day, this passage attacked not only unqualified men who got offices because of their birth but also those who got offices because of their party politics.

Another passage about the King's evil appropriation hit at another bad practice against which Cleveland fought—the huge profits of contractors and commercial centers made possible by pork-barrel laws. This Arthurian law, whereby money was handed out to all the citizens, said Hank, "was just the River and Harbor bill of that government for the grip it took on the treasury and the chance it offered for skimming the surplus."

Then, too, there was a whole chapter on the hottest issue of the day—the tariff question. Civil War tariffs, which had come in as emergency measures, had continued to apply in peacetime. All through the 1880's the government had collected an annual surplus of a hundred million dollars—a great temptation to grafters; prices had soared, and protected trusts had flourished. In 1887, Cleveland had sent a message to Congress flaying the tariff evils. In the election of 1888, protection was the most-discussed issue.

To treat this matter Mark Twain put into his fantastic yarn Hank's account of a discussion he had with a blacksmith he met during the course of a trip through the country—a long talk about wages in a free-trade district as compared with wages in a district where a tariff was in force. The smith, an utter ass, started things by smugly pointing out how high wages were in his parts compared with those in Hank's district. Hank countered by showing that, proportionately, the people in his section could buy more with what they earned. Then the Yankee pointed out that he had "knocked the stuffing out of the high wages" the smith had been so excited about. But the smith, being a fool, could not see the point—could not see it even after poor Hank had made it time after time, using all the illustrations that came to his mind:

"What I say is this. With us *half* a dollar buys more than a *dollar* buys with you—and *therefore* it stands to reason and the commonest kind of common sense, that our wages are *higher* than yours. . . . ."

It was a crusher.

But alas, it didn't crush. No, I had to give it up. What those people valued was *high wages;* it didn't seem to be a matter of any consequence to them whether the high wages would buy anything or not. They stood for "protection," and swore by it, which was reasonable enough, because interested parties had gulled them into the notion that it was protection that had created their high wages.

It was an effective kind of propaganda Mark was using here. Laughter was turned against the opponent of free trade, and the fool attitude was tied up with protectionism while the wise Yankee stood for free trade. A book that sold by the hundred thousands amused people with buffoonery and clowning while at the same time it slipped in little sermons like this on the most disputed issues of the day.

IV

Clemens' most interesting contribution to the humor of horse sense, however, came in a series of books purporting to have come from the pen of the lovable little ragamuffin, Huckleberry Finn. In these books, thanks to his consummate skill as an inventor of fiction, Clemens guided a pen which gave the voice of life to characters. Furthermore, as these characters talked over many subjects, time after time, the differences between their minds—between native wit and book learning, instinctive ways of thinking and learned ways of reasoning—made for delightful contrasts.

Early examples of this type of humor came in *Tom Sawyer*. On his first entrance into literature, Huck was shown in rags and bad-fitting clothes:

His hat was a vast ruin with a wide crescent lopped out of its brim; his coat, when he wore one, hung nearly to his heels and had the rearward buttons far down the back; but one suspender supported his trousers; the seat of his trousers bagged low and contained nothing; the fringed legs dragged in the dirt when not rolled up.

But, bedraggled though he was, Huck showed right away as he talked with Tom that he had made greater progress than book-learned Tom in the study of witchcraft and folk magic. Later in the book, as Tom discoursed on pirates or robbers and Huck commented, the contrast between the two minds yielded more comedy.

Huckleberry Finn showed this sort of humor developing.

When Tom, carried away by his exciting findings in books, imagined that a raid of little boys on a Sunday-school picnic was a foray against Spaniards and Arabs, Huck's mother-wit pierced through the pretense, and he would have none of it. Later, jockeyed by his instinct of sympathy into helping Negro Jim escape from slavery, Huck's muddled brain could not cope with a struggle between what his heart told him to do and what the unjust law said he should do. When Tom, seeing a chance to engineer a romantic escape, decided to help him, he was even more baffled:

> Well, one thing was dead sure, and that was that Tom Sawyer was in earnest, and was actually going to help steal that nigger out of slavery. That was the thing that was too many for me. Here was a boy that was respectable and well brung up; and had a character to lose; and folks at home that had characters; and he was bright and not leather-headed; and knowing and not ignorant; and not mean, but kind; and yet here he was, without any more pride, or rightness, or feeling, than to stoop to this business, and make himself a shame, and his family a shame, before everybody. I *couldn't* understand it no way at all. It was outrageous, and I knowed I ought to just up and tell him so; and so be his true friend, and let him quit the thing right where he was and save himself.

This was the old, old device of the lunkhead pondering a question and coming to the wrong conclusions. The method worked well in other parts of Huck's tale of his ponderings, and the boy's pappy got off some good fool speeches on education and the free Negro. Elsewhere in the book the comic conflicts of different levels of intelligence which Clemens handled so well were developed. They developed in the talks Huck and Jim had about King Sollerman and the French language as their raft drifted down the freshet-swelled river in starlight, and Huck's mind and Jim's primi-

Huck Finn

"Huckleberry was always dressed in the cast-off clothes of full-grown men, and they were in perennial bloom and fluttering with rags. His hat was a vast ruin with a wide crescent lopped out of its brim . . . . but one suspender supported his trousers; the seat of the trousers bagged low and contained nothing; the fringed legs dragged in the dirt when not rolled up."—*The Adventures of Tom Sawyer* (1876).

tive imagination coped with problems of astronomy. Said
Huck:

We had the sky up there, all speckled with stars, and we used to lay on
our backs and look up at them, and discuss about whether they were
made or only just happened. Jim he allowed they was made, but I allowed they happened; I judged that it would have took too long to *make*
so many. Jim said the moon could 'a' *laid* them; well, that looked kind of
reasonable, so I didn't say nothing against it, because I've seen a frog
lay most as many, so of course it could be done. We used to watch the
stars that fell, too, and see them streak down. Jim allowed they'd got
spoiled and was hove out of the nest.

Toward the end of the story, burlesque pulled the book
down from its high level of achievement; but the talk was
still good when the two boys and the slave argued over the
elaborate ways of helping Jim to escape that Tom had
filched from romantic novels. Tom was a formalist, eager to
follow exactly the examples of his romantic heroes; Huck
had certain common-sense doubts but usually yielded to his
friend's higher learning; Jim saw all the arguments against
doing things Tom's way, but, being used to the queer quirks
of white men, he followed instructions—but grumbled.

The comedy in which these three assorted minds argued
with one another reached its best development in a book
neglected or scorned by most critics—*Tom Sawyer Abroad*,
published ten years after *Huckleberry Finn*, in 1894. Critics
who have had no trouble with the ridiculous skeleton of *Don
Quixote* have been sadly annoyed because this American
book had as its central thread a wild fantasy which told how
Tom and Huck and Jim went to the far corners of the earth
in a balloon. But the balloon story has great value in piling
incongruities one on top of the other—an impossible situation calmly accepted by three plausible characters. More-

over, anyone who has delighted in the good talk Huck and Jim had while their raft drifted downstream, in the earlier volume, will perhaps not be too stern with any yarn that strings together a whole series of talks which equal or surpass the dialogues in the earlier book. Mr. Bernard De Voto, almost the only modern critic who has seen the good things in this novel, has greatly enjoyed the way it shows Huck's village, "St. Petersburg, trying to grapple with an enlargement of its thinking," and has pointed out that here "there can be no doubt that Mark's deliberate effort was to explore the mentality of the common man."

Again, the levels of intelligence were amusingly different. Tom, at the top, was able to defend and explain the findings of scholars as he understood them with his partly educated and sometimes naïve mind. Huck, vaguely respectful toward learning, was nevertheless willing to take a wallop at anything foolish or useless that his common sense helped him discover. Jim was brashly ignorant, his horse sense and his out-of-door lore his chief keys to ·knowledge—these and sundry other instruments, notably a childishly beautiful Negro religion, which sometimes gave him light. The three talked by the hour; Huck and Jim had as much to contribute that was worth while as Tom had, and the clash of their opinions made for contrast after contrast of an amusing sort.

The talk ranged over many topics from the way the Sahara Desert was formed (Jim thought it was a dumping-ground for stuff left over when God made the earth) to the intelligence of the flea (Tom figured that if this brilliant insect were large enough it would make a good president). Sometimes Tom said true things without thinking, as when, on being asked if "countries always apologized when they had done wrong," he said, "Yes; the little ones does." Sometimes he thought things out carefully, piled the statistics into his talk, and then came up with strange findings.

Huck could get off a leather-headed opinion which echoed the stodgy beliefs of man through the ages, as he did when he said of a great inventor:

He was a good enough sort of cretur, and hadn't no harm in him, and was just a genius . . . . which wasn't his fault. We can't all be sound: we've got to be the way we're made. As near as I can make out, geniuses think they know it all, and so they won't take people's advice, but always go their own way, which makes everybody forsake them and despise them, and that is perfectly natural. If they was humbler, and listened and tried to learn, it would be better for them.

He could rejoice because he had bested Tom in an argument when all he had done was misunderstand everything Tom had said. But not many lines later, he could put into a sentence such horse sense as, "I reckon the best way to get a sure thing on a fact is to go and examine it yourself and not take anybody's say-so."

Jim, struggling to understand with a shrewd child's mind all the problems met with on an amazing journey, was the most delightful of the three travelers. Sometimes he was beaten by complex facts beyond his comprehension, as he was when Tom carefully explained to him the differences in time between one part of the globe and another, pointing out, finally, that "when it's one o'clock Tuesday morning in England, it's eight o'clock the night before in New York." Jim first marveled and then shook with fear when he tried to cope with "two days in one day." "Den dat Monday," he moaned, "could be de las' day, en dey wouldn't be no last day in England, en de dead wouldn't be called. We mustn't go over dah, Mars Tom. Please . . . . turn back. . . . ."

Other times his knowledge of nature made him fail to catch a meaning, as when Tom said, "Birds of a feather flock together." "But dey *don't*, Mars Tom," said Jim. "No, sir, 'deed dey don't. Dey ain't no feathers dat's more alike den a bluebird en a jaybird but if you waits till you catches *dem* birds together, you'll. . . . ." Or his superstition gave him a poor explanation of something new to him—as when he saw a mirage and said:

"Mars Tom, hit's a *ghos*', dat's what it is, en I hopes to goodness we ain't gwine to see it no mo'. Dey's *been* a lake, en suthin's happened, en de lake's dead, en we's seen its ghos'; we's seen it twiste, en dat's proof. De desert's ha'nted, it's ha'nted, sho; oh, Mars Tom, le's git outen it; I'd ruther die den have de night ketch us in it ag'in en de ghos' er dat lake come a-mournin' aroun' us en we asleep en doan' know de danger we's in."

Or he might be misled by his poor mathematics, as he was when he argued against Tom's asking him, the strongest of the three, to dump out three-fifths of the sand blown into the basket of the balloon by a storm while the boys dumped out two-fifths. Tom told him to work it out his way. As Huck told the story:

So Jim reckoned it wouldn't be no more than fair if me and Tom did a *tenth* apiece. Tom he turned his back to git room and be private, and then he smole a smile that spread around and covered the whole Sahara to the westward, back to the Atlantic edge of it where we come from. Then he turned around again and said it was a good enough arrangement, and we was satisfied if Jim was. Jim said he was.

So then Tom measured off our two-tenths in the bow and left the rest for Jim, and it surprised Jim a good deal to see how much difference there was and what a raging lot of sand his share come to, and said he was powerful glad now that he had spoke up in time and got the first arrangement altered. . . . .

However, the Negro, with all his limitations, could pierce with his thought, at times, to the very core of a problem.

When Tom told him he ought to join a crusade against the pagans in the Holy Land, he said, "De hard part gwine be to kill folks dat a body hain't been 'quainted wid and dat hain't done him no harm."

Each, then, was wise in his own ways and stupid in his own ways—and a method of thinking that sometimes led to idiotic conclusions at other times brought out brilliant findings. And when two of the travelers—or all three of them—got into an argument, the interplay of minds became something worth watching. Of the eleven big arguments in the book, Tom won five, while one or both of his friends managed—to Huck's way of thinking—to win the other six. Always, however, it was a hard-fought battle, with the loser, even at the end, sometimes failing to admit he had been outmaneuvered.

A typical argument arose when a scheme to carry Sahara Desert sand back to America for sale by the bottle had to be dropped because Tom remembered that high tariff duties would lop off all profits. The duty, he allowed, was likely to be particularly large because Sahara sand was something that could not be raised in America—an arrangement that both he and Huck saw made no sense. When Tom claimed that there was a high duty on everything which could not be raised in the United States, Jim saw his chance:

"Mars Tom, ain't de blessin' o' de Lord de mos' valuable thing dey is?"

"Yes, it is."

"Don't de preacher stan' up in de pulpit en call it down on de people?"

"Yes."

"Whah do it come from?"

"From heaven."

"Yassir! you's jest right, 'deed you is, honey—it come from heaven, en dat's a foreign country. *Now*, den! do dey put a tax on dat blessin'?"

"No, they don't."

"Course dey don't; en so it stan' to reason dat you's mistaken, Mars Tom. Dey wouldn't put de tax on po' truck like san', dat everybody ain't 'bleeged to have, en leave it off'n de bes' thing dey is, which nobody can't get along widout."

Tom Sawyer was stumped; he see Jim had got him where he couldn't budge. He tried to wriggle out by saying they had *forgot* to put on that tax . . . . but that was a poor lame comeoff. . . . . He said . . . . they wouldn't be consistent without taxing it, and to be consistent was the first law of politics. So he stuck to it that they'd left it out unintentional and would be certain to do their best to fix it before they got caught and laughed at.

The exchange had several nice touches. It was clever to have Tom and Huck and even Jim see right away that taxing something that could not be raised in the country made no sense. It was naïve of the Negro to assume that, since a law did not make sense, there could be no such law. Sure of himself and proud of his reasoning power, Jim swooped down on his victim with a series of Socratic questions. It was natural for the devout black man to think of an exception in the world of spiritual blessings, because his mind was stored with religious teachings. Tom, instead of seeing that the exception Jim cited was in a different class from other importations, reluctantly agreed that the Negro had stumped him. Out of his wisdom, though, he was able to prophesy that politicians, paragons of consistency, would fix everything up at the next legislative session.

Anyone interested in the vagaries of the average mind and the reach of common sense, in short, will find Mark Twain has made the most of their comic possibilities in *Tom Sawyer Abroad*. Naturally, when America's greatest humorist exploited this vein, he had an amusing contribution to make to the humor of horse sense.

CHAPTER X

Josh and Samantha

Americans love caustic things; they would prefer turpentine to colone-water, if they had to drink either. So it is with their relish of humor, they must have it on the half-shell with cayenne. . . . . Don't forget one thing, you have got to be wize before you can be witty; and don't forget two things, a single paragraph has made some men immortal, while a volume has bin wuss than a pile-driver to others. . . . .

—JOSH BILLINGS

You have to hold up the hammer of a personal incident to drive home the nail of Truth and have it clench and hold fast.

—SAMANTHA, JOSIAH ALLEN'S WIFE, JONESVILLE

I

ONE thing about literary history which students find bothersome is that it does not break up neatly into periods. Presumably, for example, in English literature, the Elizabethan period ended at a certain date; but a number of authors, annoyingly enough, kept writing Elizabethan poetry after that date. Or the Puritan period ended—so it is said—in 1660; but a number of years after that date Milton wrote the greatest of all Puritan poems. This is awkward for students, but it is hardly mysterious. Authors are likely to write, in manhood, like the authors whom they admired in childhood and youth, and a large

218

proportion of the public is likely to prefer the older ways in literature—especially humorous literature—to the newer. Josh Billings and Samantha Allen are two of several humorists who offer proof that old ways and old tastes in humor thrived in a period of change. Both were affected, of course, by the new ways of writing; but essentially both were old-fashioned comic writers who flourished in the latter half of the nineteenth century.

About 1859, Henry Wheeler Shaw, the man who was later to gain fame as Josh Billings, had finally settled down in Poughkeepsie, New York, after a life of wide wandering. A Massachusetts Yankee by birth, Shaw had cut loose from home ties when he was still quite young and had migrated to the West. There, with stop-offs here and there and now and then to do odd jobs, he had traveled a great deal. At one time or another he had been a farmer, a coal operator, a captain, and proprietor of an Ohio steamboat. Now, aged forty-one, he was a real estate agent and an auctioneer who found time to scribble a humorous piece in spare moments. The humorous pieces came out in country newspapers, were read by a few, and were then forgotten.

One piece, called "The Essay on the Mule," was printed in the *Poughkeepsian*—printed there and nowhere else. In that day when the success of a humorous article could be gauged by the number of newspapers which picked it up and reprinted it—with or without credit—the failure of the essay to circulate showed that it had not been a hit. About a year later, looking at the papers, Shaw noticed with interest that a piece somewhat similar to his—one on the mule by Artemus Ward—had been printed by one newspaper after the other in every corner of the country.

Looking for a reason for his own failure and Ward's success, Shaw decided that one difference between the pieces stood out: Ward had used a great deal of bad spelling and grammar, while he himself had used none. Promptly Shaw re-wrote his piece, warping the grammar and the spelling out of its normal form, and sent off what he now called "An Essai on the Muel." Signing it with the pen name he had adopted—Josh Billings—he mailed it to a New York paper. Not only did he get pay for the essay (a whole dollar and a half), in addition, he had the pleasure of seeing it reprinted in three of the leading comic magazines of the day.

"I think I've struck oil," said Shaw. Still using the bad spelling, he turned out a number of pieces which he managed to peddle to the papers. His fame spread, newspapers everywhere contributing to it by using brief passages of Josh to lengthen out short columns. With the help of Artemus Ward, he won the interest of a successful New York publishing house, and books spread his fame and fattened his purse. In time, of course, like most of the thriving humorists of the day, he became established as a lecturer. His tall body, his large head with its long hair and swooping mustache, his stooping posture—all helped to emphasize the deep seriousness with which his witticisms were uttered. Starting in 1863, for twenty seasons in a row, he lectured

. . . . in every town on this continent that has 20,000 people, and in hundreds that have not got 1,000 in them; read it [the lecture] in every town in Texas and California, and in all the Canadian towns, and then down South, from Baltimore to Palatka, Florida, and still across to Memphis, and then down into new Orleans, reading each season from fifty to over a hundred nights.

Beginning in 1869, Shaw started a venture which spread his fame even wider than did his newspaper writings, his books, or his lectures—the publication of a series of comic almanacs called *Josh Billings' Farmer's Allminax*. Each year for a decade a new issue of this publication came out, with sales running almost always to more than a hundred thousand. The author netted thirty thousand dollars on these almanacs before they were put together and published as a book.

The humor which this writer turned out and which sold so widely was shaped in several ways by the humor which was fashionable at the time he started to write it. The poor spelling, of course, and queer phrasing to which he was forced to turn were early tricks of the school of the latter half of the nineteenth century. Like most other writers of the time, Shaw steered clear of violent party attitudes in politics.

But long after misshapen words and sentences had gone out of fashion in most humor, Shaw kept using them in the greater part of his work (though he did produce a four-year series of pieces headed "Uncle Ezek's Wisdom," properly spelled and grammatically phrased, for the *Century*). And he was a throwback in another way—a way suggested when he wrote for a friend a recipe for success as a lecturer. He said the author ought to give his listeners the characters they had enjoyed when they had read his books; Shaw himself had done this: "What little success I have gained, I think has been got by sticking close to Billings, not leaving him long, and always believing him to be my best friend." The point was that Josh was a character—that, unlike many humorous writers of the day, Shaw saw to it that his spokesman was not thrust out of the limelight.

Josh Billings, to be sure, was not so localized or so individualized as a Downing, say, or a Major Jones. But like his creator, he was clearly from Way Down East—a Yankee farmer. He had a family almost as large and about as queer as a modern radio comedian, Bob Burns, has invented for himself—Jehossaphatt Billings, "a very close man who died at the age of 63 . . . . from an overdose of clam chowder drank at a free lunch"; Jamaika Billings, "the laziest man that ever visited this world"; Zephemiah Billings, "a fiddler by birth and perswashun"; Adam Billings, the first of the family, "born, as near as I can figure, about the year 1200, more or less"; and others. However, these were not people who wandered in and out of stories, as the members of the Downing clan had earlier in the century. As a matter of fact, Billings wrote very few narrative passages except in the brief histories of his kinfolk.

For Billings was primarily an essayist, in the Addison-Steele-Goldsmith tradition, writing about all sorts of subjects in a fashion which was formal except in two respects: he did not follow grammatical rules, and the letters he used to form his words were not those generally in use. A piece typical in length and general quality of hundreds of such pieces (with a large share of the bad spelling repaired) was one he wrote on "Hoss Sense":

There is nothing that has been discovered yet, that is as scarce as good Hoss sense, about 28 hoss power.

I don't mean race hoss, nor trotting hoss sense, that can run a mile in 1:28 and then brake down; nor trot in 2:13 and good for nothing afterwards, only to brag on; but I mean the all-day hoss sense, that is good for 8 miles an hour, from rooster crowing in the morning, until the cows come home at night, clean to the end of the road.

I have seen fast sense, that was like some hosses, who could git so far in one day that it would take them two days to git back, on a litter. I don't mean this kind nuther.

Good hard-pan sense is the thing that will wash well, iron out without wrinkling, and take starch without cracking.

Many people are hunting after uncommon sense, but they never find it a good deal; uncommon sense is of the nature of genius, and all genius is the gift of God, and can't be had, like hen's eggs, for the hunting.

Good, old-fashioned common sense is one of the hardest things in the world to out-wit, out-argue, or beat in any way, it is as honest as a loaf of good domestick bread, always in tune, either hot from the oven or 8 days old.

Common sense can be improved upon by edukashun—genius can be too, some, but not much.

Edukashun galls genius like a bad setting harness.

Common sense is like biled vittles, it is good right from the pot, and it is good next day warmed up.

If every man was a genius, mankind would be as bad off as the heavens would be, with every star a comet, things would get hurt badly, and nobody to blame.

Common sense is instinct, and instinct don't make any blunders much, no more than a rat does, in coming out, or going into a hole, he hits the hole the fust time, and just fills it.

Genius is always in advance of the times, and makes some magnificent hits, but the world owes most of its tributes to good hoss sense.

A book by Billings or an almanac or a lecture would be a gathering-together of many essays like this one. He would write on the virtues ("Love," "Fear," "Beauty"), on various fauna ("The Mouse," "The Poll Cat," "The Striped Snaik"), on kinds of men ("The Honest Man," "The Kondem Phool," "The Model Man"), on carrying out important tasks ("How To Pick Out a Dog," "On Courting," "How To Pick Out a Horse"), on miscellaneous subjects ("The Fust Baby," "Billiards," "Habits of Grate Men," "Spring and Boils," "Tight Boots").

A lecture by Josh Billings would be a series of such bits following on the heels of one another. The synopsis of his

CIRCULAR ADVERTISING A LECTURE BY JOSH BILLINGS

last lecture, as he gave it out, shows how it leaped from one topic to another:

1. Remarks on Lecturing—General Overture
2. The Best Thing on Milk
3. The Summer Resort
4. Josh on Marriage
5. Josh on the Mule
6. The Handsome Man: A Failure
7. The Dude: A Failure
8. What I Know about Hotels
9. The Bumble-Bee
10. The Hornet
11. The Quire Singer
12. Josh on Flirting
13. Courtin'

He introduced a lecture by saying:

I don't propose this evening to speak of the "Lost Arts" nor the "Rise and Fall of the Roman Empire" . . . . nor touch on the Darwinian Theory—nor the probable purchase of Great Britain by Secretary Blaine—Nor allude in any way to the Third Term Question—But rather to deal with the Probabilities of Life, wrought out in Short Essays—monographs—Bits of Natural History, Answers to correspondents, and Proverbial philosophy.

Back of his books or lectures would be a personality which gave these wide-ranging compositions whatever unity they had. The personality was not notable for anything so much as its averageness in outlook, its sense of humor, and, finally, its pointed way of putting things. His closest approach to social reform was a hit now and then at feminism and a number of hits at intemperance ("Rum is good in its place," he said, "and hell is the place for it"). For the most part, though, when he wrote about the problems men had to solve, he was satisfied to put into his queer language sentences which spoke well of old-fashioned virtues and the joy they brought—a good home life, an honest (though shrewd) business career, and simple but strong religion. These passages—and those which simply explained the characters of

men and women of different sorts—showed his knowledge
of human nature and his thorough acceptance of old ideas
about it. Perhaps his greatest individual quirk was his fascination with animal life of many sorts—a fascination which
showed itself in essay after essay about insects and snakes
and animals of all kinds. In these essays Josh was interested
in turning over in his mind the strange facts about animal
life, phrasing his findings in a humorous way, and decorat-
ing his remarks every now and then with a moral the dis-
course had suggested to him. A sample of Billings on biology
was a piece called

STRIPED SNAIK

The striped snaik is one of the slipperyest jobs that natur ever turned
loose.

They travel on the lower side of themselfs, and can slip out of sight like
blowing out a candle. They were made for some good purpose, but I
never have been informed for what, unless it was to have their heads
smashed.

They are said to be innocent, but they have got a bad reputashun, and
all the innocence in the world won't cure a bad reputashun.

They live in the grass but seldom git stepped on, because they don't
stay long enough in the right place. . . . .

How on earth Eve was seduced by a snaik, is a fust class mistery to me,
and if I hadn't read it in the bible, I would bet against it.

I beleave everything there is in the bible, the things I can't understand,
I beleave the most. . . . .

Snaiks are all sorts, and all sizes, and the smaller they are, the more I
am afraid of them. . . . .

I never could account for a snaik or a cat hateing to die so bad, unless
it was because they was so poorly prepared for death.

Always, whatever the subject, Josh Billings showed a
great gift for squeezing much lore into a few words. Shaw
did not take pains to give Josh Billings a home or much of a

family circle; he did not give him adventures. Instead, he gave much time to his way of boiling down thoughts. A fellow-humorist, Eli Perkins, once came upon Shaw, seated in the corner seat of a New York streetcar and staring out so thoughtfully over his spectacles that he did not seem to recognize even his friend. Of a sudden he raised his hand and said:

"I've got it, Eli!"

"Got what?"

"Got a good one. Let me read it."

Shaw read one of the Billings pithy sentences—fourteen words: "When a man tries to make himself beautiful, he steals a woman's patent right." Perkins asked how long he had worked on it. "Three hours," Shaw told him, "to get it just right." Another time he said: "With me, everything must be put in two or three lines."

An English critic said of Shaw: "He is a writer of comic aphorisms—a Solomon in cap and bells." "He," said the creator of Bill Arp, "was Aesop and Ben Franklin, condensed and abridged." Turn anywhere in the writings of Josh, and you will find, every few lines, single sentences as good to quote as you will find anywhere in American literature. The long run of Billings is pretty tiring, but the short sentences are sparkling gems of bright expression. Often whole pages of proverb-like sentences were dumped into Josh's books, labeled with titles like "Sayings," "Remarks," "Yankee Notions," "Pepper Pods," "Hooks & Eyes," or with similar headings. Here were gathered sentences like these:

A pet lamb always makes a cross ram.

"The law of nations;" iron clad gun boats.

I have worked on a farm just long enough to know that there is no prayers so good for poor land as manure, and no theory can beat twelve hours each day (Sundays excepted), of honest labour applied to the sile.

The Live Yankee never gits sick at the stummuk in a foreign land, or grows sentermental; the beauty of a river to him is its capacity for a steamboat; its sloping banks checker into building lots, and its poetry waters might do the drudgery of a cotton mill.

There is only one good substitute for the endearments of a sister and that is the endearments of some other fellow's sister.

A learned fool is one who has read everything, and simply remembered it.

I love to see an old person joyfull, but not kickuptheheelsfull.

I never knew but one infidel in my life, and he had no more courage than a half drowned kitten just pulled out of a swill barrel, and was as afraid to die as the devil would be if he was allowed to visit this earth, for a short seazon to recruit himself.

Pride lives on itself, it is like a raccoon in winter, kept fat by sucking its claws.

It would be hard to say just what—aside from the spelling (most of which I have corrected)—makes these aphorisms differ from the general run of such sentences. Mr. Max Eastman, looking at Billings' writings, makes much of the way he would "set down on his page . . . . a series of verbal pictures, and leave them to stand for what they might be worth." It may be true that, more than other creators of proverbs—the literary ones, at any rate—Josh had a habit of getting his ideas into picture form, as several examples in the sentences just quoted will show. The sentence about pride is like many he wrote: it makes its point by using a vivid figure of speech rather than by simply saying anything general, like: "He who has pride will have more, for pride increases even though there is no reason for its growing." But, aside from this talent for vividness, aside from a few quirks of opinion and a comic way of abusing rules of spelling and grammar, this maker of almanacs in the last half of the nineteenth century was a sort of a throwback to the days of Poor Richard, many decades earlier.

II

Though women did not loom large in the history of horse-sense humor in America, there were enough of them in the literature to show that the writing of such humor was not restricted to males. Franklin's Widow Dogood was quite early in the field, and in the 1830's a few of the Downing letters were penned by the women of Downingville, notably Cousin Nabby and Jack's mother.

In the fifties, Benjamin P. Shillaber, writing down snippets of the talk of Mrs. Ruth Partington, won such a wide following for this lady that for many decades readers who believed in her were to send in requests for her autograph. Mrs. Partington was set against a vivid background, in which a number of her friends and her mischievous nephew Ike, a forerunner of Tom Sawyer, were prominent. The woman was the foreshadower of at least two radio characters very popular in 1942—Vera Vague and Mrs. Jane Ace. Muddled in her thinking, so much in love with big words that she was always dragging them into her talk, usually quite incorrectly, she was a fool character in everything of the mind, though her good intentions and her tender heart made her, at times, take the right side. The sketch called "Mrs. Partington in Court" will show how she told of a typical experience:

"I took my knitting-work and went up into the gallery," said Mrs. Partington, the day after visiting one of the city courts; "I went up into the gallery, and, after I had adjusted my specs, I looked down into the room, but I couldn't see any courting going on. An old gentleman seemed to be asking a good many impertinent questions,—just like some old folks,—and people were sitting around making minuets of the conversation. I don't see how they made out what was said, for they all told different stories. How much easier it would be to get along if they were all made to tell the same story! What a sight of trouble it would save the lawyers! The case, as they call it, was given to the jury, but I couldn't see it, and a gentleman with a long pole was made to swear that he'd keep an eye on 'em, and see that they didn't run away with it. Bimeby in they came agin, and then they said somebody was guilty of something, who had just said he was innocent, and didn't know nothing about it no more than the little baby that had never subsistence. I come away soon afterwards; but I couldn't help thinking how trying it must be to sit there all day, shut out from the blessed air!"

Starting earlier than the Partington papers and remaining famous as long were the Widow Bedott papers, which first began to come out in the 1840's and, in book form, sold twenty-three editions in the nine years after 1855. New editions of these papers, as late as 1883 and 1893, found many purchasers, and late in the century a drama about the widow was played to good houses in the East and the Middle West. The talk of this loquacious dame, set down at great length, had to do with all sorts of domestic happenings and with the story of the ruthless pursuit of a man. Bad poetry from her pen from time to time added to the humor of what she had to say.

In a way, these feminine chatterboxes were forerunners of the humorists who, later in the century, fought shy of political controversies. As was fitting for females (according to respectable thought in their day), they shrank from soiling their fingers with politics or social questions—social questions larger, that is, than the kind dealt with nowadays by Mrs. Emily Post.

III

When, however, in 1873, Marietta Holley came along with one of the most popular characters in American humor, male or female, she had some important preaching to do. Miss Holley had been born in rural New York, the daughter of a farmer. After a little work at the public school, she had been tutored at home in art and music, doing well enough to get some students of the piano in the neighborhood. She had somehow managed to acquire a number of ideas during her first thirty-seven years. These she expressed not only in her first book but in a long series of books which followed, the last coming out in 1914. Issued by the same company that published Mark Twain's early volumes and sold by that company's high-pressure agents, her works had an enormous sale. In 1905 a writer in the *Critic* said: "She has entertained as large an audience, I should say, as has been entertained by the humor of Mark Twain." That, perhaps, was a little strong; but there is no doubt that she had a tremendous following.

The books which made Miss Holley famous in America and in some of the countries of Europe as well were supposed to be written by a woman who called herself "Samantha" or "Josiah Allen's wife." Samantha was in the old tradition of firmly drawn characters rather than in that of the alternately wise and foolish humorous writers of her time. Not a few of the comic habits of funny females which had caused laughter long before were her habits, too. Like Mrs. Partington, she often used a word that sounded like another word but made less sense. Though less free with such malapropisms than the earlier chatterer, Miss Holley's heroine could say "formally" for "formerly," "adulteration" for

SAMANTHA IN THE ART GALLERY

"But there was some Italian statues that instinctively I got between and Josiah, and put my fan up, for I felt that he hadn't ort to see 'em."—*Samantha at the Centennial* (1878).

"adultery," and "Michael Angelico" for "Michael Angelo" within a few pages. She had a little trouble with her spelling which led her to similar mistakes: usually "their" was written "thier," "prey" might turn up in place of "pray," and "fare" might be used for "fair." At times she sounded more than a little like the Widow Bedott, as she dealt with the same kinds of things that took up so much of the widow's attention—and now and then in her talk a reader with a good ear might catch echoes of the voice of the beloved Artemus Ward.

Still, as the publishers said: "Never was a character's lines drawn more distinctly than that of Josiah Allen's wife." Nee Samantha Smith, she had married Josiah Allen, a widower with two small children, about fifteen years before she started to put her adventures on the printed page. When the good woman took up writing, the family was living in Jonesville, which was in about the middle of the United States. A few pages of any book she wrote were enough to make plain to any reader that she was—as her publishers said—"cute, wise, shrewd and observing, with a vein of strong common sense."

As long as she stayed on the farm, aside from her uneducated language, few signs of anything but her gumption showed themselves; but, as soon as she got away from home, it was clear that she could make the same sort of mistakes hicks had been making ever since humor had become American. Thanks to the advice of helpful friends, she did not blow out the gaslights in her hotel; but she behaved at other times exactly as a rural visitor to the city was supposed to do. On the train she thought the conductor reaching for her ticket was trying to shake hands. At the station, after leaving the train, she frowned fiercely at a man who asked her if she wanted a bus. On the street, bewildered by all the traffic, she thought a funeral was passing and waited for it to go by. At the hotel she offered to help do the breakfast dishes.

Whenever she did any thinking, though, Samantha showed no sign of awkwardness. Practically all her ideas, her notions, her prejudices, according to the standards of her day, were beautifully right. She was a wonderful housekeeper, a tolerant wife, a wise stepmother, a good Christian. What she had to say, for example, about the subject of home was an excellent summary of prevailing Victorian sentiment:

As I have said more'n a hundred times, if it is spelt right there haint another such word as home in the English language. The French can't spell it at all, and in my opinion that is jest what makes them so light minded and onstiddy. If it is spelt wrong, ... it means the horrors, and the very worst kinds of discomfort and misery. In fact love is the only school-master, that can put out that word worth a cent. And if it is put out by him, and spelt, for instance, by a couple who have loved each other for goin' on fifteen years, with a firm and almost cast iron affection, why it stands for peace and rest and comfort, and is the plainest picture God has give us below, kinder like we put painted pictures in children's story books, of that great Home above, where the colors won't never rub off of the picture, and peace and the rest are everlasting.

One comes upon many little sermons just as full of beautiful or striking thoughts scattered through Samantha's pages.

Miss Holley found this character very useful for the expression of her own views—her prejudices against the liquor traffic, foolish fashions, religious hypocrisy, white slavery, divorce, corruption in government, and, especially, the inequality of women. The title-page of her first book read *My*

Opinions and Betsey Bobbet's: Designed as a Beacon Light, To Guide Women to Life, Liberty, and the Pursuit of Happiness; But Which May Be Read by Members of the Sterner Sect without Injury to Themselves.

In this volume the author worked out a formula which fits practically every one of her books. The opening pages showed what a paragon of gumption Samantha was, in spite of little mistakes she made in arranging letters, in using words, or in forming sentences. Then followed a few comic stories—not to preach anything in particular but simply to amuse. After which was introduced the first of the long line of characters who, turning up at intervals in the narrative, made it possible for Samantha to blast them with her superior opinions.

Samantha, in Jonesville or wherever she went—and in this first book she told of a trip to New York—had clustered around her a fine collection of fools. In her first book the chief of these stooges was Betsey Bobbet—the type spinster of low comedy—skinny, toothless, hairless, and, in the words of Josiah Allen's wife, "awful sentimental." "I have seen," says the author, "a good many that had it bad, but of all the sentimental creeters I ever did see Betsey Bobbet is the sentimentalist, you couldn't squeeze a laugh out of her with a cheeze press." Mrs. Allen snorted at her affected way of pronouncing words, her textbook grammar. "I don't know much about grammar," said Samantha, "but common sense goes a good ways." Poor Betsey spent all her time (1) trying to track down a man and (2) writing horrible poetry about her soul.

Like the worst fools Samantha met, Miss Bobbet was against women's having the right to vote; and every few pages she got off some featherbrained opinion on the subject—and then calm, collected Mrs. Allen slapped her down with an answer. For example:

. . . . Betsey resumed, "It is so revoltin' to female delicacy to go to the poles and vote; most all the female ladies that revolve around in the high circles of Jonesville aristocracy agree with me in thinkin' it is real revoltin' to female delicacy to vote."

"Female delicacy!" says I, in a austere tone. "Is female delicacy a plant that withers in the shadder of the pole, but flourishes in every other condition only in the shadder of the pole?" says I. . . . . "Female delicacy flourishes in a ball room, where these sensitive creeters with dresses on indecently low in the neck, will waltz all night with strange men's arms round their waists," says I. "You have as good as throwed it in my face, Betsey Bobbet, that I haint a modest woman, or I would be afraid to go and vote; but you ketch me with a low neck dress on, Betsey Bobbet, and you will ketch me on my way to the Asylum, and there haint a old deacon, or minister, or presidin' Elder in the Methodist church, that could get me to waltz with 'em, let alone waltzin' with promiscuus sinners. . . . ."

The fact that Josiah got into this argument on Betsey's side shows where he stood in the books his wife wrote. He, too, was the object of his wife's attacks, particularly useful because it was no trouble at all to have him turn up whenever a numskull was needed to prod Mrs. Allen into a mother-wit lecture about something or other. Samantha was a plump matron weighing about two hundred and ten pounds; her spouse was a little bald-headed shrimp of a man weighing less than a hundred. It was good fun to have this mite talk about feminine weakness and delicacy to a woman like Samantha.

Not only did gigantic Mrs. Allen meet and pulverize the nitwits who were wholeheartedly against women's suffrage; she also had the pleasure of meeting and whacking a number of supporters of what seemed to her dangerous movements on behalf of females. Betsey, on being kissed—after years devoid of kisses—by a lecturer on free love, naturally became an advocate of free love. Samantha took care of her. Not satisfied with this triumph, Josiah's wife traveled all the way to New York to tell Victoria Woodhull, the chief advocate of divorce of the day, how wrong she was.

In New York, Samantha met a kind of person who turned up less often than fools in her books but was useful, nevertheless—the noble, wise character who had views like her own. At Victoria's house, so she said, she met Elizabeth Cady Stanton. As Josiah Allen's wife described this famous leader of the cause of women's rights, she

. . . . had jest about as noble a lookin' face as I ever see, with short white curls a fallin' all round it. The beholder could see by the first glance onto that face, that she hadn't spent all the immortal energies of her soul in makin' clover leaf tattin', or in cuttin' calico up into little pieces, jest to sew 'em together agin into blazin' stars and sunflower bedquilts. It was the face of an earnest noble woman, who had asked God what He wanted her to do, and then hadn't shirked out of doin' it. Who had gripped hold of life's plough, and hadn't looked back because the furrows turned over pretty hard, and the stumps was thick.

She knew by experience that there was never any greensward so hard to break up, as old prejudices and customs; and no stumps so hard to get round as the ridicule and misconceptions of the world. What made her face look as calm then, when she was doin' all this hard work? Because she knew she was makin' a clearin' right through the wilderness that in future was goin' to blossom like a rose. She was givin' her life for others, and nobody ever did this since the days of Jesus, but what somethin' of his peace is wrote down on thier forwards.

Of intentional humor there was absolutely none in a passage as poetical and eloquent as this one was intended to be.

This, then, was the pattern of *My Opinions and Betsey Bob-*

bet's—enough humor of an obvious and usually a time-tested sort to get a laugh every few pages; the huge, calm, housewifely Samantha giving her quaint accounts of the goings-on with horse-sense comments; nitwit characters met at Jonesville or during trips and shown up by the wise heroine's arguments against them; a few famous people who agreed with her and thus showed how clever she was. With variations it was good for a number of books—books which ranged from Jonesville to the great world's fairs in America (Philadelphia, Chicago, St. Louis) and beyond the sea to Europe and Hawaii.

If new styles in humor were what the reader wanted, these books were not, for the most part, very rewarding. But they were, in some ways, new enough in their appeal to win deep affection. Their message was—for humor in America—a rather new one: the feminist movement, which for decades had been a stand-by for broad comic attacks, in these writings became the policy vigorously supported. And, of all the humorists of the last century, Miss Holley most definitely wrote for the great host of feminine readers. By a woman whom these readers would admire, largely about women, these books evidently lured more dollars out of purses than out of pockets. The author avoided collisions with feminine prejudices as relatively few male humorists—excepting good Major Jones—had managed to do. Her triumphs and her opinions were those women liked to share.

Back of the books was shrewd Marietta Holley, friend of the great leaders of the women's-rights movement of the day—Susan B. Anthony and Frances E. Willard—spreading their teachings. The propaganda was brilliantly handled, and I think that there can be no doubt that Samantha did more for the cause than many hard workers ever accomplished by serious speeches and arguments.

To me, Miss Holley's writings are interesting not only as preachments but also as biographical documents. Here was a spinster in a day when spinsterhood was generally thought of as a sad misfortune. In the role of Samantha she was a married woman with a family, contemptuous of spinsters, proud of her wifehood, often becoming very emotional about household joys. No one has made public enough about the life of Miss Holley to settle the point, but we cannot help wondering whether her Samantha did not gain a great deal in vitality because a certain amount of envy and admiration entered into her creation.

CHAPTER XI

Imported Horse Sense
Mr. Dooley

There's only three books in the world worth readin'—Shakespeare, the Bible, and Mike Ahearn's histhry of Chicago. I have Shakespeare on trust, Father Kelly reads the Bible for me, and I didn't buy Mike Ahearn's histhry because I seen more than he could put into it. . . . . Life, says ye! There's no life in a book. If you want to show thim what life is, tell thim to look around thim. There's more life on a Saturdah night in the Archey Road than in all the books from Shakespeare to the rayport of the drainage trustees. . . . .

—MR. MARTIN DOOLEY, SALOONKEEPER, ARCHEY ROAD, CHICAGO

I

THE humor of common sense was carried on without definite breaks well into the 1930's. Always before the death of the author, at the moment supreme in writing of this sort, another had started his career. Thus, though the number of humorists in the homespun school declined in the years after the 1870's, Americans who liked their laughter mixed with horse sense had no trouble at any time in finding productions to suit their fancy. Three very successful authors spanned, between them, the period from the end of the nineteenth century to the middle of the fourth decade in the twentieth century—Finley Peter Dunne, Kin Hubbard, and Will Rogers—all of them still remembered

240

with great love. Dunne's hero, Mr. Dooley, will be considered in this chapter, Kin Hubbard's hero and Will Rogers in the next.

Finley Peter Dunne, Chicago born and reared, was a journalist in the Windy City when the idea came to him that he might do well to start expressing his notions about contemporary affairs through the lips of an Irish saloon-keeper, who, in time, was to be known to hosts of readers as Mr. Dooley. Whether Dunne was aware of it or not, his hero was one of a long line of humorous characters who had talked not in the American language but in the dialect of recently Americanized foreigners.

Back in the 1850's and thence forward until the last decades of the nineteenth century, the German-American talk of Hans Breitmann had been a gold mine for his creator, Charles G. Leland. Hans had been a German-American Falstaff, living largely for food and drink, enjoying himself hugely in all sorts of situations in all sorts of places—a bummer in the Civil War, a riotous romper in the Far West, a happy visitor to foreign lands. Hans had a good deal, off and on, to say about politics. In his broad German dialect, for example, he told of his adventures in this field—how he lined up with a man named Twine—

> . . . . a Connedicut man
> In whom we haf great hopes,
> Who hat shange his poledics fifteen dimes,
> Und therefore knew de ropes

—how he decided

> Dat any man who gifs me his vote
> Votefer his poledics be—
> Shall alvays be regartet
> As polidigal friendt py me

and how he worked out a way of satisfying any critics who might not agree with him:

> Dese ish de principles I holts,
>   And dose on vitch I run:
> Dey ish fixed firm and immutaple
>   Ash the course of de 'ternal sun:
> But if you don't abbrove of dem—
>   Blease notice vot I say—
> I shall only be too happy
>   To alter dem right avay.

Hans, though a little hard to read, had a gusto and animal healthiness which made him pleasant company. In England as well as in America he delighted a large number of readers.

In the days of the Civil War, a series of verses had made the talk of Private Miles O'Reilly known to many patrons of humor. O'Reilly, the brain-child of Charles Graham Halpine, was the chief figure in a few rather uninteresting wartime adventures—among them a visit to the guardhouse and a secret mission to the Confederate government. He was best remembered, however, for his verse, of which this piece—a soldier's unheroic remarks about the use of Negro soldiers in the Civil War—is a fair sample:

SAMBO'S RIGHT TO BE KILT

Air—"The Low-Backed Car"

> Some tell us 'tis a burnin' shame
>   To make the naygers fight!
> And that the thrade of bein' kilt
>   Belongs but to the white;

> But as for me, upon my sowl!
>   So liberal are we here,
> I'll let Sambo be murthered instead of myself
>   On every day in the year.
>
> . . . .
>
> So hear me all, boys darlin',
>   Don't think I'm tippin' you chaff,
> The right to be kilt we'll divide wid him
>   And give him the largest half.

The best thing about this is the refreshing realism of a soldier about the glory of war—but it is pretty tepid stuff, at best. The German dialect of Yawcob Strauss, as put down by Charles Follen Adams, had carried humor of this sort into the seventies and eighties. These were some of the more famous of the scores of humorists who used comic dialect. It is perhaps worth noting that all these dialect comedians wrote in verse.

On the American stage in the years just before Dunne put an Irish brogue to work for him, the paddy was a type character. As Mr. Franklin P. Adams says:

> And the stage was full of Irishmen; every vaudeville house had one or two Irish acts on its bill; the Russell Brothers, John W. Kelly, Bobby Gaylor, Johnny Ray, Ferguson and Mack, Maggie Cline, and Johnny Carroll; there were still echoes of Harrigan and Hart; and the tenor voices of Chauncey Olcott and Andrew Mack, in Irish plays written for them, were heard in the land.

Doubtless these stage figures helped develop the American taste for Irish dialect humor.

II

Dunne, a young Chicago journalist, was much impressed by the personality of Irish saloonkeeper James McGarry, who, in the nineties, wetted the whistles of most of the reporters of the city in his handsome place on Dearborn Street. Plump, red-cheeked, blue-eyed, McGarry said little but had a talent for making his few remarks impressive. When he heard McGarry say some amusing things about Jay Gould the day the great financier went to his heavenly reward, Dunne decided they might be worth a little skit for his paper. Attributing the sayings to a mythical Colonel McNeery, he published them and, for a time, forgot them.

The memory of this piece came back to the writer, however, somewhat later, when he and his managing editor were waging a war against the customary corruption in the Chicago city government. The publisher, according to Dunne's account,

. . . . was nervous about libel suits and loans at banks that were interested in the franchises for sale in the council. It occurred to me that while it might be dangerous to call an alderman a thief in English no one could sue if a comic Irishman denounced the statesman as a thief. So I revived Col. McNeery and used him to bludgeon the bribe-taking members of the council. I think the articles were effective. The crooks were ridiculed by their friends who delighted in reading these articles aloud in public places, and, as they were nearly all natural Irish comedians, doing it well. If I had written the same thing in English I would inevitably have been pistolled or slugged, as other critics were. But my victims did not dare to complain.

When Jim McGarry failed to enjoy the way his customer made use of his character and a name much like his own, the humorist made some changes in his articles. His hero became old Martin Dooley, and the Dooley saloon out on Archer Avenue—the scene of his talks—became a very different place from the Dearborn Street public house. Every week from 1893 on, a Dooley article came out in the *Post*, and the Irishman's name became known to some, at least, not only in Chicago but in other parts of the country as well.

What really made a national figure of the Sage of Archey Road (as he called Archer Avenue) was the way he talked about the Spanish-American War in 1898. There was plenty of material for good satire in that contest. Americans, after many decades of coveting Cuba, decided that they had a holy inspiration to go to the aid of that downtrodden island. There were amusing discrepancies between the contempt in this country for the Spaniards and the fear that, after all, the American army and navy might be as inefficient as the American government in general. There was a laughable contrast between the desperate valor summoned up before the fighting and the ease with which what John Hay called "a splendid little war" was won. Finally, there was the contrast between the holy aims of the United States and the imperialistic plunder they gained by fighting.

All these matters were grist for Mr. Dooley as he chatted in his saloon on Archey Road with his old friend, Mr. Hennessy. Dunne thought that the pieces setting down the talk possibly were as popular as they were because they "reflected the feeling of the public about this queer war," and his guess was probably a pretty good one. Having caught the attention of a large audience, the Irish saloonkeeper chattered on in piece after piece for many years, and his remarks were printed in numerous newspapers and magazines. Although the period, roughly, from 1898 to 1910 was the time of his greatest success and although the articles and books came less often as the years passed, Dooley kept commenting on all sorts of contemporary subjects down into the 1920's. The issues of four decades, therefore, were discussed over the counter in his humble saloon.

III

Dooley's creator gave a good characterization of the old fellow in the Preface to the first book about him. He was, said Dunne, a

traveller, historian, social observer, saloon-keeper, economist, and philosopher, who had not been out of the ward for twenty-five years "but twict." He read the newspapers with solemn care, heartily hated them, and accepted all they printed for the sake of drowning Hennessy's rising protests against his logic. From the cool heights of life in the Archey Road, uninterrupted by the jarring noises of crickets and cows, he observed the passing show, and meditated thereon. His impressions were transferred to the desensitized plate of Mr. Hennessy's mind, where they could do no harm. . . . . He was opulent of advice, as became a man of his station; for he had mastered most of the obstacles of a business career, and by leading a prudent and temperate life had established himself so well that he owned his own house and furniture, and was only slightly behind on his license. . . . . He has served his country with distinction. His conduct of the important office of captain of his precinct (1873–75) was highly commended, and there was some talk of nominating him for alderman. . . . . But the activity of public life was unsuited to a man of Mr. Dooley's tastes; and while he continued to view the political situation with interest and sometimes with alarm, he resolutely declined to leave the bar for the forum. His early experience gave him wisdom in discussing public affairs. "Politics," he often said, "ain't bean bag. 'Tis a man's game; and women, children, and pro-hybitionists would do well to keep out of it."

This was the man who gave Mr. Hennessy the low-down on everything as it happened. Hennessy, a fool character "who had at best but a clouded view of public affairs" and who suffered badly from credulity and horrible logic, asked an innocent question now and then to get the Sage started and to keep his tongue wagging, and Dooley held forth on anything close to his heart.

The old Irishman was in many ways a victim of his limited environment. Since Archey Road was his universe, he reduced every problem to the terms of life in that bedraggled section of Chicago—and in his mind a major general or a queen was as easy to understand as a shanty Irishman who now and then came to the saloon. Since life on Archey Road was friendly and informal, he did not see anything strange about calling President McKinley "Mack" and Admiral Dewey "Cousin George." Even the czar of Russia was pictured with great familiarity when the barkeeper said:

The Hague conference, Hinnissy, was got up by the Czar of Rooshya just before he moved his army against the Japs. It was a quiet day at St. Petersburg. The Prime Minister had just been blown up with dinnymite, the Czar's uncle had been shot, and one of his cousins was expirin' from a dose of prussic acid. All was comparative peace. In the warm summers afternoon the Czar felt almost drowsy as he sat in his royal palace and listened to the low, monotonous drone of bombs bein' hurled at the Probojensky guards. . . . . The monarch's mind turned to the subjeck of war and he says to himself: "What a dreadful thing it is that such a beautiful world should be marred by thousands of innocent men bein' sint out to shoot each other for no cause whin they might better stay at home and work for their royal masters," he says. "I will disguise mesilf as a moojik and summon a meetin' of the Powers," he says.

This Dooleymorphism was matched by other limitations on his knowledge. Entirely unread in anything but the newspapers, knowing nothing of the world of books, he was likely to call an acolyte "an alkali," an encyclopedia "a bicyclopedia," and when he quoted what he thought was the German national anthem, it came out "Ich vice nit wauss allus bay doitan." His ignorance of books led him to ascribe all sorts of fine sayings to his friend Hogan, giving him credit for all the phrases he had quoted. "Oh," Dooley would say,

"as Hogan says, why should the spirit of mortal be proud?"
or "Onaisy, as Hogan says, is the head that wears the
crown." His ethical standards, worked out during a rough
life in his ward, were those of the wrong side of the tracks—
he might use loaded dice or pass bad money at times to cheat
a neighbor he disliked; he had a liking for a good hard brick
to settle an argument; he accepted vote-buying and crook-
edness as normal parts of politics. An Irishman from the top
of his white head to the tips of his toes, he had all the prejudices, whether justifiable or not, of his race.

But in his long life he had seen men come and go, and he
was well acquainted with their ways. Hence he knew much
of human nature—both its grandeurs and its depravities.
His democracy was a fine thing, and so was his tolerance and
sympathy. Sometimes his heart worked better than his
head, as when he practiced charity on the sly, although his
thinking had caused him to condemn it.

William Dean Howells, well read though he was in the
great literatures of Europe, paid high compliments to the
way Dunne made his hero a believable character:

Dooley's characterization is . . . . through his own talk, and the art
of the author is felt in nothing so much as in his sensitive respect for
Dooley's personality. Dooley is wise and shrewd and just for the most
part; but from time to time he reaches a point when he is neither. . . . .
Mr. Dunne knows Mr. Dooley's limitations, and he does not force him
beyond them in the interest of the best purpose. He knows that there are
moments when his philosophical spectator of events must lapse into a
saloon keeper, and he guards the precious integrity of his creation from
the peril of perfunctory humanity.

As a personality, then, a richly complicated character in
spite of resemblances to older characters, he stood out from
the hosts of humorous figures who had preceded him. There

were two other things about him which made him different
from most of his predecessors—his sense of humor and the
doctrines which (often without knowing it) he preached.

Strange though it may seem to casual readers of comic
writings, his sense of humor was an unusual gift for an
American humorous character to enjoy. Jack Downing,
Major Jones, and almost the whole army of their followers
had been as solemn as owls and as blind to the funny sides of
things they were saying as they were to the knowledge contained between the covers of books. Artemus Ward, on the
lecture platform, saying excruciatingly funny things but
looking as woebegone as an undertaker, was a type of the
average hero of native humor.

But Dooley could crack a joke with a point to it. He had a
liking for a pun—as when he said that all the powers of Europe sent delegates to a peace conference "and a great many
of the weaknesses did so too" or that "Gin'ral Miles is pre-
parin' to destroy the Spanish at one blow—and he's the boy
to blow." He had a flair for a phrase which painted a funny
picture, as when he told how a drunken man was "comin'
home a little late and tryin' to reconcile a pair of round feet
with an embroidered sidewalk." At times he could be ironic.
When he had told how an Irish revolutionary plot had
failed because newspapers had been notified of it and how
the leader, Tynan, had then led a parade of conspirators
and unloaded explosives in the sight of everyone, the dumb
Hennessy said brightly, "There must have been a spy in the
ranks." Then—

"Sure thing," said Mr. Dooley, winking at Mr. McKenna [another
customer]. "Sure thing, Hinnessy. Ayether that or the accomplished de-
tictives at Scotland Yards keep a close watch in the newspapers. Or it

may be—who knows?—that Tynan was indiscreet. He may have dropped a hint of his intintions."

At times this talent of the Irishman for fun gave the Dooley papers passages in which there were amusing contrasts between the minds involved—Dunne pretending to be Dooley, and Dooley acting like a fool.

IV

The doctrines the good-natured saloonkeeper gave voice to were also distinctive. He evidently had an interest in almost everything that got into the columns of the daily press, so his talk was far from specialized. He treated not only war but political battles of all sorts, family life, sports, literature, education, and enough other subjects to make his collected monologues quite encyclopedic. Wittingly or unwittingly he threw light on this great variety of subjects in such sayings as:

There's only one thing that would make me allow mesilf to be a hero to the American people, and that is it don't last long.

If a man is wise, he gets rich and if he gets rich, he gets foolish, or his wife does.

There are no friends at cards or world politics.

Here's the pitchers of candydates I pulled down from the window, and just knowin' they're here makes me that nervous for the contints of the cash drawer I'm afraid to turn me back for a minute.

I guess a man niver becomes an orator if he has anything to say, Hinnessy.

The Supreme Court follows the iliction returns.

In a gineral way, all I can say about golf is that it's a kind of a game of ball that you play with your own worst inimy which is yourself, and a man you don't like goes around with you and gloats over you, and a little boy follows you to carry the clubs and hide the ball after you've hit it.

As far as Martin Dooley was concerned, this wide variety in his talk was inspired by his great interest in the many things he found in newspapers. As far as his creator was concerned, Dunne could put pertinent remarks into the saloonkeeper's words because he himself had more than average interest in the affairs of the day and more knowledge of them than most men. The wry wisdom and the scorn for sham that so often stir in the minds of big-city reporters were his. In addition he happened to fall in with a crowd of people in Chicago who were beginning to become excited over social and political changes. He was a member of the newly organized White Chapel Club, which a fellow-member, George Ade, said, is

. . . . still remembered as a collection of harum-scarum irresponsibles who scorned the conventions and shared an abiding enthusiasm for alcoholic liquors. It was more than that. It was really a round-up of interesting intellectuals whose opinions and doctrinal beliefs were far in advance of the Chicago environment of that time, although they have since come into favor and received governmental endorsement. Not all of what they stood for will ever be approved by popular vote, because they were irreligious and probably might have been classified as agnostics. They had such scathing contempt for the self-seeking political bosses and the stuffed shirts of the millionaire aristocracy of their own town, and such a tyranny of wealth, that they probably might be called socialists, with a leaning toward outright anarchy.

Mr. Ade thought the Dooley articles were "merely truth concealed in sugar-coated idiom and dialect"; and it is true that they said more harsh things about the United States and its people in general than a writer could have said—and have remained popular—a few years before Mr. Dooley started to make his pronouncements. But though Dunne adopted the device he did because he wanted a safe way to say biting things about certain politicians without risking libel suits, it is wrong to think that the sugar coating was necessary for the expounding of doctrines such as the humorist wanted to preach. The period of Dooley's reign in humor was one during which social revolt flourished. After 1896, William Jennings Bryan (on whom Dooley at times affectionately bestowed the Irish name O'Brien) was a beloved leader of dissatisfied common people of the prairies and the mining country. William Allen White was shouting his Kansas version of liberal doctrine. Such a poem as Edwin Markham's "The Man with the Hoe" (1899), complaining about the woes of the worker and dimly hinting at the possibility of revolution if things did not straighten out, could, in those days, stir the nation. It was the time of the rise of Teddy Roosevelt (Rosenfelt to Dooley), who lashed out fiercely at "the malefactors of great wealth." The early 1900's saw, too, the great success of the muckrakers—popular magazine writers whose fame was based on sensational attacks upon graft and corruption in the city, the state, and the nation. Mr. Dooley, in other words, was a humorous ally of a group of crusaders who shared many of his liberal views and made good money by putting them into print.

Yet it is striking to see how many of the old Irishman's comments, in the light of discoveries made by historians long after the days of his talking, have turned out to be sound. As Mr. John Chamberlain has pointed out,

Certainly a dandy course in pre-war American history could be taught by taking Mr. Dooley as a three-times-a-week plain English text. His comments on the conduct of the Spanish-American War, for example, anticipated Walter Mills' sanely comic *The Martial Spirit* by some thirty years. His description of William McKinley, the praying President who got the tip direct from Jehovah that the United States owed it to Christianity to take the already Catholic Philippines, turned up a generation later in Thomas Beer's *Hanna* as the "mature" judgments of the nineteen-twenties. His title for Theodore Roosevelt's book on the Rough Riders—*Alone in Cubia*—made Hermann Hagedorn look silly even before Hermann Hagedorn had constituted himself chief T. R. hagiographer. And his remarks on the Dreyfus case might have served as the text for Matthew Josephson's *Zola*.

Some proof of the aptness of the Archey Road sermons is the number of times they turn up in good histories of the Dooley era—especially in one of the best of them, Mr. Mark Sullivan's *In Our Times*. There is at least some justice in the claim of Thomas L. Masson: "If all the newspaper files and histories were destroyed between the years 1898 and 1910 and nothing remained but Mr. Dooley's observations, it would be enough."

And it is also striking to note how much of the talk, early and late, of Mr. Dooley, without change or, at most, with that of a few names, has the sting of satire on the affairs of the present day. Professor Pattee's claim that "satire . . . . , no matter how biting or sparkling, perishes with its own generation" does not hold good for the Irishman's talk—for much of it, at all events—if touches of dialect too hard for modern readers are deleted.

The experience Martin Dooley had when he visited Mary Ellen Cassidy's kindergarten has more than a little lasting value as comment on various contemporary educational fads. The children were sitting around on the floor, or sleeping, or dancing, and he noticed one lad pulling another lad's hair.

"Why don't you take the coal shovel to that little barbaryan, Mary Ellen?" says I. "We don't believe in corporeal punishment," says she. "School should be made pleasant for the childer," she says. "The child whose hair is bein' pulled is larnin' patience," she says, "and the child that's pullin' the hair is discoverin' the futility of human indeavor," says she. . . . . "Put them through their exercises," says I. "Tommy," says I, "spell cat," I says. "Go to the devil," says the cherub. "Very smartly answered," says Mary Ellen. . . . . "They don't larn that till they get to college . . . . , sometimes not even then." . . . . "And what do they larn?" says I. "Rompin'," she says, " and dancin'," she says, " and independence of speech, and beauty songs, and sweet thoughts, and how to make home home-like," she says.

Mr. Dooley's talk about the value of the crusader to political reform also has lasting value:

As a people, Hinnissy, we're the greatest crusaders that iver was—for a short distance. On a quarter mile track we can crusade at a rate that would make Hogan's friend, Godfrey the Bullion look like a crab. But the trouble is the crusade don't last after the first sprint. The crusaders drops out of the procession to take a drink or put a little money on the ace, and by the time the end of the line of march is reached the boss crusader is alone on the job and his former followers is hurlin' bricks at him from the windows of policy shops. The boss crusader always gets the double cross. If I wanted to send my good name down to the ginerations with Cap. Kidd and Jesse James I'd lead a movement for the suppression of vice. I would so.

What he thought about the cost of the Spanish-American War does not seem dated yet:

"And so the war is over?" asked Mr. Hennessy.

"Only part of it," said Mr. Dooley. "The part that you see in the pitcher papers is over, but the tax collector will continyoo his part of the war with relentless fury. Cavalry charges are not the only ones in a real war."

Nor is his account of his harrowing experiences during the horrible conflict without a good deal of point:

This war, Hinnissy, has been a great strain on me. To think of the suffrin' I've endured! For weeks I lay awake at nights fearin' that the Spanish armadillo'd leave the Cape Verde Islands, where it wasn't, and take the train out here, and hurl death and destruction into my little store. Day by day the pitiless extras came out and beat down on me. You hear of Teddy Rosenfelt plungin' into ambuscades and Sicrity of Wars; but did you hear of Martin Dooley, the man behind the guns, four thousand miles behind them, and willin' to be further? . . . . I'm what Hogan calls one of the mute, inglorious heroes of the war; an' not so dam mute, ayther.

How long Mr. Dooley will continue to sound as apt as he does now it is, of course, impossible to say. So far, however, as Hogan says, age has not withered nor custom staled his infinite variety.

CHAPTER XII

Abe Martin and Will Rogers

Th' safest way t' double your money is t' fold it over once an' put it in your pocket.

— ABE MARTIN, BROWN COUNTY, INDIANA

Two hundred years from now history will record: "America, a nation that flourished from 1900–1942, conceived many odd inventions for getting somewhere, but could thing of nothing to do when they got there."

— WILL ROGERS

I

PLENTY of people in 1930 were ready to swear that, in Kin Hubbard and Will Rogers, the twentieth century had produced two figures the like of which America had not seen in the past. But anyone who looks back through the years at the scores of homespun philosophers who said things as Americans liked to have them said will see that the resemblances between these writers of our own day and the men who went before them are much more important than the differences—that a good old pattern in humor is often better than a new one and the popular literary memory is short.

Kin Hubbard, born in Bellefontaine, Ohio, in 1868, went for a short time to public school and then broke into writing just as Artemus Ward, Petroleum V. Nasby, and Mark Twain had done—taking off as a typesetter on a country newspaper. In 1891 he began working for the *Indianapolis News* as a cub reporter who illustrated many of his news stories. He took about fourteen years, after that, to find himself as a humorist. It was in 1905 that, making use of some of the rural local color he had picked up while covering Indiana political campaigns, he began to phrase his ideas in the words of a Hoosier bumpkin, Abe Martin.

The formula he used then and for about a quarter of a century thereafter was a simple enough one. In the part of the paper assigned to Hubbard, there would be a picture of the musing Abe, perhaps working away at some farm chore or, perhaps, sitting or standing and thinking. The old farmer, with his floppy hat, his old shirt, his striped pants, and his old boots, had a scarecrow-like figure. His face had the button eyes, the one-line mouth, and the careless nose of a cartoon, and he had the chin whiskers of a low-comedy farmer. James Whitcomb Riley did some verse which captured very well the spirit of the drawing:

> The artist, Kin Hubbard, 's so keerless
> He draws Abe 'most eyeless and earless;
> But he's never yit pictured him cheerless
>   Er with fun 'at he tries to conceal—
> Whuther onto the fence er clean over
> A-rootin' up ragweeds er clover,
> Skeert stiff at some "Rambler" er "Rover"
>   Er new fangled automobeel.

Underneath such a picture would be written, as a rule, two sentences, usually sentences which had no connection except that they happened, both of them, to have been said by Abe in his Brown County dialect. Thus:

There was a ole fashioned one-ring weddin' at th' Tilford Moots home t'day. Some folks git credit fer havin' hoss sense that haint ever had enough money t' make fools o' themselves.

At the end of every year a collection of these sayings would be made in a little book sometimes called *Abe Martin's Almanack* and decked out with monthly calendars, but usually given a title like *Abe Martin's Back Country Sayings* or *Abe Martin's Home-cured Philosophy*. In such a book the previously wedded sentences would be divorced—separated by spaces between them. In addition to these daily skits, Hubbard now and then wrote an essay, usually in language rather like that which Abe used but as a rule signed by one of Abe's Brown County neighbors.

No one who knows the humor of Josh Billings can fail to see that, whether Abe Martin knew it or not, he had in Josh his nineteenth-century prototype. The strange spelling had given away to a more restrained dialect, and many of the topics—automobiles, fashions in dress and entertainment, farm woes and city woes—were not of the nineteenth century but of the twentieth. But the appeal was to lovers of the aphorism phrased in homely rural language, and when a longer passage of humor was written it was an old-fashioned essay, with aphorisms playing the chief part in causing laughter. Even the "almanacks" remind one of Billings. The character back of the talk is just as sketchy as Billings was, an embodiment simply of good horse sense with a vague quirk or two. Many of his sayings might easily have been written by Josh Billings—sayings such as these:

Don't be fooled on purrin'. A cat would attack us in a second if it wuzn' afraid.

Christmas jewelry often turns green in the spring.

Lots o' people insist on eatin' with a knife that wuz born with a silver spoon in their mouth.

Ther's somebody at ever' dinner party that eats all th' celery.

Of all th' home remedies a good wife is th' best.

But, of course, the fact that the author belonged to this century rather than to the last one makes him appeal more strongly to readers of today. Many of his sayings, even those written many years ago, have point today; for example:

I wish somebuddy would make a new Republican speech.

Ther's some folks standin' behind th' President that ought t' git around where he kin watch 'em.

Our unemployment parade yisterday wuz a big success, some three hundred an' thirty-three cars bein' in th' procession.

Hubbard as an essayist had rather more organization than Billings; but, like Billings, he depended on good sayings to give his essays their zest. "Th' Use o' th' Nut" is a typical essay:

Nine-tenths o' th' people go thro' this life without usin' ther nut. Lots o' folks die at seventy-five with bran' new, unscuffed brains, brains that have jest been cuddled up an' forgotten fer years, brains in ther original wrappers. In other words, most people tackle all th' great transactions o' life without stoppin' t' think, or if they do stop it's because o' cold feet, an' not thro' any exercise o' th' nut. Th' feller that drives a car should have his nut at his toes' tips at all times, an' th' feller that's importuned t' go int' somethin' where he kin double his $700 should consult his nut at once, retire t' a room, or water plug, an' think. Some folks talk fer hours without thinkin', or they'd never begin. "It never dawned on me," "I never once thought," "I never dreamed o' such a thing," are all familiar expressions that come from people with dormant thinkin' apparatuses. Results have showed that th' average voter don't use his nut any more than th' widows who invest ther money. "I wish I'd thought," says th' feller or widow, who's lost ever' thing. "It never occurred t' me," is another common stock expression very pop'lar with fellers who have missed rare opportunities, or lost out on th' chance of a lifetime. We all go too fast an' bust int' things too freely. The sober second thought allus comes mopin' along after th' car's ditched, or we've made a mess o' marriage, or th' savin's of a lifetime have gone glimmerin'. Then fer th' first time most of us discover that we've got a nut. This would be some country if ever' one used his nut instead o' lettin' a few glib, affable handshakers with brief cases do ther thinkin'. Pick up any-buddy an' try t' git his nut t' workin' an' see how you come out. He may say, "I never thought o' that before," but that's th' best you'll git. We don't believe eight fellers out o' ten even think they'll play golf. We

ABE MARTIN
One of the typical drawings of Abe by his creator, Kin Hubbard

believe they jest automatically neglect ther work an' play. Occasionally some feller really uses his nut an' still shows poor judgment, but that's due t' a faulty nut. Life is filled with tight places, an' at no time in all history wuz ther ever an age like t' day's, an age when we depend almost entirely on quick nut work lest we git skinned, or shot, or maimed—or poisoned.

It was in the short aphorisms, however, rather than in the

longer essays on subjects like "Salesmanship," "Speedin'," "Th' Circus," "Popularity," and "Farmin'," that Abe was at his best. Kin Hubbard had tricks of his own that were worth something. His combination of two unrelated aphorisms into a single paragraph piled up disparities. He used some queer names of fellow-Hoosiers for allusions and quotations and tended to make them type characters—Miss Fawn Lippincott, a village belle; Young Lafe Bud, a dandy; Mr. and Mrs. Tilford Moots, who had domestic trouble; Miss Tawny Apple, who was rather brash in her dress and her sex life; Tell Binkley, the village failure who thought he knew about finance, and others who came into his talk every now and then down through the years. Finally, he had a way of putting together slowly unfolding sentences, the meaning of which was hidden to the last: " 'I'll be glad when I'm found guilty, an' git a new trial, an' go free, an' have this mess over with,' said Mrs. Tilford Moots' niece, whose late husband wuz insured for eighteen thousand dollars." This rambling sentence came out in 1928, a year when a number of self-made widows were cleared of murder charges. Again: " 'If she comes in t' night I'll try t' catch her in th' mornin' an tell her,' said Mrs. Tipton Bud, when somebuddy left a message for her daughter." This tragic story, with its poignant contrast between the old and the new generation, is developed in a similar way: "Uncle Mort Hickman, nearly ninety-eight, after cuttin' and splittin' four cords o' wood yisterday afternoon, wuz found frozen stiff in th' lane leadin' t' th' house by his four sons, who had been attendin' a billiard tournament."

These stories compressed into a sentence, with the climax falling neatly in the last word, were Hubbard's chief contribution to the art of expressing ideas humorously. Other-wise, this writer, who Will Rogers said "is writing the best humor in America today," did very well with little more than Billings had used many decades earlier.

II

"Ther's at least one instance," said Abe Martin, "where havin' enough rope didn' end disastrously, an' that's Will Rogers." It was natural that Hubbard and the cowboy humorist should admire each other, because the success of the humor of Rogers as well as that of Hubbard was largely the result of an ability to squeeze a great deal of good sense into a funny sentence.

Rogers was the more successful of the two. His life-story was a fantastic triumph of the sort that has made America an amazing country. Born in 1879 in a ranchhouse in Indian Territory, as he put it, "halfway between Claremore and Oologah, before there was a town in either place," he grew up in the cow country. He went to a country school and then to Kemper Military Academy, "a little while"— and his formal schooling was ended. His informal schooling included working in the Texas oil fields, punching cows for a number of years, service in the Boer War, travel with a circus in the Antipodes and the Orient, and vaudeville work in America.

He was in vaudeville, staging a lariat-whirling act, when he discovered that if he mixed talk with his roping tricks, the audience liked him better. Bit by bit he added anecdotes and sallies to his act, until he became famous as a wisecracking cowboy. In Ziegfeld's Follies, in 1914, he became a star, partly because he added comments on national and international affairs to his humorous monologues. From then on, the way was easy: by leaps and bounds he mounted to such prominence that when he died in an airplane accident in August, 1935, many felt his death to be a national calamity. Newspapers used column after column to rehearse his life-story, a coast-to-coast radio hookup carried a memorial program, and in the Senate, Majority Leader Robinson rose and said: "Probably the most widely known citizen in the United States and certainly the best beloved met his death some hours ago in a lonely and faraway place."

It is interesting to guess at the reasons for this great fame Rogers had. Undoubtedly, one thing that helped it a great deal was the novelty of a cowboy humorist. Perhaps even more important was the fact that he embodied for Americans a type which in some ways at that time seemed more representative of the life of the country than the farmer type did. And the way the screen plays of some decades had portrayed heroic western cowboys certainly had built up a friendly attitude—if not a worshipful one—toward the type.

Rogers' tremendous popularity doubtless was also partly the result of his getting to the people of America in more ways than any humorist had ever before used to reach the public. He became known first as a trouper with vaudeville companies swinging around the country. Then came Broadway engagements, with the metropolitan press giving him all the publicity usually given to a man who is an unusual kind of a stage celebrity. The silent moving pictures made his face and his gestures known to millions, and some of the lines he wrote to be flashed on the screen gave this huge audience samples of his wit. Then came the talkies, and the hesitant Rogers drawl charmed crowds who went to see him play Bill Jones in *Lightnin'*, Hank in *A Connecticut Yankee*, Lem Morehouse in *Young as You Feel*, and other roles just as well suited to him. A fine contract lured him to the lecture circuit—and, like Artemus Ward, Mark Twain, and others, he traveled across the continent, appearing before many delighted audiences. The radio, too, carried his voice to hundreds of thousands of chuckling listeners. Meanwhile, he had begun to write—books at first, newspaper columns and magazine articles later. The take from these many activities was impressive—at its height about $20,000 a week. At the time he died 350 daily newspapers and 200 Sunday newspapers from coast to coast were using his pieces, and it was believed that he had about 40,000,000 readers. Never, even in the Gilded Age—the golden age for humorists—had any American jester reached such a huge audience.

Mr. Jack Lait, old-timer in the world of journalism, saw signs of the humorist's great popularity in the way the news of his death struck the world. He said:

Never in my lifetime have I seen a whole world so stunned and sorrow-stricken. . . . . In the years that went before, I have reported and handled for newspapers and press services the tidings of the passing of monarchs, ecclesiastical heads, dictators, saints. But never had or has anything approached the myriad human soul-reactions of the final "fade-out" of this . . . . man. . . . .

An editorial writer on one of the intellectual magazines noted with some wonder that on the day Rogers died everyone—waitress, garage man, white-collar office worker, professor, financier—was talking about his death, grieving about it.

III

Mr. H. S. Canby, an editor of the *Saturday Review of Literature* better acquainted than most people of the time with the history of American humor, was interested in the way Rogers followed old paths. Said he:

> We Americans have had a long tradition of philosophers in homespun. . . . . Homespun in mind they have all been, which means, that whatever the source of their wisdom, its form and pressure was distinctively local to this continent, and many of them have been homely also in speech, self-made in knowledge, and blatantly provincial. . . . . The type has varied . . . . , although Will Rogers bred true, and was the perfect upcountry philosopher who would have been at home in Lincoln's law shop, or Red Gulch, or Down East on a Gloucester wharf. To the last dash and comma, his tricks were the same,—that combination of shrewd human philosophy as broad as human nature with a fundamental distrust of everything not made in America which has made us a trial to Europe and sometimes to ourselves.

The notion that Rogers wrote and thought like the great mass of philosophers in homespun before him had a solid basis. In several ways, of course, he was unique. His cowboy background, his experiences on the stage and in Hollywood, the fact that he lived in an age of airplanes and skyscrapers—all made him diverge somewhat from the exact pattern of earlier humor. But he had the old-fashioned horse-sense kind of a mind, and he won laughs in old ways.

Back of his humor, as almost everybody said who wrote about him, was a philosophy. When, in 1930, he was criticized because of the huge sum he was to be paid for a series of brief monologues on the radio, *World's Work* said, in his defense: "It seems to be his mission, under the guise of genial raillery, to tell us the hard, blunt truths about ourselves—truths about our politics, our civic standards, and our social habits. They are the sort of truths we do not always like to hear, but we will take them with a contagious chuckle. . . . ."

He himself thought that ideas made his humor what it

was. When someone spoke to him about the poor grammar in his newspaper articles, he said, "Shucks, I didn't know they was buyin' grammar now. I'm just so dumb I had a notion it was thoughts and ideas." His feeling, he said, was that "A gag to be any good has to be fashioned about some truth. The rest you get by your slant on it and perhaps a wee bit of exaggeration, so's people won't miss the point." He started many of his pieces by saying, "Well, all I know is just what I read in the papers"; but he believed, as most of his readers did, that he had better thoughts concerning his reading than the average person did. He put it this way:

> I'm just an ignorant feller, without any education, so to speak, but I try to know what I'm talking about. . . . . I do a lot of studying . . . . read editorials a lot . . . . when I go to a national convention I have to know what they're talking about to know what's funny. If I was just a clown, Borah and Read and Mellon and all those fellows wouldn't take the trouble to explain what they're drivin' at to me.

His mind worked in a way that appealed to his countrymen. He liked the ways of thinking he had learned in the cow country, feeling that they were good enough to carry him to success if he continued to stick to them. "I am just an old country boy in a big town trying to get along," he said. "I have been eating pretty regular, and the reason I have been is because I have stayed an old country boy." On the basis of his experience and what he saw had worked, he judged anything and everything—all the way from a little political squabble to international affairs. The Republican Convention of 1932, for him, was "kind 'er like a country picnic—you meet a lot of old friends from everywhere and see all the newspaper boys again." His remarks about the greatest Chinese philosopher showed his brain at work:

Confucius had some mighty pretty Sayings, but none of 'em have ever kept a Foreigner from coming in and gobbling up what he wanted. . . . . Now, I am not taking anything away from Confucius. He must have been a wonderfuly smart man. From reading some of his sayings, I would judge him to have been a cross between our Abraham Lincoln, Elbert Hubbard and H. L. Mencken. But the things he said was for the Chinese; they wasn't meant for a half-baked Chinese that had a conglomeration Night Club and Tammany Hall political-method background. I bet if Confucius had known his people would adopt a lot of this modern-world foolishness, he would have written a different book, telling 'em to stay at home. He had life figured out for 'em better than any man in the world for any Nation, and to prove it, it worked for two thousand years; but he naturally thought they was going to stay Chinese.

It was typical of Rogers, the provincialist, to suggest the nature of the writings of an Oriental sage by comparing him with three American writers known to ordinary men, just as it was typical of him to call Paris "the Claremore, Oklahoma, of France." Like Franklin, he was able to test a moral system not by general principles but by the way it worked. Like Lincoln, he took for granted that even rules for living thought up by a sage had to be discarded after changes in conditions had made the old rules lose their usefulness.

IV

The results of such thinking on all sorts of subjects he made amusing by using many of the tried tricks of old-time American humorists. When he started out as a talker, he made use of a manner much like that of the old-time humorous lecturers. He did not wear the funereal expression so many of them had found valuable, but his loose-lipped, shy grin, his slow drawl, and his shambling walk on the platform gave him an appearance of diffidence, even of humorlessness, like that of many earlier lecturers. He had Artemus Ward's and Mark Twain's way of looking innocently surprised when the audience chortled at one of his bright remarks. On the whole, then, he posed as much simpler than he really was.

When he turned to writing, he often continued to use the old-fashioned device of acting like a fool. "The only pose in Will Rogers," said Mr. Lowell Thomas, "was the pretense that he was an ignorant and illiterate fellow." He was in the habit of saying, "I studied the fourth reader for ten years." He dotted his pages with poorly spelled words, thus getting back to a device which had not been used by most humorists since the time of the Civil War. Another way he had of showing his illiteracy—one not often used by American humorists before him—was the lavish misuse of capital letters. His grammar was bad, and he let on that he had little respect for it. "Grammar and I," he said, "get along like a Russian and a bathtub" and, again, "Maybe ain't ain't so correct, but I notice that lots of folks who ain't usin' ain't, ain't eatin'."

He used many of the kinds of expression that had long been useful to humorists. The old habit of linking together in one sentence a group of queerly assorted articles—a habit useful to Ward, Twain, Nye, and others—made possible such a remark as "Russia's a country that used to have four exports—dukes, grand dukes, princesses and whiskers." He had a liking for puns and malapropisms, as hosts of humorists had had before him: "Now the President says we're going to recognize the Czecho-Slovaks. We may recognize them but we will never pronounce them." The old device of the comic simile cropped up in sentences like "Americans are getting like a Ford car—they all have the same parts, the same upholstery and make exactly the same noises" and like "Eskimos are thicker here [in Alaska] than rich men at a save-the-Constitution convention."

Most of the pains he took with his writing went on polishing his lines until they did two things, both important: (1) they phrased a humorous idea in a way that *seemed* very casual and (2) they phrased the idea in just the way to make it most amusing.

The guys that tell you they can be funny at any minute, without any effort, are guys that ain't funny to anybody but themselves [he claimed]. I depend on the newspapers for most of my inspirations. Some days there is material for several good lines. Then there will be a week when there isn't a little thing worth mentioning. About once a month I turn out a gag that I get a big kick out of myself. That's a pretty good average.

He used the same sort of care Josh Billings did on phrasing. Often he wrote eight or ten versions of a sentence before he got one that suited him. But his expressions, for all their working-over, had to seem offhand, spontaneous, accidental.

Many of the things he did were in the character of a simpleton who behaved as foolishly in the presence of fame or greatness as only a very impudent person—or a fool— could be expected to do. On the stage in New York at the start of his career he found that if he made joking attacks on celebrities in the audience, both the celebrities and the audience enjoyed them, and he never forgot the formula. At a time when the Prince of Wales was getting much notoriety because he had tumbled off his horse in a number of steeplechases, the American met him in London.

"Hello, old-timer," Rogers greeted him. "How are you falling these days?"

The Prince won the humorist's approval by saying, "quick as a flash": "All over the place. I got my shoulder broke since I saw you last." "I hear you are a journalist now," the Prince went on. "This is no interview, remember; just renewing old acquaintanceship."

"Anything you say to me is just *ad lib*," Rogers told him, "and nobody will ever know it but President Coolidge and America."

Or he was introduced to Coolidge, and the pucker-faced President said something through tight lips as they shook hands. Rogers leaned over as if he had missed some words and said:

"Pardon me. I didn't catch the name."

He thought it was a good joke, on a radio program, to announce that he would now introduce the President of the United States, and to mimic Coolidge's Yankee twang, saying: "It gives me great pleasure to report on the state of the nation. The nation is prosperous on the whole, but how much prosperity is there in a hole?"

Not long afterward he met Mrs. Coolidge, who told him that she could imitate her husband's voice better than the comedian did. "Well, Grace," he said to her, "you can imitate Cal's voice better'n me, but look what you had to go through to learn it." After an overnight stay at the President's mansion with the Coolidges, he reported, as if with the greatest innocence:

I am the only Democrat who has slept in the White House for a long time. . . . . Of course, the President's not understood. He's a nice fellow with a sense of humor. We spent last night swapping yarns. About eight o'clock the President began to yawn and at ten he fell asleep on me.

Like Jack Downing, therefore, Rogers told of his talk with

great men in public affairs. Like him, he made fun of both sides, but like Jack's contemporary, Davy Crockett, he told stories which were not merely figments of the imagination but were based on actual experience. In the boom days of beautiful nonsense during which he thrived, a clown famous throughout the nation could actually turn into realities some of the fantasies which, in the 1830's, it had been mildly shocking even to imagine. In the 1830's, for example, no one would have thought of having Crockett stand up on the stage before a national convention and get off witticisms about the leading politicians, as Rogers did more than once. Like both the two earlier heroes, Will received many votes in various elections, and he was nominated for the presidency. Unlike the earlier men, Rogers was a candidate who really was given more than passing consideration by a number of people. Once, at least, his name was seriously suggested on the floor of the House of Representatives. Said Representative Everett B. Howard, "Rogers is a statesman, experienced, courageous, safe, and sound, and offers excellent material for the Presidency."

There were times, though, when the cowboy comedian took on, in his writings, a fictitious governmental job. Traveling abroad, he posed as "a self-made diplomat," writing reports to either the chairman of the Senate Committee on Foreign Affairs or to the President. In the assumption of this ignorant man that he, in his old blue serge suit, could and should do a better job than the diplomats, there was amusing evidence of almost sublime conceit. "Of course we have foreign Ambassadors over there," he said, "but they are more of a Social than a Diplomatic aid to us." Readers laughed at the frank and democratic way this traveler chatted with rulers. People were amused, too, by the way this diplomat, in contrast to those who were not self-made, kept his thoughts, findings, and conversations secret by publishing them first in the *Saturday Evening Post* and later in widely sold books. Finally, what he said about Europe had about as little diplomatic tactfulness as anyone could imagine.

"You know, of course," he said, for example, "or perhaps you have had it hinted to you, that we stand in Europe about like a Horse Thief. Now I want to report to you that this is not so. It is what you call at Amherst 'erroneous.' We don't stand like a Horse Thief abroad. Whoever told you we did is flattering us. We don't stand as good as a Horse Thief."

This cynicism about the relationship between America and other countries came out in many passages in the letters. The common sense of Rogers, as he believed, usually led him to favor our isolation from foreign affairs.

> Let a nation do like an individual [he wrote]. Let 'em go through life and do and act like they want to, and if they can't gain friends on their own accounts, don't let's go out and try and buy it. . . . . If we would stay at home and quit trying to prowl around to various conferences and conventions somewhere, we would be better off.

Undoubtedly he was a great force in behalf of isolationism, and probably such preaching, despite its sincerity, was his greatest disservice to his country.

Rogers' suspicion of Europeans and his democratic way of sizing up things with his humble mind and confidently making known what he had decided carry back one's memory to a time when another Westerner, Mark Twain, had looked at Europeans and European things and had made unflattering remarks with just as much confidence. Clemens, too, had been a sort of an unofficial ambassador, seeing the great men of many lands and chatting with them easily. Toward the end of his life, Twain had become almost as much of an oracle as Rogers, with reporters clamoring to hear his opinions about all sorts of subjects.

When Rogers died, not a few commentators thought of comparing him with Mark Twain. But there was one great difference between the two, a very significant one. The earlier humorist turned against whatever he disliked with a hate that was ferocious; Rogers had no hate. "When I die," he said, "my epitaph or whatever you call those signs on gravestones, is going to read, 'I joked about every prominent man of my time but I never met a man I didn't like.' I am proud of that. I can hardly wait to die so it can be carved." And again: "You folks know I never mean anything by the cracks I make on politics. I generally hit a fellow that's on top because it isn't fair to hit a fellow that's down." This meant that, though many people thought Rogers was a sort of unofficial preacher-at-large to the United States, the sermons he preached did not attack the popular sins of the day as ferociously as they might have done. Perhaps, though, more ferocity would have spoiled his humor—as it sometimes spoiled Mark Twain's; perhaps this funnyman, the latest of a long line of towering philosophers in homespun, went as far as anyone could who was as true to the traditions of his craft as Will Rogers was.

CHAPTER XIII
Crazy Men

It is a little terrifying, with all that I have to do this week, to discover that I have a dementia praecox into the bargain. "What next?" I often ask myself.

—ROBERT BENCHLEY

Sixty minutes of thinking of any kind is bound to lead to confusion and unhappiness.

—JAMES THURBER

I

PEOPLE who went to the Egyptian Hall in London in 1866 to hear the lecture of Artemus Ward had a high time roaring at the queer American humorist. The lanky New Englander with the long, hollow-cheeked face, the drooping mustache, and the sad eyes stood quietly before his audience and went through a rigmarole about Mormons. The sentences in his speech were put together in the vague style of a stream-of-consciousness novel, except for the fact that they were somewhat less sexy. Mental associations, no matter how phrenetic, decided what kind of a word, a phrase, or a sentence would follow another.

A delighted writer for the *London Spectator*, fumbling to find words to describe the lecture of this American funnyman, in time decided that the whole trick of his humor was to give

. . . . the impression . . . . that his confusions of thought and speech are all inevitable on his own part, that his mind drifts on hopelessly from one

274

of those grotesque ideas or expressions to the next, as the creature or victim of some overruling power, which chooses his thought and language for him, so that he is not even a party to the transaction, though he has an earnest and rather melancholy interest in the result. . . . .

The critic gave some examples of the weird way the humorist's mind wandered around. At the start of his speech he would say, with great earnestness, that he himself had no very high opinion of his lecture—that all he wanted was to earn enough money to go to New Zealand. He thought a little while, then added, "If I could only go to New Zealand, I should feel that I had not wholly lived in vain." When the audience laughed at this queer recipe for avoiding a wholly vain life, he rushed on, with childish eagerness, to say, "I don't *want* to live wholly in vain." More than once he was enslaved by a rhythm, as he was when he told how some women, when he had left New York, had told him: " 'Base man, leave us, oh, leave us!'—and I left them, oh, I left them." Clearly, though he tried, he could not break off his own sentence before it had echoed the final cadence of the women's remarks. He told how he had once asked the question, "Why is this thus?" and the audience saw him worry about two words like "this" and "thus" getting so close together, then heard him stammer out a sentence with the vague hope that he might fix things up—the sentence, "What is the cause of this thusness?" Said the critic:

The art with which he gives the impression that he is floundering along in his choice of words, the victim of the first verbal association which strikes his memory, and yet just familiar enough with language to feel uncertain as to his ground, and to wish to get hold of some clearer term, is beyond praise. . . . . He cannot evidently help developing at length those subtle suggestions of verbal confusion which so often strike everybody's ear with an idiotic jingle of fascination. This is closely analogous to his curious habit of floating feebly down the chain of intellectual association, however grotesque. . . . . When he points out the lion on

Brigham Young's gate, he says . . . . "Yonder lion, you will observe, has a tail. It will be continued *for a few evenings longer*." The humor of all this is the humor of helplessness, the humor of letting your thoughts drift idly with the most absurd association that crosses them, and never rescuing yourself by an insurrection of common sense.

Passages in which there was a similar kind of wild-eyed linking of ideas by a befuddled fool turned up pretty often in the work of humorists who flourished after Ward. Charles Heber Clark, for instance, had his character, Max Adeler, tell about an unhappy time at a political rally. New to public speaking, poor Max had been pushed into making a date to speak at a near-by town. Full of fear, he had pieced together his little speech, largely made up of a series of jokes which he managed to drape around his political notions. On the platform the trembling Max had heard one orator after another use his own arguments and tell his own anecdotes, until only two feeble jokes remained unused. Introduced by the chairman, he stood up, and, to his utter horror, heard his voice saying:

Fellow-citizens: It is so late now that I will not attempt to make a speech to you.

(Cries of "Yes!" "Go ahead!" "Never mind the time!" etc., etc.)

I say it is so late now that I can't make a speech as I intended on account of its being so late that the speech which I intended to make would keep you here too late if I made it as I intended to. So I will tell you a story about a man who bought a patent fire-extinguisher which was warranted to split four cords of wood a day; so he set fire to his house to try her, and—No, it was his wife who was warranted to split four cords of wood—I got it wrong; and when the flames obtained full headway, he found she could split only two cords and a half, and it made him—What I mean is that the farmer, when he bought the exting——courted her, that is, she said she could set fire to the house, and when he tried her, she collapsed the first time—the extinguisher did, and he wanted a divorce because his house—Oh, hang it, fellow-citizens, you understand that this man, or farmer, rather, bought a—I should say courted a—that is, a fire-ex——(Desperately.) Fellow-citizens! IF ANY MAN SHOOTS THE AMERICAN FLAG, PULL HIM DOWN UPON THE SPOT; BUT AS FOR ME, GIVE ME LIBERTY OR GIVE ME DEATH!

Bill Nye created a similar kind of bewilderment-bothered character, who with his tiny mind tried to cope with the great subject of Space, saying:

Space is very large. It is immense, very immense. A great deal of immensity exists in space. Space has no top, no bottom. In fact, it is bottomless both at the bottom and at the top. Space extends as far backward as it does forward, and *vice versa*. There is no compass of space, nor points of the compass, and no boxing of the compass. A billion million of miles traveled in space won't bring a man any nearer than one mile or one inch. Consequently, in space, it's better to stay where you are, and let well enough alone.

Put alongside of these a few extracts from a modern humorist, Mr. Robert Benchley in one of his pieces, this present-day sufferer tells of the trouble he had when, like Ward, he became worried about grammar and the sound of words. It all started when he tried to figure out the present tense of the verb of which "wrought" is the past participle:

I started out with a rush. "I wright," I fairly screamed. Then, a little lower: "I wrught." Then, very low: "I wrouft." Then silence.

From that day until now I have been murmuring to myself: "I wrught—I wraft—I wronjst. You wruft—he wragst—we wrinjsen. . . . ."

People hear me murmuring and ask me what I am saying.

"I wrujhst," is all that I can say in reply.

"I know," they say, "but what were you *saying* just now?"

"I wringst."

This gets me nowhere.

It is easy to see why this writer claims that "One of the easiest methods of acquiring insanity is word-examining. Just examine a word you have written, and then call up Dr. Jessup and tell him to come and get you. Tell him to wear just what he has on."

Mr. Benchley—in his role as a humorist, at any rate—has the same sort of random associations Ward had when he was on the platform in the sixties. Riding on a train, he sights a dust storm, which calls to his mind the fact that "a dust-storm . . . . is a lot like life. It has its entrances and its exits, and it is the strongest team that wins. And by 'the strongest team' I do not mean the team with the most muscle, or sinew, or brawn. I mean the strongest team." Weirdly his mind maunders on, from the strongest team, to the lives of people in shacks, to mountain trout, to old miners and what they might have thought, to what trout have thought, then to Indians and what "they think when they see sand-storms and mountain trout."

Again, like Max Adeler, this fellow is faced with the job of getting up before an audience and making a speech. Hear him galumphing around:

Now in connection with reading this report, there are one or two points which Dr. Murnie wanted brought up in connection with it, and he has asked me to bring them up in connec—to bring them up.

In the first place, there is the question of the work which we are trying to do up at our little place at Silver Lake, a work which we feel not only fills a very definite need in the community but also fills a very definite need—er—in the community. I don't think that many of the members of the Society realize just how big the work is that we are trying to do up there. For instance, I don't think that it is generally known that most of our boys are between the age of fourteen. We feel that, by taking the boy at this age, we can get closer to his real nature—for a boy *has* a very real nature, you may be sure—and bring him into closer touch not only with the school, the parents, and with each other, but also with the town in which they live, the country to whose flag they pay allegiance, and to the—ah—(*trailing off*) town in which they live.

ROBERT BENCHLEY

"Every time I pay a hotel bill by check, I feel and look like a forger, embezzler and potential firebug."—ROBERT BENCHLEY.

Here there is both the snakelike fascination of rhythms and phrases that worried Ward and the jittery uncertainty that scrambled the phrases of Adeler. A humorist at work today, in other words, is nicely carrying on with one of the good old devices of American humor.

II

Mr. Robert Benchley is one of the most popular men in the business of being funny today. He has syndicated his skits, at various times, to a large number of newspapers; his books have sold well above 120,000 copies; he has done well on the stage, on the screen, and on the radio.

Son of a New England family and graduate of Phillips Exeter Academy, Mr. Benchley began to show a knack for humor when he was an undergraduate at Harvard. There he made college mates laugh by giving a burlesque lecture which had qualities closely akin to those of his later comic writings—one which, by the way, used many tricks like those which had been used by Artemus Ward, when that old-timer had given his burlesque lecture in London. Young Benchley's talk was on the woolen-mitten industry, and he used a napkin for a screen and an umbrella for a pointer. Part of it went like this:

Our first slide shows that in 1904, it took 1487 man hours to produce 1905, which, in turn, required 3586 man hours to hold its own. This made 3,000,000 foot-pounds of energy, a foot-pound being the number of feet in a pound. This is, of course, all per capita. . . . . Next slide, please! . . . . I'm afraid my assistant has it upside down. . . . . There! that's better!

Inevitably, some years after graduation, the man who had made such an analysis of industry as this, having found that the world of business was not for him, turned to humor.

The pages of the books he wrote, as has been suggested, often remind one of the humor of his forerunners. Many times he shapes his paragraphs and sentences as they did: instinctively, probably, he hits on tried and true ways of making people laugh. But there is a difference between his writings and the older ones which, in this history, seems significant.

This difference is suggested by a look at the kind of a character who woefully makes his way through the strange happenings set down in Mr. Benchley's writings. Any of the books shows the chief thing about this poor devil—that his whole life is a series of humiliations and frustrations. He is constantly bedeviled by all sorts of petty little things which a masterful man would easily be able to take in his stride. As a critic of this writer, Mr. Bryant, says,

.... he sees himself .... not the master of high comedy, but the victim of low tragedy. King Lear loses a throne; Benchley loses a filling. Romeo breaks his heart; Benchley breaks his shoelace. They are annihilated; he is humiliated. And to his humiliations there is no end. His whole life has been spent as the dupe of "the total depravity of inanimate things." To-day a knicknack leaps from his hand and shatters to the floor. Tonight his slippers will crawl away and wheel around backward. ....

Happier men could laugh little troubles like these off—but they happen so often to the fellow who appears in the Benchley pieces that he develops a persecution complex about them.

A book of his, aptly called *My Ten Years in a Quandary*, shows this character sloshing around in a sea of troubles. Furious, eager to take arms—as Shakespeare puts it—against the waves, he finds himself unable to do anything. All the time he is bothered by frustrations—in general and in particular. He cannot leave a party at a decent time, cure hiccoughs, wear a white suit, smoke a cigarette, or read while eating—though he wants passionately to do all these things. Pathetically, this victim of suppressions looks forward to a total eclipse, when darkness will give him "a chance," as he says, "to do a lot of things I have planned to do, but have been held back from." And what are these daring deeds to be? Simply these—he will put on a white suit, pick some flowers, waltz, exercise on a rowing machine, read some books, and make some faces. All these innocent little diversions he has been afraid to enjoy in the bright light of day.

Plainly, the difference between this victim of fate and healthier men is that the healthier men would not want to do such things or—if they did—would do them. But the man in a Benchley sketch, paralyzed by these tremendous frustrations, worries and worries about them. A chronic worrier, he is tormented by other things besides those which have been mentioned—fur-bearing trout, a bird which breaks down his morale, a ghost which worries him into spending a whole night in the Grand Central Station, meteorites, a Scottie (to which he feels inferior), the Younger Generation (which he fears is hatching a sinister plot), and dancing prairie chickens.

Read on in the book and you will find that even more serious troubles pester him. When this poor creature lies down to sleep, his throat closes up and he stops breathing. He has dementia praecox and a phobia for barber chairs, and he goes crazy in a lonely shack on the seashore. All these psychopathic woes are made known in one volume. Read the rest of his volumes, and it will be clear that the man—if his books are to be believed—is just a mess of frustrations and phobias. As Mr. Bryant has said, "Madness so dominates the landscape of his humor that a second reading is necessary to recognize its other features." When another humorist not long ago published a volume called *A Bed of Neuroses*, he might well have used a picture of Mr. Benchley's four-poster for a frontispiece.

III

Any one of three humorists who, like Mr. Benchley, were long on the staff of the best comic magazine of these days— the *New Yorker*—might be classified with him in this chapter. A good companion might be Mr. S. J. Perelman, whom Mr. Benchley has dubbed a king of "the dementia praecox field." Said Mr. Benchley, admiringly: "He did to our weak little efforts at 'crazy stuff' what Benny Goodman has done to middle-period jazz. He swung it. To use a swing phrase, he took it 'out of the world.' And there he remains, all by himself." Or the chapter might treat at length either Mr. E. B. White or Mr. James Thurber. These latter two, in most of their attitudes and methods, are very much alike. Each has spoken most highly of the other, and each has written many passages that it would not be hard to show were characteristic of his friend. I shall write about Mr. Thurber, simply because he is the most versatile and most popular of the trio and because there are more data available about him than about either of the others.

Mr. Thurber, born and reared in Columbus, Ohio, went to the Ohio State University for his formal education. His informal education included work as a code clerk in Washington in wartime, followed by drudgery on several newspapers—in Columbus, in New York, and in Paris. In 1927 he got his start as a humorist, when Mr. White, meeting him and liking him, engineered his appointment to the *New Yorker* staff.

In the next thirteen years he proved to have a good many talents which were salable. He could write amusing parodies, he could do stories, and he could draw strange but emotion-stirring pen-and-ink sketches which made people laugh. In 1939, with the help of a collaborator, he managed to write a play, *The Male Animal*, amusing enough to run for some time on Broadway and later to be turned into a popular moving picture.

During most of his career, in spite of the fact that Mr. Thurber has expressed himself in several mediums, he has kept on saying practically the same thing. In a preface to his comic autobiography, he has written some keen things about humorists in general which apply very well to him in particular when he writes in the first person. Of humorists, he says:

They lead . . . . an existence of jumpiness and apprehension. . . . . In the house of Life they have the feeling that they have never taken off their overcoats. . . . . Authors of such pieces have . . . . a genius for getting into minor difficulties: they walk into the wrong apartments, they drink furniture polish for stomach bitters, they drive their cars into the prize tulip beds of haughty neighbors. . . . .

Such a writer moves restlessly wherever he goes, ready to get the hell out at the drop of a pie-pan or the lift of a skirt. His gestures are the ludicrous reflexes of the maladjusted; his repose is the momentary inertia of the nonplussed. . . . . He talks largely about small matters and smally about great affairs.

The point is that, like the "I" in Mr. Benchley's pieces, the character in this humorist's skits has insomnia in a bed of neuroses. He, too, has the sort of trouble Artemus Ward had with expression—so much of it that he has tried to help others similarly worried in a "Ladies' and Gentlemen's Guide to Modern English Usage." In this treatise, after bringing all the learning he has to bear on the subject, he contents himself with telling people to surrender or make strategic retreats. When one has to decide between using "who" and using "whom," he says, "it is better to re-word the statement." Has the need to use "which" come up? "Never," he says sternly, "monkey with 'which.'" Since many people are routed by the word "whether," "The best advice is make up your mind and avoid doubt clauses." The perfect infinitive is rambunctious, too, so "Avoid the perfect infinitive after the past conditional as you would a cobra." His talk about one tough construction shows typical defeat; it also shows that he has the old humorists' trouble with random association and, what is more, he has a fancy name for it. He points out:

Another adverbial construction which gives considerable trouble, or will if you let it, is the adverb ending in "-lily." The best thing to do with the adverb ending in "-lily" is to let it alone. You can say "he plays lovelily," but even if the word is perfectly proper, it won't get you anywhere. You may just get by with it at a concert; but try shouting it at a ball game. . . . . It is especially advisable to avoid this construction because of its "Thematic Potentiality." The Thematic Potentiality is the quality which certain words and phrases have of suggesting a theme song—that is, some such thing as "Heavenly Lily O' Mine," "Ruffian Lily, Come Back to Me," "Love Vo-deo-do Lily," and so on. Think of something else.

Furthermore, as his analysis of a humorist shows, Mr. Thurber—like Mr. Benchley—is victimized by inanimate things; he lives a life which is ruined by tremendous trifles.

The man's suffering is complicated in other ways. If his

autobiography, properly called *My Life and Hard Times*, is to be trusted, he grew up in the midst of a family which was as fine a group of psychopathics as one will find outside the pages of a grim, old-style Russian novel—a cousin who (like poor Mr. Benchley) believed that "he was likely to cease breathing when he went to sleep," an aunt who went to bed nightly expecting a burglar to blow chloroform through a tube under her door, a grandmother who "lived the latter days of her life in the horrible suspicion that electricity was dripping invisibly all over the house," a father who had nightmares—"usually about Lillian Russell and President Cleveland," and other nerve-wracked Thurbers.

Growing up in that family and suffering from insomnia himself now and then when he could not remember the name of Perth Amboy, Mr. Thurber naturally in time was well equipped with various neuroses. As his friend Mr. White points out,

In his New York existence, ... more than any other thing he was concerned with the relation between the sexes. . . . . Appalled at the grave thrumming of sex itself in the metropolis, he was at once amused and frightened by its manifestations among his friends, many of them married. This was the "household" phase of the Thurber ordeal, the phase in which he vainly tried to rationalize the physical equipment of an apartment occupied by two people, and establish the position of kitchenware in relation to eroticism, children, and dinner engagements. That he was afraid is obvious from the drawings in the book, the bent or "stooped" postures of the males contrasting strongly with the erect and happy stance of the females. . . . . Above the still cool lake of marriage he saw rising the thin white mist of Man's disparity with Woman.

Thus the pitiable fellow suffered because he was victimized not only by chairs and clocks but also by women. In the battle of the sexes, he saw, males were doomed to helpless and ignoble defeat. In an essay, "Women Go On Forever," noting the way females outlived males, he bravely pushed on to the inescapable conclusion that "Man's day is indeed done; the epoch of Woman is upon us." Look at a man, he says, and you will see signs of a crack-up—"an air of uncertainty, an expression of futility, a general absence of 'hold.' " Look at a woman, though, and you will see that she is strong exactly where he is weak.

It seems clear, too, thát Mr. Thurber has a good deal of trouble with machines. "No man," he says, "who has wrestled with a self-adjusting card table can ever be quite the man he once was." He shows fear of all the mechanical devices he meets "because he recognizes the menace of the machine as such." His descendants, it is likely, will inherit

a desire to jump at, and conquer, mechanical devices before they have a chance to turn into something twice as big and twice as menacing. It is not reasonable to expect that . . . . children will have entirely escaped the stigma of such traumata. I myself will never be the man I once was, nor will my descendants ever amount to much, because of certain experiences I had with an automobile.

When Mr. Thurber writes not in the first person but in the third, he is likely to take as his hero—in the broad sense of the term—a pestered little man much like the "I" who appears in his essays. In a whole series of stories about one Mr. Monroe, that gentleman proves that in him—to quote his creator—

we have . . . . the makings of a character study—or would have except for the fact that Mr. Monroe didn't really have any character. He had a certain charm, yes; but no character. He avoided difficult situations; he had no talent for firm resolution; he immolated badly; and he wasn't even very good at renunciation, except when he was tired and a little sick.

Time after time, one sees Mr. Monroe forming a high opinion of himself, only to have it flop down when he fails to
justify it. When, for example, he took charge of some mov-
ing-men at work in his apartment, he started with confidence to issue orders. But shortly he had so much trouble
making up his mind how they should be directed that "the
'chief' and 'mister' with which they had first addressed him
changed to 'buddy' and 'pardner' " and finally, as Mr.
Monroe strove desperately for an air of dignity and authority, to "sonny." Or, just when he had managed to make
himself believe that he was a great one to get along in a
summer cottage, he was driven into a panic by his fear that
there was a bat in his room. Always, insignificant little
things made a shambles of his dignity and self-respect.

He was humiliated not only by such minor things but
also by the two great forces which had so often scared his
creator—the Machine and the Woman. He had a way, it
seems, of attacking machinery, then having it go wrong on
him, and then yelling "Woo! Woo!" as loud as he could.
The machinery, even if it was a simple shower-bath spray,
always went wrong on him. As for the Woman, that would
be Mrs. Monroe. When this little wife came back from a
trip to France, smuggling in a dozen bottles of Benedictine,
her spouse sneaked away from the inspection station and
acted as if he were a stranger to her, while she triumphantly
handled the officials. When the couple had a dog shipped to
them, the husband had to give up the idea of finding it, but
his helpmeet solved the problem neatly. She called him
"My great big wonderful husband," but he could not help
knowing in his heart of hearts that she was being ironic.

In the play Mr. Thurber and Mr. Nugent wrote together,
the hero, Tommy Turner, a bedeviled associate professor of

English in a stodgy American college, is another Mr. Monroe. When Joe Ferguson, an old-time football hero who had been Mrs. Turner's sweetheart years ago, returned to the little college town for the big game of the year, Turner was fortune's stooge. Sensing that the heroic Ferguson and Mrs. Turner were going to revive their old romance, Tommy felt that he ought to do one of two things—(1) be "modern" and reasonable and talk things out or (2) be forced by the tiger in him, if any, to smite Joe cheek and jowl. But he was as unable to deal with this situation as with others—a fumbler bogged down in futility. Mrs. Turner, however, like Mrs. Monroe, was the Triumphant Female, in the end able to handle in her own sweet way not only her jittery husband but also the ex-athlete.

IV

Messrs. Benchley, Perelman, Thurber, and a number of humorists in the same group are enemies of common sense. When they try to make terms with it, their humor is likely to go haywire. Consider a little further the case of Tommy Turner when, in *The Male Animal*, he differed from the usual Thurber character in that he not only took a firm stand but managed to hold it. Except in this instance, Tommy behaved according to the usual Thurber pattern, that is, he had high visions of himself in a heroic role, but, when the time came to act, he bungled things. When, however, he once decided to read Vanzetti's last letter to his English class, he stuck to his plans, come hell or high water. This was admirable of Dr. Turner, but it was also inconsistent with the rest of his doings in the drama. Though it was not an ideological flaw in the play, it definitely was an artistic one.

The artistic flaw was important because it did things both

to Mr. Thurber's characterization and what, in the past, had been his philosophy. If the patterns in his past writings meant anything, they meant that, in his opinion, the funny thing about man is that, though he thinks he is heroic, his deeds always prove that he is a football of fate. When, not long ago, he wrote seriously of his philosophy, the humorist put the idea in these words:

For some curious reason Man has always assumed that he is the highest form of life in the universe. There is, of course, nothing with which to sustain this view. Man is simply the highest form of life on his own planet. His superiority rests on a thin and chancy basis: he has the trick of articulate speech and out of this, slowly and laboriously, he has developed the capacity of abstract reasoning. Abstract reasoning, in itself, has not benefited Man so much as instinct has benefited the lower animals. . . . . In giving up instinct and going in for reasoning, Man has aspired higher than the attainment of natural goals; he has developed ideas and notions; he has monkeyed around with concepts. The life to which he was naturally adapted he has put behind him; in moving into the alien and complicated sphere of Thought and Imagination he has become the least well-adjusted of all the creatures of the earth, and hence the most bewildered. . . . . Man . . . . is surely farther away from the Answer than any other animal this side of the ladybug.

Clearly, therefore, when Tommy Turner solved his big problem, he was doing something that took him out of the world as his creator had seen it in the past.

In typical pieces of writing, then, Mr. Thurber has not been likely to espouse common sense. Since, according to the way he has been looking at it, no man is wise except in his own foolish daydreams, the humorist usually has found it impossible to picture a character who, with plain horse sense, finds the answers to the questions life puts to him. A Davy Crockett or a Hosea Biglow, if he happened to stray into one of Mr. Thurber's typical pieces, might think he knew the answers—probably would be cocksure about knowing them, but the whole point of a story about either of them, as Mr. Thurber told it, would be to show that the character had too high a notion of himself. Thus he would write humor of a pattern very different from that in the earlier humor.

His "I," his Mr. Monroe, and his Tommy Turner, in other words, are related not to the horse-sense characters but to the fool characters of the old homespun tradition. However, they contrast even with these—contrast sharply. It is obvious, of course, that they have nothing like the same rural background. Moreover, as Mr. Bernard De Voto has said, "The literary comedians . . . . after the Civil War presented themselves as Perfect Fools, whereas our comedians present themselves as Perfect Neurotics." In other words, these humorous figures are more than stupid: they are close to insanity.

The difference goes even deeper. When Mark Twain sentimentalized over the tomb of Adam, the joke was that Mark the fool was set off against the canny horse-sense character (Clemens) who knew all the time that Mark was making a dunce of himself. The fool was funny largely because the reader realized that his creator was a wise man who amusingly contrasted with the fool because he knew the answers. But Mr. Thurber is superior to his creation only in one thing—that he knows that his hero is foolish in the belief that there are any answers. This gives Mr. Thurber a chance to stand back somewhat from the poor suffering fool and laugh at him. "Humor," this comic writer has said, "is a kind of emotional chaos, told about calmly and quietly in retrospect." The chaos comes about because the character struggles against inevitable frustration. The calmness, possibly, is the result of the knowledge that the struggle naught availeth.

What students of Mr. Thurber's life and writings stress is that the humorist writes of sufferers who are like him. Says Mr. Robert M. Coates:

One of James Thurber's virtues as a writer . . . . is his ability to distil his personal escapades, even the most fantastic of them, into convincing literary form. . . . . Some writers, of course, make up their misadventures out of hand, but their work lacks the smack of the real thing. Thurber has rarely had to descend to such methods. Nature has provided him with an infinity of source material. Tall, shy, lean, loose-jointed, and absent-minded, he has the physical equipment for getting into involuntary mischief. . . . . He has a knack for losing things or leaving them in hotel rooms, for forgetting to pay his hotel bills. . . . .

Instead, then, of developing a chump character unlike himself, Mr. Thurber develops one like himself and, what is more, like all mankind.

When Mr. Bryant tries to get at the basis of Mr. Benchley's humor, his conclusions show that it has much in common with Mr. Thurber's. "Benchley," he says, "is misfortune's fool. . . . . Like Ben Turpin, he makes capital of his handicap. A Benchley short is simply the refinement of Benchley humiliation. It is commotion recollected in tranquillity. Yesterday's tragic ineffectuality has become today's comic effect." Not only is this the definition of all humor; in addition it makes plain that "I" is the same person as his creator. More, it makes clear that the humor does not depend upon a contrast between an utterly stupid man in the foreground and a sufficiently wise man in the background.

In the writings of these two modern writers, in other

words, satire has been expanded so far that it has lost a great deal of its sting. Old-timers made fun of only a small group of men—the ones who did not use their gumption to arrive at sound opinions. These modern humorists make fun of all mankind, and of all its opinions except one—the opinion that no ideas are very sound. Mankind is made up, they hint, of Benchleys and Thurbers who lack their skill to record its follies in tranquillity.

To such negative philosophers, horse sense becomes folly. When, under the title "Chips from an Old Philosopher," Mr. Benchley writes his closest parallel to the stuff Josh Billings turned out, he dishes up a series of aphorisms which either contradict one another or are sheer nonsense. Thus:

How true it is that opposites attract each other. It is Nature's way, I guess, of making her wishes known.

How true it is that opposites repel each other. I suppose it is Nature's way of making her wishes known.

It isn't so much what you put *into* a pudding as it is when you trip yourself up.

The passage concludes: "I could go on looking at life like this forever, just a-sittin' and a-dreamin', with only an occasional attack of nausea." Naturally a man who gets no closer to insight by using his head than Mr. Benchley does would be a little squeamish when he sat alone with his thoughts.

Mr. Thurber, too, has carried his attack upon horse sense (or any other kind, for that matter) to the camp of the enemy. His series of studies, *Let Your Mind Alone*, batters down one principle after another set forth in such recent "Bibles of Common Sense" as *Wake Up and Live!*, *Streamline*

Your Mind, and *How To Win Friends and Influence People*. His basic idea, he says, is "that man will be better off if he quits monkeying with his mind and just lets it alone." His recent collection called *Fables for Moderns* has as its burden that common-sense truisms in a large number of instances just do not work out.

Such futilitarians as these two humorists, in short, take little stock in Josh Billings' old-fashioned claim that "you hav got to be wize before you can be witty." Their point seems to be that nobody is wise, and nobody can be.

CHAPTER XIV

Modern Survivals

The prophets chant and the prophets chatter,
But somehow it never seems to matter,
For the world hangs on to its ancient sanity
And orders another round of vanity.

—OGDEN NASH

I

AMONG the writers of humorous poetry today, undoubtedly the most popular is Mr. Ogden Nash. People hunt out poems of his in the *New Yorker* or the *Saturday Evening Post* and read them to guests. His books have now and then made best-seller lists. At times, too, he has been starred—as a reader of his own pieces—on radio programs which entertain millions of people.

One of the pieces in Mr. Ogden Nash's book, *I'm a Stranger Here Myself*, deals with a lawyer named Ballantine, whose life was blighted by his failure ever to receive any valentines. Talking the matter over with his law partner, Mr. Bogardus (who got plenty of valentines and found them boring), Mr. Ballantine bitterly pointed out that, come St. Valentine's Day, all he found on his desk were a pile of affidavits. "Affidavit," said Mr. Bogardus, "is better than no bread." Then—to quote Mr. Nash—"Mr. Ballantine said that af-

fidavit, affidavit, affidavit onward rode the six hundred."
Some more chitchat followed, during the course of which
Mr. Bogardus mentioned that he did not know "who was
the king before David, but Solomon was the king affidavit."

The style of talk here is the sort of thing that might easily
turn up in the writings of the dementia praecox school—a
good example of what Mr. Thurber has called "Thematic
Potentiality." The story ends on a similarly deranged note:
having met Herculena, the strongest woman in the world,
who also was bothered by never getting any valentines, Mr.
Ballantine seemed to have solved his sex problem. "Thematic Potentiality," however, ruined his love affair. In a
coy moment, mighty Herculena, proud of her biceps, asked
him to pinch her muscle. As Thurber puts it, "He thought
she said bustle"—Herculena misunderstood the poor man,
and it took him some time to recover consciousness.

In many poems in various volumes Mr. Nash shows that
he is like other modern humorists in having his words shaped
by a mind not completely under control. When, for example, a taxi driver about whom he is writing turns out to be
both adamant and an eavesdropper, he is impelled to call
him "an Adam-ant-Eves-dropper." The very titles of his
poems now and then show a victim of associated sounds—
titles like "To Bargain, Toboggan, To-Whoo!" "Roulette
Us Be Gay," "Curl Up and Diet," and "A Ride on the
Bronxial Local." His rhymes often seem to be the haunting
echoes of sounds which pester random associations. If, say,
a line ends with "exhausted," he is driven to end the next
with the ungrammatical "losted." Again and again, too,
parallel sounds force him to use parallel but incorrect spellings—"kitchens" and "obstetritchens"; "King Midas" and
"tonsilidas"; "rhinoceros" and "prepoceros"; and so on.

Snatches of old poems come to his memory as he writes, and he cannot help putting them down, even though they jangle with the songs he is singing. Cursing fancy appetizers, he irrationally recalls Wordsworth's famous ode on immortality—and into his verse slips the line, "My heart leaps down when I behold gadgets with cocktails." Or he is writing about debt, and unaccountably he turns "You-were-a-creditor-in-Babylon-and-I-was-a-Christian-debtor" into an unwieldy adjective.

At times, too, his acts—like those of a Thurberite—are in the fell clutch of circumstances beyond his control. One poem gives an instance of his slavery to inanimate objects, telling how, if he steps out of bed, he gets a splinter in his foot; another tells how his sleep is ruined by a failure to keep covered at night; a third bewails the havoc in his life wrought by bad plumbing in a summer cottage. Like a Benchleyite, he makes humorous capital of the fact that he cannot file tax returns or make reservations on time and that he cannot keep resolutions. He gets into a couplet the despair of a stooge of fate:

> The things I want to do, I won't,
> And only do the things I don't.

Again he carols:

> Heavens, how happy I could be
> If only I were sure of me.

But, as a matter of fact, more than half the time, Mr. Nash *is* sure of himself.

For in spite of the things in his writings which ally him with modern humorists, Mr. Nash is often reminiscent of the humorists of an older time. Aphorisms which might have found their way into the pages of Ben Franklin or (with worse spellings) into those of Josh Billings dot many of his verses, for example:

One way to be very happy is to be very rich.

Why doesn't everybody that goes abroad stay abroad?

The reason for much matrimony is patrimony.

A man is very dishonorable to sell himself for anything less than quite a lot of pelf.

Other lines can easily be translated into horse-sense sayings, for instance:

You wouldn't be in so much danger of being cheated by strangers if your kinfolk were better fun.

People seem to be proudest of their infirmities.

Parents were invented to make children happy by giving them something to ignore.

Why did the Lord give us so much quickness of movement unless it was to avoid responsibility?

The poem phrasing the last of these ideas is called "Common Sense," and many a poem by Mr. Nash might come out under that title without shocking anyone who has the old-fashioned notion of what common sense is. Such poems are simply a putting into verse of some horse-sense ponderings of this world-wise author. "Hush, Here They Come" points out that "I don't care how unkind the things [are] people say about me so long as they don't say them to my face." "Golly, How Truth Will Out!" which notes how lying helps one get along in the world, is based on the author's painful experience. "How Long Has This Been Going On? Oh Quite Long" declares that horse races are "safe to go to as long as you fail to begin to win." "I Know You'll

Like Them," on the basis of several of the poet's experiences, leads to the saying "Most people are only vocal when talking local." "I'll Take a Bromide, Please" plumps 100 per cent for such platitudes as "It's not the heat, its the humidity," "It never rains but it pours," and others, and intones:

> Ah, Youth, Youth!
> It is well to remember that the mighty platitude is made
>   up of little drops of experience, little grains of truth.
> Do not seek to acquire the wisdom of the ages
> From the philosophers and sages;
> You will not find it in any old ism or any new ism;
> Truth doesn't lie in the well, it lies in the truism. . . . .

Here is as good a statement of the basic doctrine of horse sense as one can find anywhere in verse. It is doubtful if any plain dementia praecox writer could speak so favorably of the gumption of olden times.

Even the verse form Mr. Nash uses has its counterpart in horse-sense comic writing. Much of the hayfield humor all along was laughable, because naïve language—slang, bad spelling, lame grammar—was used to express wisdom. When, even a number of decades ago, a horse-sense humorist essayed poetry, the naïveté which set off his wisdom showed itself in strange rhymes and rhythms. Keen-minded Hosea Biglow, though his meter was on the whole better than the modern poet's, rhymed "presume we" and "Montezumy"; "Californy" and "scorn ye," "innercent" and "sinner sent"; "patience" and "insinuations"; "horrid" and "forrid" (forehead); "balance" and "talence" (talents); "messiges" and "pessiges" (passages)—and his rhyming showed the illiterate side of his character. In the 1870's many Americans chuckled at the poems of Julia

Moore, called "The Sweet Singer of Michigan." This was a farm woman who, when she wrote poetry, showed her ignorance by using rhythms which limped and rhyming words which could be linked only by violence. Mr. Nash, in his first volume, spoke of his debt to "the Sweet Singer of Michigan, without a complete and handy set of whose works this book could not have been written so quickly."

Critics of Mr. Nash's work have seen in it both aspects of his genius. Mr. William Soskin has found his verses "a compendium of bitter insanity, wry foolishments and considerably inspired lunacy." When, in January, 1941, the poet appeared for the fourth time on Dr. Bing Crosby's popular radio program, Mr. Bob Burns of that program, whose role was that of an unlearned hillbilly, spoke highly of the combination in the poems of good sense and plain speaking—and the studio audience howled at gumption embodied in Mr. Nash's stumbling verse. The blurb writer for his book of collected poems, *The Face Is Familiar*, sees both "Nash the nonsensical and Nash making very good sense indeed." Mr. Louis Untermeyer thinks the author's work "is interesting to brows of all altitudes."

II

The duality of Mr. Nash's nature emphasizes the duality of today's American humor. As in his books horse sense stands cheek-by-jowl with a mild sort of lunacy, so in the comedy of the day the old-style and the new-style humor are found existing side by side. Anyone who looks around a little will find many reminiscences of the older strain.

Spring of 1942 saw not a few newspapers in the country reprinting a series of the sayings of Abe Martin, culled from the works of the late humorist to satisfy the taste he had created for his shrewd comments. But newspapers did not have to depend merely upon the old files for the humor of gumption. Each day they could print bits from the thoughts of some of Abe's modern descendants.

In some papers, for instance, little Todd Tuttle—his picture and his remark for the day—appeared. A pen-and-ink drawing showed Todd in the foreground, a baldish man with a face vaguely like that of a cartoon Calvin Coolidge, staring, leering, or winking at the spectator. He wore a large stiff collar which bulged out beyond his Adam's apple, a string bow tie, a black coat which did not match his gray vest and trousers, spats. Always he was smoking a cigarette in a fancy, long holder; always he carried an umbrella. Backgrounds in the pictures of him give modern touches, showing skyscrapers, perhaps, or a trailer camp. Like old Abe Martin, at times he would quote the wise saying of a fellow-townsman. For instance: " 'Th' way some fellers work I don't believe they'll have any trouble killin' time if they do lose their jobs,' snorted constabule Abe Sprosby." Again, the idea he voiced was his own. For example: "Too many fellers pop up with 'I think I know' when they hain't capable of either thinkin' or knowin'."

In the columns of other newspapers a daily feature called "Poor Pa" was published. Again a drawing accompanied each remark—a picture of the bald-headed, skinny average citizen, peering through spectacles and saying something like: "My brother Ed has got better table manners than the rest of us brothers. He married a bossy woman an' she got the upper hand from the very start." A feminine counterpart of his who also appeared daily (and who was the brainchild of the same author, Mr. Robert Quillan) was "Aunt

Het," pictured as a plump, wholesome woman in a black skirt and a white waist, usually looking fixedly at the person—in the background—about whom she made her discerning comment. "Cousin Jim knows the secret of sellin'," she was saying in one typical example. "If you act humble and anxious, folks act haughty and turn you down; if you seem rich and indifferent, they grab for the hook."

Another aunt was quoted at length within recent times in a series of advertisements for Lipton's tea. She was pictured, under the headline, "Aunt Abby Says," as a little old-fashioned lady who kept her spectacles on the end of her little pointed nose. The column quoting her alternated short wise sayings about human nature with paragraphs of praise for the product she was advertising. Two horse-sense bits of Aunt Abby's talk were:

Used to be only young folks took up roller skatin'. Now there's no age limit on breakin' your neck.

Jim's wife raised so many o' her mother's children, she's lettin' Jim raise their one and only.

The foreign element in America was also represented by a daily feature. "Ching Chow," a smiling, pig-tailed Chinaman who had been invented by the creator of Andy Gump and who now was drawn by his successor, Mr. Stanley Link, daily grinned at the public and spoke wisely. "This useless person believes," he said one day not long ago, "the only secret a woman can keep is that of her age." Ching was not unlike the Oriental sage who had been the hero of many jesting sayings—and even a popular song—in 1939. "Confucius say," the man on the street would remark to a friend, and then would follow a horse-sense remark (often scatological), phrased in what sidewalk humorists believed was Sino-

American dialect. But Ching's sayings both preceded and survived these inventions.

These horse-sensible characters—a few of the many like them which might be cited—had little to say about politics. They were commentators on human nature who harked back to such oldsters as Poor Richard, Josh Billings, and Abe Martin among males and Mrs. Partington among the womenfolk. There were others contemporaneous with them, however, who, like Jack Downing, Davy Crockett, Major Jones, and others, were able to tell their contemporaries how to vote.

The presidential campaign of 1940 had a number of touches of the old-fashioned sort. Mr. Wendell Willkie, the Republican candidate, was pictured by his backers as one very close to his farm in Indiana. An attempt was made, in other words, to give him some of the aura which, in the 1840's, had proved so useful to a winning presidential candidate. Down in Berkeley, California, a Willkie parade used a float which tried to reproduce a scene in an old-time country grocery store. Two men dressed in farm clothes sat on cracker boxes and carried on an argument in rural language. Loud speakers amplified rustic remarks, pointing out that the man with gumption could not help but vote for Mr. Willkie.

When the Democratic Convention was held in Chicago, some anonymous Associated Press writer did a series of letters reproduced throughout the country. "A letter back home from a delegate to the Democratic Convention," read the introduction. Then Henry, writing to "Dear Mom," would tell what was happening. It appeared that Henry, like Jack Downing, was a bumpkin from the rural districts (from Texas, as it happened) and that, like Jack, he combined hayseed ignorance with some horse sense. Said he in one passage:

I met a very interesting man this morning. His name is Charley Michelson and his job is publicity director of the Democratic national committee. This may be a hard title to understand, but it's something like what that fellow who comes through home every year with the circus.

In addition to that he writes speeches.

I heard a newspaperman say he was the man behind the man behind the man, whatever that means. Anyhow, he's a nice fellow.

I told him I had to make a speech at the Lion's Club when I get home and I might need his help, but he says no. He says he can write a speech that would tear the hide off an elephant, but that lions is out of his line. I think by an elephant he was talking about the Republicans.

Reminiscent of the distant past, too, in this campaign, were the candidacies for the presidency of two comedians—Miss Gracie Allen, nitwit of the radio, and Mr. W. C. Field, fool of the screen.

III

Today, of course, new mediums bring the old-fashioned type of wit to the people. The comic strips, though they have, in many instances, discarded most of their comedy in favor of melodrama and sentimentality, often use horse-sense characters. Both Andy Gump and Rudolph Nebb, in the past, have satirized politics by running for office. The strip called "Orphan Annie" puts into the mouth of the red-headed urchin who is its heroine a great deal of homely moralizing, based on her own wide experiences. "Little Annie Roony," a similar strip, has a moppet who can say the same sort of acute things. Mr. Percy Crosby's "Skippy" has talked sensibly not only in the funnies but also in a book supposed to have come from his hand. "Apple Mary" is also wise in the traditional homespun way. A glance at other comic strips will quickly furnish other examples.

The popular radio programs go in even more heavily for this sort of comedy. An advertisement for one suggests its flavor: "Uncle Ezra: A hilarious half-hour of homespun humor and music with Rosedale's cracker-barrel philosopher." Like the newspapers which have dug up Abe Martin's sayings, the radio has drawn on the past for wise men and women: "Mrs. Wiggs of the Cabbage Patch" and "David Harum" are programs exploiting two characters which date back some years. The names of other programs suggest their nature—"Neighbor Nell," "Lorenzo Jones," "Lum and Abner," "Ma Perkins," and "Just Plain Bill." Listening in on some of the family programs will prove that a large share of them win wide followings by giving prominent roles to men and women who use man-on-the-street speech to voice the wisdom won by living in the everyday world— programs like "The Goldbergs," "One Man's Family," "The Story of Bob Barton," "The Story of Mary Marlin," and "The O'Neills."

In a number of instances, horse-sensible characters are available to the public in more than one medium. "Little Orphan Annie" is not only a character in a cartoon but also in a daily radio broadcast which carries her bright thoughts to listening thousands. "Lum and Abner" and several others are in motion pictures as well as on the radio. "Scattergood Baines," created by Mr. C. B. Kelland, has been the hero of a series of stories which have appeared in various magazines—a plump storekeeper who helps less sage people out with his practical advice. In the *American Magazine*, he has been holding forth in a column called "Scattergood Says," of which this passage is representative:

> Nobody never accomplishes suthin' by doin' nothin'. If your cow gits lost, you're nearer to findin' him if you look north of taown, when the cow's wandered south, than you be if you jest set and repine.

> Brains was put inside the skull so as the feet could carry 'em around handy. The skull hain't nothin' but a satchel you can use to carry your intellect to places where you kin put it to use. The' never was a day when I wouldn't swap twenty theories fur one set of calluses.

In spite of his unusual conception of the sex of a cow, Scattergood here is preaching very orthodox common sense. He is a hero, too, on a radio serial, wherein time after time he has carried around the satchel containing his intellect to the great gain of young lovers in dire circumstances. In 1941, played by Mr. Guy Kibbee, he made his appearance in two moving pictures. Like the humor of other characters of today, his humor is often soft-pedaled because he is involved in sentimental or melodramatic happenings. Between tears and thrills, though, Scattergood can talk exactly like an old-fashioned comic cracker-box philosopher.

IV

Now all these characters, evidently, are quite popular. It appears that thousands of people enjoy the wit of gumption as it is embodied in their sayings. Nevertheless, there is a problem connected with their fame. For at least a hundred years—from 1835 to 1935, say—there always were, in America, one or more characters of this sort, towering head and shoulders above the rest. Jack Downing, Davy Crockett, Artemus Ward, Petroleum V. Nasby, Bill Arp, Mark Twain, Josh Billings, Samantha Allen, Mr. Dooley, Abe

Martin, Will Rogers (to mention only the most eminent) in their day had a respect that approached reverence, an influence that was nation wide.

Compared with them, the horse-sense wits of today have microscopic fame and negligible influence. Not one of them can hope to be quoted as the old-timers were. Not one can jump into a political argument with any hope that what he says will carry any real weight. In short, after playing a major role in America all these years, the comic figure with gumption or his opposite, the fool character, has come down greatly in the world. This, of course, suggests a problem—why?

No simple answer to this question, of course, is possible, and any answer must be speculative. Three suggestions may be hazarded: (1) that this homespun, traditional humor may be suffering merely from a temporary decline, (2) that it is now played out because American life has changed so much in recent years, and (3) that a little tinkering to adapt its devices to modern ways may still bring it back to something like its former importance.

There are arguments in favor of each of these views. It might be argued, for example, that, after all, we have lacked a homespun oracle of towering height only about seven years. This may mean simply that in this brief period, no genius has happened to survive or to arise who could say things with old-time authority and that as soon as one comes along the old pattern will be resumed.

Anyone favoring this view might argue: Suppose Will Rogers had not died in an accidental airplane crash in 1935. Is it not very likely that he would still be as popular, as influential, as he was in the days of his life? With the radio to carry his voice to more millions than ever, with newspapers and motion pictures augmenting his fame, could not the cowboy humorist carry on the tradition beautifully? And if someone as effective as Rogers came along, would not the public give ear to his pithy comments? Perhaps such a humorist may show up any day.

V

It may be claimed, though, that Rogers—like Samantha Allen and Josh Billings, whom he so greatly resembled— was only a lucky survival of a type of humor which was on the wane and that, by the time his career ended, America had so altered that not even the best of luck could lift such a person to fame again. Anyone believing this might point to several changes in the American scene which began a long time ago and were speeded up dizzily in the last years of Rogers' life.

One such change was in the way Americans lived. When horse-sense humor first became both popular and effective, a large proportion of the people of this country were of the rural districts—old-time farmers or people who had daily contacts with them. Well into the nineteenth century the old-style farmer was felt to be a typical American; and even at the end of the century enough people were farmers of this sort or had been brought up on farms to make the farmer seem a good American symbol. But in recent times the city has bred generations who know nothing of country life and who are, moreover, very dubious about the knowledge of those who might be called "hicks." For these city folk a modernized Jack Downing or Hosea Biglow might hereafter have little appeal. Even if the city folk were willing to grant that experience brought wisdom, they might be dubious about the value of experience gained in a hayfield or a barnyard.

And countryfolk themselves have changed. Mr. Westbrook Pegler, in his column for February 19, 1941, shrewdly argued that the Republican campaigners of the previous year had made the great mistake of being far behind the times in their appeal to rural voters in the Middle West. Said the columnist:

The Hoosier remains a distinct breed . . . . but the scene has changed . . . . , and anyone who still thinks of Hoosiery in terms of simple and honest but shrewd rusticity is living in the past. . . . . Indiana has become an industrial state with an industrial population which is urban even in the country. The factories and works have spread out beyond the old city lines, which used to be the demarcation between soft comfort and hardy misery, sophistication and chew-tobacco innocence, way up into Michigan and over Ohio and Illinois.

Hence Mr. Pegler believes that even country people might be leery about the oracles of cracker-box philosophers—and he may be right.

Another change which may have been important was in education. More and more people, as the years passed, went to high school or even to college. The old-time suspicion of book learning, which had been so important in the past, tended to be replaced by a trust in scholarship, perhaps in all fields, certainly in many. The specialists came to be more respected than the man who, simply because he had been a practical man, presumed to tell people what they should do. For many educated folk the bad grammar and the colloquial ways of talking, which once had been the distinguishing marks of a horse-sense oracle, actually may have come to be regarded as signs of inadequacy.

Education was important in causing, also, a split in the American reading public. Once the people of this country, since they had similar backgrounds, had tended to read—all of them—very much the same things. Now there was common talk of "highbrows" and "lowbrows"—a general recognition of differing literary tastes. Other splits resulted from the sort of specialization which was becoming a wide-spread phenomenon.

Still another change was the development of skepticism about truth and about virtue. Somehow more and more people came to conclusions something like those of the futili-tarian dementia praecox humorists—the suspicion that the world was so complex that the only thing one could be certain about was uncertainty. It became fashionable, whenever anyone tried to advocate any belief, to point out that there were hosts of exceptions to rules and everything was relative. Thus not only the horse-sense process but also the possible results of the process fell under suspicion. It may be argued that all these changes, as Mr. Pegler believes, have made the humorists of gumption outmoded beyond recall.

VI

Others may claim that all that homespun humor needs to get something like the same sort of hearing it had in the past is a few possible adjustments here and there in American attitudes and in the way they are humorously voiced. This happens to be my own guess, based on the study of the way adjustments of this sort have been made in the past. Several factors in the present situation seem to me to point to this possibility.

When Mr. Thurber showed the chief character of *The*

Male Animal overcoming futility, rising above fear and ineptitude, and in the end acting to assert his belief in the importance of free speech, the action in the play was a symbol of something happening in America today. Like Mr. Thurber's harried little professor, Americans, after a period of doubt, despair, uncertainty, are beginning to feel that there are some things about which they share convictions. Flags and slogans stuck on windshields of automobiles of nearly all makes and ages, the sincerity with which thousands intone the song "God Bless America," the mounting hatred of naziism—all these are tokens of wide agreement about some kinds of truth and virtue.

The beginning of America's active participation in the war did much to cultivate an important democratic attitude. Said a commentator in the *New Yorker* as early as January 3, 1942:

In the weeks since December 7th, people had come through the period of shock, through the momentary personal anxieties, through the inevitable self-examinations, and had emerged, we believe, with something they felt was worth hanging onto. What they had found in themselves had turned out to be good—better than they had expected, perhaps. They had discovered a certain inner confidence, an intrinsic courage, cool and tough. Finding it in themselves, they were inclined to believe that the same thing was to be found in their fellows. It seemed to us that people began to look at each other differently, to speak differently.

The growth of such mutual esteem, recorded, of all places, in the erstwhile organ of cynical humor, is favorable to the re-establishment of a horse-sense school. This renewed faith in democracy, it is just possible, may renew faith in the democratic idea which, carried to an extreme, suggests that even the humblest man can discover and voice great truths.

The common-sense process, in other words, may shortly command more respect than it did in the recent past.

There is some chance, too, that a symbolic figure may soon be hit upon which will have a wide appeal. The situation is good for the creation of a fool character who will voice the attitudes hateful to a large share of the American people. He might, say, be the leader of a bund, similar to the characters in *Margin for Error* and *Pins and Needles*, who, by posturing foolishly and making untrue and wicked remarks, caused large audiences to howl with laughter. He could fall into the unpopular group called fifth columnists. His dialect is ready-made—that of a German-American having the sort of trouble with his phrasing Hans Breitmann did. Or he might be a dunderheaded Japanese, sinning in his peculiar way against the American language and against good sense.

Such a fool character would hark back to some of the American humorous figures who sublimated hate in other periods when it ran high. Franklin's fool advocate of the reduction of a great empire has been cited for the period before the Revolution. A poet named Trumbull in the days of the Revolutionary War exhibited in a poem the Tory McFingal saying the unpopular things Tories were saying in those days, and finally delighted his readers by making honest American Revolutionists treat the rascal to a coat of tar and feathers. Birdofredum Sawin, enlisting in the army and becoming a rascal as a result, was a butt of laughter in the days of the Mexican War. The Civil War, as has been seen, produced such muddle-headed and genial traitors as Sut Lovingood and Petroleum V. Nasby. Nothing exactly comparable came along during the Spanish-American War or

World War I, though there were, at the time of each of these struggles, comic picturings of German dunderheads which Americans found amusing. It is possible that modern times may bring a rebirth of a type of humor often enjoyed in periods of stress.

The invention of a horse-sense symbol of national appeal, though it would be harder, is not inconceivable. The sort of person who naïvely gave an account of our history and then told his ancestry and name, "America," in "A Ballad for Americans"—very popular in 1940, 1941, and 1942—a vague, synthetic figure, might just possibly do. Probably, though, he would have to have somewhat more distinct characteristics to satisfy people or to get the variety into his remarks necessary if he were to last very long.

Two characters hint what he might be. One of them is a certain "John Q. Public," who investigates civic affairs and reports on his findings to readers of the *Chicago Daily News*. Each story about him is illustrated with a drawing by Cartoonist Vaughan Shoemaker which shows the frail, bald, and bespectacled little man, dressed in rather old-fashioned clothes, talking with the mayor, the chief of police, or some other civic leader. He cuts through baffling talk about problems of government with his common-man's insight.

A second character is one who holds forth now and then in Mr. Westbrook Pegler's syndicated column—a George Spelvin, American, self-styled "a 100 per cent American." George, a man with a half-pint mind, often mistakes a cliché for an idea, as when he says, in all seriousness, "A good wife is everything in a man's life," often voices a prejudice as if it were a profound truth, and at other times is satisfied with the vague idea that simply if something is desirable it can be worked out easily. At times his logic is pretty badly mixed up. But he is a decent little fellow, and he has some sense to him. And Mr. Pegler gives him sentences which are couched in perfect American idioms.

Neither of these would do without some changes. John Q. Public is too narrow in his interests to appeal to an audience beyond the limits of Chicago. George Spelvin is too baffled and shares too many of his creator's peculiar prejudices not to alienate a large number of people. But some such vague character might duplicate the success of Bill Arp (in his post-war role) or Bill Nye.

Perhaps a character with a more definite background—if that background gave him a job common to city and country alike—might have a wide appeal. A skit in *This Week Magazine* has for some time set forth in a weekly box the opinions of one Wally Boren, who runs a roadside diner, patronized by all kinds of Americans. Behind his counter Wally watches the world and comes to deep conclusions about life today which he passes on in racy Americanese. Thus, he said, in part, about the time Labor Day came along some months ago:

> As near as I can tell, what this country has got to do is go back to work. . . . . What with booms and depressions, the last twenty years has got us into a lot of loafin' ways.
>
> Why I bring this up is on account of what happened to France. That was a nice country, once. But they dillydallied around with what some call socialism—which is like layin' in bed and imaginin' it's Sunday when it isn't.

In March, 1941, Wally left his lunch wagon for a trip to New York, and it was interesting to notice how, though he made childish mistakes of the sort Jack Downings, Major Joneses, and Samantha Allens had been making down through the years, these little errors only emphasized the keen insight with which he sized up metropolitan life. In 1942, Wally was still peddling hamburgers and horse sense.

Running a lunch wagon is only one of several occupations of both country and city workers which might bring to life a horse-sense character, give him the needful experience of human nature, and provide a background to make him interesting and real. Other jobs tied up with the transportation of our migrating countrymen might suggest the wise conductor, bus driver, truck driver, or airplane hostess. When, a few years ago, Mr. Thornton Wilder wrote a novel about a traveling salesman, he realized only a few of the possibilities of such a character. The gasoline company which recently ran a long series of advertisements quoting a gas-station man was using a figure who might very well be taken over by a humorist and re-worked into a great common-sense character.

The great war effort drawing upon rich and poor alike might give rise to a symbolical figure satisfactory for these times. Such a figure might be the man drafted into the citizen army forming in America in 1941 and 1942. In former times the armies of our countrymen have given commonsense humorists an appealing background. Davy Crockett was in the Indian wars. The grandson of a Revolutionary War hero, Jack Downing, in his role of major, helped to put down nullification and settle the Maine boundary dispute. Simon Suggs enrolled to fight Indians and was a captain of the Talapoosa volunteers. Major Jones was in the militia. The Civil War saw Private Miles O'Reilly and Orpheus C. Kerr battling for the North and Bill Arp (in his second guise) heroically defending the South. In World War I, the

"Dere Mable" letters of a soldier of democracy (by Ed Streeter) were sensationally successful, and a slangy creation of Ring Lardner stopped playing baseball to do battle with Germany. In *Time*, February 10, 1941, a new radio program which was designed to carry on this tradition was announced. Said *Time:*

As full of corn as a silo, *Dear Mom* recounts the adventures of an addlepated rookie named Homer Stubbs, and his highborn tough topsergeant called Monihan. Devised by stocky, moon-faced Robert Newton Brown, C.B.S. program director, and writer W. Ray Wilson, *Dear Mom* is supervised by Major Frank Collins, a morale officer on the executive staff of the 6th Corps Area. The program whips into a description of the joys of camp life, introduces Homer scratching away at a letter to his mother. Its first episode last week dealt with Homer's arrival at camp, next one will reveal him on garbage detail. . . . .

Typical *Dear Mom* chatter: "How do I feel about the Army? Boy, it's gonna be my meat and gravy. I'm sure anticipatin' it with relish. All I want is to find somebody I can cuss—you know . . . . like them two guys in the movie did . . . . Sergeant Quirt and Captain Flagg."

Rather puzzlingly, the sponsors of this program dropped it shortly after the entrance of America into the war. When this chapter was written, it was too early to know whether or not this program predicted a trend, but Mr. H. I. Phillips was collecting royalties for the sales of many copies of *The Private Papers of Private Purkey*, the poorly spelled and ungrammatical letters to "maw" of a comic draftee; a similar book called *Gone with the Draft* was doing well; the Associated Press was syndicating a daily cartoon, "Strictly Private," which made use of similar humor; and Sergeant York, World War I hero, was purveying homespun wisdom in a syndicated column.

Finally, there is a chance that one part of the old tradition may be modified to satisfy the present-day prejudice for education. In recent years some humorists of gumption have arisen who were educated, to be sure, but who made use of their education when it was useful just as they made use of their wide experience when it taught them something. Such men, while they carried on their work in the country, so that countryfolk could admire them, have had more training of the sort city people could admire than, say, a farmer. Country editors, country-school teachers, country lawyers, country doctors, they appeared in a large number of books published in 1938–42; and, if the number of publishing houses which printed such books is any indication, they were well liked.

A book which hinted what such a character could do in the field of humor was Dr. Hertzler's *The Horse and Buggy Doctor*, best seller of a few years ago. This was not without the appeals of sentiment and melodrama found in comic strips and radio programs of today, but in addition it had many passages of the wry kind of humor typical of the old school. "The patient suffered intensely," he might say, for example, "and a simple operation, of course, brought instant relief. He thought I had saved his life. In such situations the diplomatic doctor does not dispute the patient's opinion. He just looks grave and modest." Or:

The latest stunt [of the pretentious hospital] is to pin a sterile towel on the back of the surgeon. I'll bite—what is it for? I have never seen a surgeon sit on a wound, chances are they do not intend to sit on the wound, but there is nothing like being prepared for all possible contingencies.

Dr. Hertzler, of course, was a real person, writing his autobiography, and comic in his sour-pickle fashion simply because it came natural to him. However, an invented character of a similar sort, respected as a scientist but having the sort of rich experience that brings wisdom, might make a present-day humorous commentator on all sorts of subjects.

Those are some of the ways a man with a genius for comic writing might, in these days, take his place in the procession of horse-sense humorists who, for generations, have made Americans laugh and think. Doubtless, there are other ways, just now unpredictable, in which a successor of the old-time cracker-barrel commentators may arise. If, somehow, America gets another great licensed jester, however, he will, I think, do what the bulk of the authors considered in this book have done—conform to traditional patterns and prejudices but, at the same time, adapt his methods and materials to the peculiarities of his period.

BIBLIOGRAPHICAL NOTE

I have been aided a great deal in my work on this book by Mr. Clarence Faust, who has reasoned me out of some of my most mistaken ideas, and by Mr. Franklin J. Meine, who not only generously loaned me books from his fine humor collection but also answered many questions about American humor.

It has seemed to me a service both to the reader and to the authors to normalize the spelling in some of my quotations. Because footnotes and a learned style of writing seemed rather inappropriate for a study of this sort, I have avoided the former and have tried to avoid the latter. Nevertheless, I have drawn upon whatever sound and useful sources I could find. I list the most important of these below, and I shall be glad to answer inquiries about any others.

Much of the material I have covered has been treated, from a different viewpoint, by Miss Jennette Tandy, in her very helpful *Crackerbox Philosophers in American Humor* (New York, 1925). Briefer general studies which have contributed something are J. L. Ford, "A Century of American Humor," *Munsey's*, XXV (July, 1901), 482–90; Will D. Howe, "Early Humorists," *Cambridge History of American Literature* (New York, 1918), II, 148–59; Henry Clay Lukens, "American Literary Comedians," *Harper's*, LXXX (April, 1890), 783–97; E. P. Whipple, "American Literature in the First Century of the Republic," *Harper's*, LII (March, 1876), 526–27; and Napier Wilt, *Some American Humorists* (New York, 1929), Introduction.

CHAPTER I. EARLY TO RISE

The Writings of Benjamin Franklin (10 vols.; New York, 1905–7) were edited by A. H. Smyth. Biographies which were most useful were P. L. Ford, *The Many-sided Franklin* (New York, 1899); J. B. McMaster, *Benjamin Franklin as Man of Letters* (Boston, 1887); J. Parton, *Life and Times of Benjamin Franklin* (2 vols.; New York, 1864); and Carl Van Doren, *Benjamin Franklin* (New York, 1938). Two articles from which I have drawn important data are J. F. Ross, "The Character of Poor Richard:

Its Source and Alteration," *Publications of the Modern Language Association*, LV (September, 1940), 785–94, and George F. Horner, "Franklin's *Dogood Papers* Re-examined," *Studies in Philology*, XXXVII (July, 1940), 501–23.

CHAPTER II. DAVY CROCKETT: HORSE SENSE ON THE FRONTIER

Crockett's books include *Narrative of the Life of David Crockett* . . . . (Philadelphia, 1834) and *A Tour to the North and Down East* (New York, 1834). Books purportedly by him include *Sketches and Eccentricities* . . . . (New York, 1833) and *Colonel Crockett's Exploits and Adventures in Texas* (Philadelphia, 1836), both containing newspaper stories of the day. The best biography is Constance Rourke, *Davy Crockett* (New York, 1934). The best collection of the Crockett tall tales is *Davy Crockett: American Comic Legend*, edited by Richard M. Dorson (New York, 1939). Recent yarns from the Ozarks are included in Vance Randolph, *Ozark Mountain Folks* (New York, 1932). Information also came from Eugene Irving McCormac, *James K. Polk: A Political Biography* (Berkeley, 1922), pp. 21–24; Thomas Perkins Abernathy, *From Frontier to Plantation in Tennessee* (Chapel Hill, 1932), pp. 259–60; J. S. Williams, *Old Times in Tennessee* (Memphis, 1878), pp. 175–76; V. L. Parrington, *The Romantic Revolution in America* (New York, 1926), pp. 173–79; and Shields McIlwaine, *The Poor White in American Literature* (Oklahoma City, 1938). Newspapers of the time were most valuable—the *Boston Transcript*, *Washington Globe*, *New York Times*, and various others.

CHAPTER III. JACK DOWNING—COMMON SENSE IN IMAGINATION

Smith's pertinent writings include *The Life and Writings of Major Jack Downing* . . . . (Boston, 1833) and *My Thirty Years Out of the Senate* (New York, 1859). Charles Augustus Davis collected his pieces in *Letters of J. Downing, Major* . . . . (New York, 1834). The best study of these two authors is Mary Alice Wyman, *Two American Pioneers* (New York, 1927). Interesting bits about Jack and his creator occur in Ralph Waldo Emerson, "Ezra Ripley, D.D.," *Complete Works* (Boston, 1892), X, 365, and Josiah Quincy, *Figures in the Past* (Boston, 1883), pp. 363–64. I found details about J. and his creator in James Grant Wilson, *The Life and Letters of Fitz-Greene Halleck* (New York, 1869); *The Diary of Philip Hone* (New York, 1889); *The Correspondence of Nicholas Biddle* . . . . , edited by Reginald C. McGrane (Boston, 1919); and Marquis James, *The Life of Andrew Jackson* (Indianapolis, 1938), II, 658 and 876. A hint in this last book led me to study some of the Biddle papers in the Library of Congress. For permission to quote from these papers, I am grateful to the Library of Congress. The newspapers of the day had a great deal about Downing in them.

CHAPTER IV. A BRAHMIN DONS HOMESPUN

In addition to the *Complete Writings of James Russell Lowell* (16 vols.; Boston, 1904), I drew from *The Anti-slavery Papers of James Russell Lowell* (Boston, 1902) and *Early Prose Writings* . . . . (London, 1902). *A Bibliography of James Russell Lowell*, compiled by G. W. Cooke, contained data about the chronology of the writings. Volume I of *Letters* . . . . , edited by C. E. Norton (New York, 1906), contributed some details. The most valuable biographies proved to be Francis H. Underwood, *The Poet and the Man* (Boston, 1893), and Horace Elisha Scudder, *James Russell Lowell* . . . . (2 vols.; Boston, 1901).

CHAPTER V. HORSE SENSE, SOUTHERN STYLE

Johnson J. Hooper's book about Simon is *Some Adventures of Captain Simon Suggs* (Philadelphia, 1845). The best study of Hooper is Marion Kelley, *The Life and Writings* . . . . (an unpublished M.A. thesis, Alabama Polytechnic Institute, 1934). Thompson's books include *Major Jones's Courtship* (Madison, Ga., 1843) and *Major Jones's Sketches of Travel* (Philadelphia, 1847). Mr. Prentice Miller, who has been doing a doctoral dissertation about this author, graciously allowed me to draw upon his copious notes, for which I thank him. Material on the South came from Emory Q. Hawk, *Economic History of the South* (New York, 1934); R. S. Cotterill, *The Old South* (Glendale, Calif., 1937); A. E. Perkins, *The South* (New York, 1938); and W. J. Cash, *The Mind of the South* (New York, 1941).

CHAPTER VI. ABE LINCOLN

Lincoln's *Complete Works*, edited by Nicolay and Hay (New York, 1894), offered the text I used. Books drawn upon also included Emanuel

Hertz, *The Hidden Lincoln* (New York, 1938)—a valuable selection from letters and papers of Lincoln's law partner; William H. Herndon and Jesse William Weik, *Herndon's Lincoln* (2 vols.; Chicago, 1890); F. B. Carpenter, *Six Months at the White House* (New York, 1866); Ward Hill Lamon, *Recollections of Abraham Lincoln* . . . . (Chicago, 1895); C. G. Leland, *Abraham Lincoln* (London, 1879); Carl Schurz, *Abraham Lincoln* (Boston, 1871); James Bryce, Introduction to *Speeches of Abraham Lincoln*, edited by Roe (New York, 1919); L. E. Robinson, *Abraham Lincoln as Man of Letters* (New York, 1923); and Carl Sandburg, *The Prairie Years* (2 vols.; New York, 1925), and *The War Years* (4 vols.; New York, 1940).

CHAPTER VII. CIVIL WAR HUMOR—FOOLS FOR PROPAGANDA

The story of Lincoln's alleged trip with Sut comes from *Sut Lovingood Travels with Old Abe Lincoln,* edited by Edd Winfield Parks (Chicago, 1937). The only known book about Sut published during his creator's lifetime is *Sut Lovingood's Yarns* (New York, 1867). For biographical data about Harris I am indebted to Mr. Franklin J. Meine, who is preparing a biography of him. For the account of Sut's political dream, I am grateful to Mr. Donald Day, who found it printed in the *Southern Intelligencer* for November 26, 1856—copied, as he later learned, from another newspaper. Charles H. Smith's published volumes include *Bill Arp, So-called* (New York, 1866), *Bill Arp's Letters* (New York, 1868), *Bill Arp's Peace Papers* (New York, 1873), *Bill Arp's Scrap Book* (Atlanta, 1884), and *The Farm and the Fireside* (Atlanta, 1891). The best study of Smith is that by J. M. Steadman in *The Dictionary of American Biography* (New York, 1935), XVII, 248–49. Locke's writings have, most of them, been collected in *The Struggles* . . . . *of Petroleum V. Nasby* (Boston, 1872), but some of the more vicious passages have been expunged from these and must be sought out in the *Nasby Papers* (Indianapolis, 1864) and *Divers Opinions* . . . . (New York, 1865). Facts about Locke's life are presented in Cyril Clemens, *Petroleum V. Nasby* (Webster Groves, Mo., 1936).

CHAPTER VIII. LOST CHARACTERS

Browne's writings were collected in *The Complete Works of Artemus Ward* (New York, 1879). Biographical studies of note are E. P. Hingston, *Genial*

Showman (New York, 1870), and Don C. Seitz, *Artemus Ward* . . . . (New York, 1926). Nye's important books include *Bill Nye and Boomerang* (Chicago, 1881), *Remarks* (Chicago, 1887), and *Bill Nye's History of the United States* (Philadelphia, 1894). Frank Wilson Nye's *Bill Nye: His Own Life Story* (New York, 1926) is the most complete biography.

CHAPTER IX. MARK TWAIN, HANK, AND HUCK

Most of Clemens' writings, including those treated here, are in *The Writings* . . . . (25 vols., 1899–1910). The most useful biographies are A. B. Paine, *Mark Twain: A Biography* (4 vols.; New York, 1912, and Bernard De Voto, *Mark Twain's America* (Boston, 1932). I am indebted to Mr. De Voto for a chance to go through unpublished papers in the Clemens estate which yielded, among other things, the information that Mark had not seen Bellamy's book when he finished the *Yankee*. Mr. Lester Cook wrote a Master's thesis on the *Yankee* at the University of Chicago; I found it useful.

CHAPTER X. JOSH AND SAMANTHA

Shaw's writings are collected in *Josh Billings: His Works Complete* (4 vols.; New York, 1888). Cyril Clemens, *Josh Billings: Yankee Humorist* (Webster Groves, Mo., 1932), and F. S. Smith, *Adventures of Josh Billings* . . . . (New York, 1883) are biographies. Miss Holley's books include, among others, *My Opinions and Betsey Bobbet's* (Hartford, 1873), *Josiah Allen's Wife* (Hartford, 1877), *Samantha at Saratoga* (Philadelphia, 1887), and *Samantha in Europe* (New York, 1895). Mr. Cyril Clemens has a biography in manuscript which I have seen. Edwin Mims, Jr., has an article in the *Dictionary of American Biography* (New York, 1932), IX, 150, which contains the significant facts.

CHAPTER XI. IMPORTED HORSE SENSE
MR. DOOLEY

A good selection is *Mr. Dooley at His Best*, edited by Elmer Ellis (New York, 1938). Perhaps the best single Dooley book is the first, *Mr. Dooley in Peace and War* (Boston, 1898). Studies of Dunne include Harry M. Beardsley, "Finley Peter Dunne Is Dead, but Mr. Dooley Lives," *Chicago Daily News*, April 25, 1936; H. S. Canby, "Mr. Dooley and Mr. Hennessey," *Saturday Review of Literature*, XIV (May 9, 1936), 3–4; W. D. Howells, "Work of F. P. Dunne," *North American Review*, May, 1903); and F. L. Pattee, *The New American Literature* (New York, 1930), pp. 478–81. Mr. Ellis' biography of Dunne was published too late for me to draw upon it, but others will find it useful.

CHAPTER XII. ABE MARTIN AND WILL ROGERS

The picture of Abe Martin (p. 260) is reproduced with the permission of National Newspaper Service. The writings of Hubbard are available in a series of yearly books at times called *Abe Martin's Almanack* and at times given other titles. A brief autobiography of Hubbard appears in T. L. Masson, *Our American Humorists* (New York, 1922). Other information came from newspaper obituaries.

A collection of Rogers' writings is *Will Rogers' Wit and Wisdom*, edited by Jack Lait (New York, 1936). Most notable of Rogers' books are *Letters of a Self-made Diplomat* (New York, 1926) and *There's Not a Bathing Suit in Russia* (New York, 1927). Biographical studies are Jack Lait, *Our Will Rogers* (New York, 1935); P. J. O'Brien, *Will Rogers* (Chicago, 1935); and Betty Rogers, "Uncle Clem's Boy," serialized in the *Saturday Evening Post*, October 5–November 30, 1940, and later published between book covers.

CHAPTER XIII. CRAZY MEN

Mr. Benchley's most interesting books are *Of All Things* (New York, 1921), *The Early Worm* (New York, 1927), *No Poems* . . . . (New York, 1932), and *After 1903—What?* (New York, 1938). The most detailed treatment is J. Bryant, III, "Funny Man: A Study in Professional Frustration," *Saturday Evening Post*, September 23–October 7, 1939. The picture of Mr. Benchley (p. 279) is reproduced with the permission of Mr. Gluyas Williams, the artist, from *After 1903—What?* by Robert Benchley, published by Harper and Brothers.

A collection of Mr. Thurber's writings is *Cream of Thurber* (London, 1939). His books include *Is Sex Necessary?* (written in collaboration with E. B. White) (New York, 1929); *The Owl in the Attic* (New York, 1931); *The Seal in the Bedroom* (New York, 1932); *My Life and Hard Times* (New York, 1933); *The Middle-aged Man on the Flying Trapeze* (New York, 1935); *Let Your Mind Alone* (New York, 1937); *Fables for Our Time* (New York,

1940); and *Male Animal* (in collaboration with Elliott Nugent) (New York, 1940). His statement of his philosophy is in *What I Believe*, edited by Clifton Fadiman (New York, 1939), pp. 295–300. A critical article about him is Robert M. Coates, "Thurber, Inc.," *Saturday Review of Literature*, XXI (December 2, 1939), 10–11. The frontispiece, "Thurber: A Self-portrait," is reproduced with the permission of Mr. Thurber and the *Saturday Review of Literature*.

Both Mr. Thurber and Mr. Benchley are considered in Bernard De Voto, "The Lineage of Eustace Tilley," *Saturday Review of Literature*, XVI (September 25, 1937), 34; and Leonard Bacon, "Humors and Careers," *Saturday Review of Literature*, XX (April 29, 1939), 3–4.

CHAPTER XIV. MODERN SURVIVALS

Books by Mr. Nash, all published in New York except *I'm a Stranger Here Myself* (Boston, 1938), include, in addition to this book, *The Bad Parents' Garden of Verse* (1936); *Free Wheeling* (1931); *Happy Days* (1933); *The Primrose Path* (1935); and a collection, *The Face Is Familiar* (1940). He is discussed by Mr. Bacon in "Humors and Careers," *Saturday Review of Literature*, XX (April 29, 1939), 3–4. Other data for this chapter came chiefly from a variety of contemporary magazines and newspapers.

(A supplementary study to this present book, one which treats humor as fiction rather than as philosophy and propaganda, is my *Native American Humor (1800–1900)* (New York, 1937). Pages 163–96 of this earlier book contain a fairly detailed bibliography of humor and humorists of the nineteenth century.)

INDEX

[Numbers in italics indicate the most important entries. Authors and their characters, as a rule, are indexed separately. Parentheses, however, indicate the respective humorous characters created by the humorists or the respective creators of the characters.]

327

DATE DUE